Indigenous Screen
Cultures in Canada

Indigenous Screen

Cultures in Canada

Edited by
Sigurjón Baldur Hafsteinsson
and Marian Bredin

University of Manitoba Press

University of Manitoba Press
Winnipeg, Manitoba
Canada R3T 2M5
www.umanitoba.ca/uofmpress

Printed in Canada.
Text printed on chlorine-free, 100% post-consumer recycled paper.

Cover design: Doowah Design
Interior design: Karen Armstrong Graphic Design

Cover images used by permission of (clockwise from top left) APTN, Buffalo Gal Pictures, Eagle Vision, Big Soul Productions, Mushkeg Media, and APTN.

Interior images used by permission of Big Soul Productions, Mushkeg Media, Northern Native Broadcasting, Yukon, and Red Crow Community College.

Library and Archives Canada Cataloguing in Publication

   Indigenous screen cultures in Canada / Sigurjón Baldur Hafsteinsson and Marian Bredin, eds.
Includes bibliographical references and index.
ISBN 978-0-88755-718-7 (pbk.).--ISBN 978-0-88755-190-1 (bound)

   1. Native mass media--Canada. 2. Aboriginal television broadcasting--Canada. 3. Indian motion pictures--Canada. 4. Native peoples and mass media--Canada.

I. Sigurjón Baldur Hafsteinsson II. Bredin, Marian

P94.5.I532C3 2010   302.23089'97071   C2010-902851-1

The University of Manitoba Press gratefully acknowledges the financial support for its publication program provided by the Government of Canada through the Canada Book Fund, the Canada Council for the Arts, the Manitoba Department of Culture, Heritage, and Tourism, the Manitoba Arts Council, and the Manitoba Book Publishing Tax Credit.

CONTENTS

Introduction
**Marian Bredin and
Sigurjón Baldur Hafsteinsson**   1

Part I: The Cultural History of Aboriginal Media in Canada

First Peoples' Television in Canada:
Origins of the Aboriginal Peoples Television Network
Lorna Roth   17

Clear Signals: Learning and Maintaining Aboriginal
Languages through Television
Jennifer David   35

Part II: APTN and Indigenous Screen Cultures

Aboriginal Journalism Practices as Deep Democracy:
APTN National News
Sigurjón Baldur Hafsteinsson   53

APTN and Its Audiences
Marian Bredin 69

Aboriginal Media on the Move: An Outside Perspective on APTN
Kerstin Knopf 87

Regina's *Moccasin Flats*: A Landmark in the Mapping of Urban
Aboriginal Culture and Identity
Christine Ramsay 105

Part III: Transforming Technologies and Emerging
Media Circuits

Co-producing First Nations' Narratives:
The Journals of Knud Rasmussen
Doris Baltruschat 127

Wearing the White Man's Shoes: Two Worlds in Cyberspace
Mike Patterson 143

Taking a Stance: Aboriginal Media Research as an
Act of Empowerment
Yvonne Poitras Pratt 163

Selected Bibliography 183

Contributors 200

INTRODUCTION

MARIAN BREDIN AND SIGURJÓN BALDUR HAFSTEINSSON

> Communication is relational; it brings
> about relationships between people.
> — *Eric Michaels*

Theoretical Paradigms for Indigenous Media

In the sweep of global media markets, indigenous people around the world have increasing access to media technology such as print, radio, film, television, and the Internet.[1] Indigenous people participate in and compete for a place within the new international information order,[2] "negotiating with the settler nation"[3] and voicing their concerns with the help of media. Indigenous media are considered "a new dynamic" in social movements and help generate a critique of the "democratic deficits" of mainstream media.[4] Some media scholars suggest that indigenous people are now producing, using, and consuming media to trigger political, social, and cultural change, taking the initiative to represent themselves and address issues that mainstream media neglect.[5] The rise of indigenous media occurs in a larger global context where, as media theorists argue, developments in international communication place national sovereignty and nation states under new cultural and social pressures.[6] Joshua Meyrowitz first described these processes of cultural globalization in his analysis of how television has created communities with "no sense of place."[7] According to these models, nation states are losing their power over domestic media and are faced with diminished ability to regulate the flow of ideas and information within their territories.

As a result, individuals may re-evaluate forms of political participation and take advantage of new opportunities of expression and models of citizenship "free" from authoritarian control of the state. Global transnational media are thus conceived of as facilitating the creation of new citizens who derive their identity from post-national modes of participation that "supersede territorially based citizenship."[8] Within this theoretical framework, media scholars view indigenous media as products of declining government communications monopolies and as participants in a global information democracy. Indigenous media erode the power of the state to exercise its authority upon indigenous people while articulating concerns about government threats to indigenous cultural, social, economic, and political sovereignty. Other theorists take a less emancipatory view of indigenous media, seeing them as mere participants in a colonial and neo-liberal ruse to secure governmental control over information spaces without many additional benefits for the indigenous people.[9] The state's grip on indigenous people and their media is nowhere more apparent than in its control of broadcast frequencies, and in the licensing and legal limitations it imposes upon media content and ownership. Indigenous media scholars have acknowledged these competing theoretical possibilities with such terms as "Faustian contract"[10] or "primitivist perplex."[11]

Anthropologist Faye Ginsburg, a prolific scholar in the field of indigenous media, has constructed a key theoretical and interpretive paradigm for the field. She believes that indigenous media serve as self-conscious modes of cultural preservation and production, and as means of political mobilization. Ginsburg claims that this "cultural activism" permits people who have previously found themselves misrepresented by the instruments of the dominant culture to talk back to structures of power, using a range of media technologies.[12] Their goal is to use media for "internal and external communication, for self-determination, and for resistance to outside cultural domination."[13] Ginsburg and others have argued that indigenous media may be defined as processes of "transformative action." This definition helps us to see the emergence of "new social and cultural possibilities on a continuum, from the activities of daily life out of which consciousness and intentionality are constructed, to more dramatic forms of expressive culture (such as media or social protests)."[14] Ginsburg's theoretical assertions have been widely accepted by scholars of indigenous media. Models of cultural activism or transformative action show how indigenous media both produce and reproduce discursive and material practices; these models also challenge dichotomous constructs such as resistance and power, or subordinate and dominant.

Theoretical paradigms of indigenous media raise concerns about indigenous people's unequal access to mainstream society and its institutions. They examine the consequences of indigenous people's absence or misrepresentation in mainstream media outlets and criticize institutional practices within mainstream media structures that reinforce hegemonic power. Critical indigenous media research addresses the lack of official attempts to integrate indigenous people economically and/or structurally into national and global systems of media production, thus undermining popular notions of "the global village."[15] Indigenous media scholars explore key questions about who has the power to narrate and the power to suppress indigenous narratives.[16] Are indigenous media representations themselves appropriate?[17] What is the role of indigenous media in striking a balance between external interests and local constituencies?[18] This book takes up these questions with respect to indigenous media in Canada and undertakes a critical examination of the role of media in Aboriginal communities.

Indigenous Media Scholarship in Canada

In Canada, studies of Aboriginal and First Peoples' media have emerged from within communication and media studies. The earliest studies of Native broadcasting were carried out by communication scholars with an interest in the cultural impact of radio and television in Native communities. The research literature on indigenous media and Aboriginal broadcasting in Canada contains examples from a number of disciplinary and theoretical fields. These might be loosely organized into five categories: television "effects" surveys drawing upon social psychological notions of identity and assimilation; social historical approaches focusing on the political importance of indigenous media; sociological models of "development communication"; media studies using anthropological concepts of culture and ethnographic methods; and, finally, textual analyses using methods of media content analysis and concepts in film theory.

From within the fields of cultural anthropology and social psychology, researchers in the 1970s and '80s examined the influence of introduced media on individual and group behaviour, values, perceptions, and sense of identity in indigenous communities. At the same time, within the field of communication studies, researchers attempted to measure media effects on individuals and groups, seeking to establish links between consumption of certain kinds of programming and changes in norms and behaviour. These approaches were often ahistorical, paying inadequate attention to the social and cultural contexts within which media consumption took place. Nonetheless, they are important for their emphasis on subjective and collective locations of identity and culture. "Effects" research conducted in Inuit communities immediately after the introduction of television to the North examined the tensions created by extensive exposure to non-Inuit programming, in the absence of Inuktitut programs reflecting Inuit cultural knowledge. From this perspective, the effects of television can be seen as part of a broader colonial relationship that, alongside the introduction of English schools, government institutions, and wage labour, contributed to the disruption of traditional Inuit cultural knowledge and social organization.[19] However, this research also reveals that the consumption of southern television is not simply a unilateral process of passive assimilation, but an active transformation of introduced images and ideas in the contexts of Inuit norms and values. Further, an unintended effect of introduced television, at least in Inuit communities, was to trigger the demand for indigenous production.

Cultural anthropologists have conducted similar research on the impact of introduced media on Aboriginal cultures, but with less emphasis on measuring individual responses and behavioural changes, and more concern with the negotiation of meaning of electronic texts and the situation of the new medium within existing patterns of social organization and communication. This approach is useful for illuminating both the processes of consumption of externally produced media and the more recent appropriation of media technologies for internally generated production. In either case, the emphasis is on cultural differences in the interpretation and creation of texts. An early Canadian example of this approach was Gary Granzberg and Jack Steinbring's 1980 study of the introduction of mainstream television programming to three Manitoba Cree communities. Granzberg and Steinbring were concerned with the effects of television over a period of several years, and they employed standard social psychological survey instruments, "focus group" discussions, and participant observation in order to measure these effects.[20] While in this present volume we are primarily interested in the Aboriginal production of media content, some understanding of responses to externally produced media is necessary in order to establish the contexts from within which Aboriginal audiences interpret the programs produced by their own and the mainstream media.

The underlying assumption of "cultural impact" studies is that some or all of the various perceptual, discursive, or structural components of culture will be altered by a new medium of communication. The weakness inherent in such an approach is its tendency to view culture, especially the culture of non-Western Others, as a set of fixed perceptions, norms, discourses, or behaviours to which an objective measure of "change" can be applied. The connotations of "change" in this case are often those of "loss"—new media are associated with a degradation of the integrity and coherence of cultural knowledge. At the same time, the impact of electronic media on indigenous culture and social organization is often considered to be qualitatively different from the impact, for instance, of computer networks and information technologies on mainstream North American culture and society, even though there may in fact be important similarities between the two cases. Anthropological models of culture do provide considerable insight into the shifts in everyday habits, patterns of social interaction, and generation of meaning precipitated by the introduction of a medium like television. For example, Granzberg, Steinbring and Hamer argued that in the period of initial exposure, Manitoba Cree communities incorporated mainstream television into their existing conceptions of communication. Understood in relation to the traditional significance given to dreams and visions, television and radio were referred to by the same term used for the shamanic "shaking tent" ceremony.[21]

Researchers with a background in social history, sociology, or social theory tend to view the conjuncture of new communication technologies and Aboriginal cultures as part of macro-processes of contact and change. Gail Valaskakis's early research on historical shifts in communication patterns in the eastern Arctic, for example, was influenced by the social-historical methods and communication theories of Harold Innis. Valaskakis's work focused on the links between communication and control, between Euro-Canadian monopolies of knowledge and other modes of neo-colonial domination.[22] In a contemporaneous study of communication and political development in northwestern Ontario, Heather Hudson took a similar perspective. She applied models from the sociology of development to media use by Aboriginal leaders in the region.[23] Hudson and Valaskakis shared a similar concern with the influence of communication upon social interaction between groups and its role in historical relations of dependency and control between centre and margin. These researchers examined the initial links between Native-controlled media and indigenous self-determination movements of the 1970s and 1980s in Canada. As initially applied to Third World societies, development communication models proposed by Wilbur Lang Schramm, Daniel Lerner, and others viewed the exposure to mainstream modes of mass communication as a necessary component of "modernization," economic growth, and social development.[24] By situating the introduction of mass media to the North in the historical contexts of colonialism, Valaskakis and Hudson rejected this dominant theoretical paradigm in development communications. The most recent research adopting a social historical approach to indigenous media includes the work of Valerie Alia and Lorna Roth, who trace the history of First Peoples' news media and locate the origins of contemporary networks like Television Northern Canada (TVNC) and Aboriginal Peoples Television Network (APTN).[25] Roth is particularly concerned with the activist role of Aboriginal groups and indigenous media practitioners in their struggle to assert greater control over broadcasting infrastructures, policies, and program content.

Much recent Canadian indigenous media research is concerned with the productive output of Aboriginal-controlled print, radio, television, film, and digital media. Aboriginal media content can clearly be treated as a corpus of texts, interpreted using the methods of discourse analysis or film criticism. However, the search for an inherent "visual language" or for distinct formal properties and narrative structures derived from "authentic" indigenous cultural codes is sometimes problematic. Sol Worth and Eric Michaels[26] provided some early evidence that Aboriginal film and video texts diverge in significant ways from the cultural norms of Anglo-American or European visual communication. Indigenous media research in the Canadian context pursues this approach in a number of ways. In her analysis of Inuit Broadcasting Corporation (IBC) programs, Kate Madden argues that Inuit television resists the passive positioning of the viewer and rejects the construction of reporters and anchors as expert and omniscient authorities, both of which are common to dominant codes of news production.[27] She proposes that the rejection of these conventions is linked to Inuit cultural values of individual autonomy, decentralized leadership, and consensual decision making, and to its emphasis on cooperation and non-confrontational behaviour. Madden locates formal and substantive expressions of each of these values in IBC programs. Avi Santo takes a similar perspective in his analysis of the Igloolik Isuma television series *Nunavut* as a means of mobilizing Inuit cultural citizenship. He examines two specific episodes in the series, highlighting their televisual and narrative mechanisms of inscribing Inuit identity as examples of what Ginsburg refers to as "embedded aesthetics."[28] Michael Evans makes use of a related set of theoretical tools in his analysis of Inuit video as folklore.[29] Tracing intersections with other oral and material expressions of folklore, he explores Igloolik-based videomakers' distinctive use of symbols and stories and describes the local cultural significance of video production. In another form of textual analysis, Lisa Philips Valentine undertakes a discursive analysis of OjiCree community radio in her larger study of Severn Ojibwe oral discourses in northwestern Ontario. She is primarily interested in the multiplication of discursive strategies occasioned by the emergence of indigenous media, but the model of culture and the understanding of negotiated cultural change that she employs converge with Granzberg's.[30] Kathleen Buddle considers potential forms of Aboriginal cultural-capital creation in the context of urban Native community radio.[31] Unlike Valentine, she is not dealing exclusively with indigenous language use in a relatively remote community, but she explores relations of production in Aboriginal urban and off-reserve radio programming in southern Ontario. Buddle argues that Aboriginal-community radio programming and Native media activism in general ought to be read as forms of "cultural action, rather than as 'representations' that can be abstracted and analyzed apart from their authors."[32]

As this brief review of current research suggests, the "differences" associated with indigenous media production in Canada might be located in a variety of places: in the interpretations of the anthropologist/analyst who has a vested interest in seeing communal values or cultural practices as traces in the text, in the social organization of indigenous media production and the outcomes of collective decision making, or in the deliberate refusal and accidental transgression of the dominant conventions of mass media and their commercial or aesthetic production codes and values. In most cases, researchers conclude that textual analyses of indigenous media have minimal relevance without a concomitant understanding of the practical conditions of media production. Canadian research is remarkably consistent in recognizing this necessity, and in this respect it conforms to Ginsburg's view of indigenous media as embodying processes of transformative action. The contributors to this book likewise situate their readings of Aboriginal film and television texts within specific social historical and cultural contexts.

Objectives and Outline of the Book

The contributions to this volume are located between the anthropological and the historical in the existing research literature. This collection is one of the first to deal specifically with contemporary programming practices and content emerging from Aboriginal media organizations. The authors combine a focus on the political economy of Aboriginal media in Canada with a close critical reading of its visual and textual content to explore the presence and importance of Aboriginal media in the changing domestic and global media environment. The volume includes contributions from within the disciplines of anthropology, sociology, film and media studies, and Native studies. Each chapter provides a concrete example of how mass media permit increasing cultural and social agency among indigenous groups and how Aboriginal media producers conceive of traditional knowledge, languages, and practices as vehicles of modern culture. The primary objective of *Indigenous Media in Canada* is to understand each case presented in the following chapters as a local instance of cultural practice within global mediascapes, and at the same time as an example of contemporary indigenous cultural expression in Canada.

This book emerged from a panel chaired by Sigurjón Baldur Hafsteinsson at the Society for Cinema and Media Studies annual conference in Vancouver in March 2006. The original conference presentations focussed on programs, practices, and audiences at the APTN, and the resulting publication sustains that interest in the world's first national network operated by Aboriginal people with predominantly Aboriginal content. In collecting these essays here, we hope to highlight how APTN builds on an extensive history of Aboriginal media use and indigenous television production while generating rich new possibilities in broadcast, digital, and online media content. The focus on APTN was broadened to include chapters on the historical evolution of First Peoples' television, its place in the wider project of Aboriginal-language broadcasting, and comparative perspectives on the experience of indigenous film production and the creation of information infrastructures for Native cyber-communities. The chapters thus present wide-ranging analyses of three key aspects of Canadian indigenous media: their textual and discursive content, their use of technology and modes of production, and their audiences within and beyond Aboriginal communities. The book provides fresh insights from both established and emerging scholars of Canadian indigenous media studies.

The collection is divided into three parts, beginning with two essays that situate Aboriginal media in Canada within their cultural and social history. Lorna Roth's opening chapter, "First Peoples' Television in Canada's North: Origins of the Aboriginal Peoples Television Network," provides a social, historical, and political framework for understanding what we might call the "conditions of possibility" for indigenous media in Canada. She traces the origins of APTN and its precursor, TVNC back to their roots in the policy interventions and broadcast "experiments" of the 1970s. Roth outlines six discrete phases in this history, each marked out by distinctive changes in representational practices and technological infrastructures, and a corresponding expansion of target audiences. Roth's comprehensive historical analysis of Aboriginal media policies and practices is widely cited in the literature on APTN and on Aboriginal media in Canada and around the world. In this chapter, she describes the trajectory of indigenous television, from early local satellite communication projects, to the creation of regional Native communications societies, to a pan-northern network, which led to the creation of a national network carried on cable across the country. Roth provides valuable insight into the public perception of APTN, its popular support among viewers, and the initial resistance of other players in the Canadian television industry. This chapter lays important groundwork for readers unfamiliar with the history of Aboriginal broadcasting while guiding us skilfully through the field of Canadian broadcasting policy.

In her adaptation of a report originally commissioned by APTN, Jennifer David places the network within larger analyses of the role of Native broadcasting in sustaining Aboriginal language use. Her chapter, "Clear Signals: Learning and Maintaining Aboriginal Languages through Television," presents a survey of the state of Aboriginal language broadcasting. David describes the current availability of indigenous language content on federally funded northern Native radio and television production, on local community radio stations predominantly in southern Canada, and through independent film and video productions that provide language material for APTN. Her findings demonstrate that Aboriginal language content depends heavily on financial assistance, as a function of the relatively high costs of production in relation to a small audience. David highlights the importance of Aboriginal language use in media to its acquisition by children and youth. She argues convincingly for more substantive research into the role of media in creating employment opportunities for indigenous language speakers and in encouraging Aboriginal youth to maintain their language.

The four chapters in Part II narrow the focus from the broader historical and social terrain of Aboriginal media to develop case studies of media practice, televisual content, and audience consumption at APTN. As a cultural anthropologist, Sigurjón Baldur Hafsteinsson moves from the terrain of policy analysis and media history to a detailed ethnographic study of news production at APTN during its first licence term (1999–2006). In his contribution, "Aboriginal Journalism Practices as Deep Democracy: APTN National News," he makes use of interview material to describe the creation of a news production team and weekly news programming at the network. This chapter explores the APTN news team's need for a careful balance that both addresses the general neglect of Aboriginal issues by most other Canadian news outlets and answers the demand for journalist independence from Aboriginal politicians and political organizations. Hafsteinsson traces the cultural specificity of news narrative and production practices at APTN, showing how the democratic principles underpinning the news department extend not only to relations of production among journalists, but also to specific practices of representation within APTN's news discourse.

The fourth chapter shifts from a focus on the history, structure, and internal practices at APTN to a more sustained look at the network's audience. In "APTN and Its Audiences," Marian Bredin proposes a triangulated analysis of the ideal, active, and actual viewer of APTN programs. The ideal viewer emerges from interview accounts of how APTN producers and hosts imagine their audience; the active viewer can be understood by looking at informal feedback and dialogue generated by APTN's online forum and the call-in portion of its current affairs program, while the actual viewer (Aboriginal or non-Aboriginal) can be delineated through qualitative and quantitative audience research conducted by the network and commercial ratings services. Relying on theoretical perspectives on the audience drawn from media studies, this chapter attempts to locate APTN's audience within shifting relations between the three elements of text, reader, and community. In her chapter, "Aboriginal Media on the Move: An Outside Perspective on APTN," Kerstin Knopf focuses on program schedules, acquisition policies, and specific content at APTN to demonstrate how the network fosters new political and cultural perspectives shaped by Aboriginal cultural needs. Looking mainly at examples from its initial licence period, Knopf suggests that while APTN works toward the decolonization of Canadian airwaves, the shortage of good quality indigenous content sometimes results in program choices that contradict the decolonizing process. With a close reading of APTN's televisual texts, including news, documentary, drama, children's programs, and advertising, Knopf demonstrates how these programs produce and reproduce Aboriginal cultural discourses while also at times recirculating stereotypes from dominant discourses about Aboriginal people.

Christine Ramsay, a film scholar at the University of Regina, examines the local production of the APTN series *Moccasin Flats*. This landmark program was the first North American television drama series to be created, written, produced, and performed by Aboriginal people. In her critical reading of the show's first season (2003), Ramsay seeks to locate the series within global youth culture and the urban 'hood genre, while establishing how it speaks to the cultural experience of young Aboriginal people growing up in Canadian cities. Ramsay suggests that the program evokes North Central Regina as a "place image" in the Canadian national imagination and as both urban dystopia and utopia for its Native residents. This chapter, "Regina's *Moccasin Flats*: A Landmark in the Mapping of Urban Aboriginal Culture and Identity," gives a detailed account of how the series' creators, the young non-professional Aboriginal cast, and the narrative itself negotiate the cultural borderlands of race and class and the tensions between elders and youth.

Essays in the third part of the collection engage the transformation of screen technologies and changing circuits of media distribution by looking at film, Internet, and digital media in indigenous communities. In her contribution, "Co-producing First Nations' Narratives: *Journals of Knud Rasmussen*," Doris Baltruschat explores the community origins of indigenous media in her examination of the most recently released film from Igloolik Isuma Productions, an Inuit-controlled independent film and video production company. The company's first film, *Atanarjuat, the Fast Runner*, garnered international awards for its compelling adaptation of local Inuit stories of shamanic intrigue and family conflict. A co-production with a Danish film company, *The Journals of Knud Rasmussen* follows the same community through the early period of European contact. Baltruschat considers the role of digital video technologies, the influence of co-production agreements, and the emphasis on key values of community-based media in this example of indigenous filmmaking

The book's final two chapters move from the terrain of what are now increasingly referred to as "traditional" media into the world of new digital media and online communication. In his chapter, "Wearing the White Man's Shoes: Two Worlds in Cyberspace," Mike Patterson demonstrates how the internet and online media are being used by Native peoples to overcome marginalization and resist colonization. He traces the emergence of Aboriginal communities in cyberspace, arguing that, as with earlier adaptations of European technology, indigenous people are using new media tools to occupy new cultural territory. In a series of case studies, from FrostysAmerindian and the Fighting Whites websites to the use of online media in Aboriginal education initiatives, Patterson explores the potential of the Internet as a virtual space both for indigenous community-building and for intercultural dialogue. He highlights the pressing need for improved local broadband access if Native people are to overcome the digital divide in Canada. In the final chapter, "Taking a Stance: Aboriginal Media Research as an Act of Empowerment," Yvonne Poitras Pratt echoes this call in her participatory study of plans for information infrastructure in Aboriginal communities, while reiterating this book's central focus on the social conditions within which media—new and old—are deployed. Poitras Pratt reminds readers that indigenous strategies of decolonization still face considerable social, political, and economic resistance from governments and within Canadian society at large. She explores the emerging paradigms of action research to show how indigenous scholars are making important new inroads into participatory and ethnographic research. Pratt describes how she was influenced by these models in her own research on the extension of

Alberta SuperNet to three Aboriginal communities. Her reflection on her experience as indigenous ethnographer and her role in the empowerment of the communities she studied points to vital future research directions in the study of indigenous media in Canada.

Each chapter in this book considers the use of indigenous media in their combined potential to enable cultural persistence while raising political cal awareness and generating social change. Taken as a whole, the studies presented here show that the historical origins and contemporary status of indigenous media in Canada can clearly be understood as forms of what Ginsburg calls "transformative action." The examples documented in this collection, especially the major achievements of APTN, contribute to a greater understanding of Aboriginal people's demand for cultural sovereignty while situating the Canadian case within larger global movements for information democracy. While media alone cannot provide the means of decolonization and economic parity, they occupy an increasingly central place in processes of change within Aboriginal communities and in relations between Aboriginal and non-Aboriginal people in Canada.

NOTES

1   Arjun Appadurai, *Modernity at Large: Cultural Dimensions of Globalization* (Minneapolis: University of Minnesota Press, 1996).

2   Kaarle Nordenstreng and Herbert I. Schiller, *National Sovereignty and International Communication, Communication and Information Science* (Norwood, NJ: Ablex Publishing, 1979).

3   Faye D. Ginsburg, "Resources of Hope: Learning from the Local in a Transnational Era," in *Indigenous Cultures in an Interconnected World*, ed. Claire Smith and Graeme K. Ward (Vancouver: University of British Columbia Press, 2000), 46.

4   William K. Carroll and Robert A. Hackett, "Democratic Media Activism through the Lens of Social Movement Theory," *Media, Culture and Society* 28, 1 (2006): 83.

5   Studies of indigenous media and their relation to social change and cultural identity have focused on a number of specific case studies around the world, including Valerie Alia, *Un/Covering the North: News, Media, and Aboriginal People* (Vancouver: University of British Columbia Press, 1999); Donald R. Browne, *Electronic Media and Indigenous Peoples: A Voice of Our Own* (Ames: Iowa State University Press, 1996; Patrick J. Daley and Beverly A. James, *Cultural Politics and the Mass Media: Alaska Native Voices* (Urbana: University of Illinois Press, 2004); Faye D. Ginsburg, "Mediating Culture: Indigenous Media, Ethnographic Film, and the Production of Identity," in *Fields of Vision: Essays in Film Studies, Visual Anthropology, and Photography*, ed. Leslie Devereaux and Roger Hillman (Berkeley: University of California Press, 1995), 256–91; Faye D. Ginsburg, "Resources of Hope: Learning from the Local in a Transnational Era," in *Indigenous Cultures in an Interconnected World*, ed. Claire Smith and Graeme

K. Ward (Vancouver: University of British Columbia Press, 2000), 27-48; Faye D. Ginsburg, "Screen Memories: Resignifying the Traditional in Indigenous Media," in *Media Worlds: Anthropology on New Terrain*, ed. Faye D. Ginsburg, Lila Abu-Lughod, and Brian Larkin (Berkeley: University of California Press, 2002), 39–57; George Marcus, ed. *Connected: Engagements with Media* (Chicago: University of Chicago Press, 1996); Hans Henrik Philipsen and Birgitte Markussen, eds. *Advocacy and Indigenous Film-Making* (Aarhus: Intervention Press, 1995); Harald Prins, "Visual Media and the Primitivist Perplex: Colonial Fantasies, Indigenous Imagination, and Advocacy in North America," in *Media Worlds*, 58–74; Gail Valaskakis, "Communication, Culture and Technology: Satellites and Northern Native Broadcasting in Canada," in *Ethnic Minority Media*, ed. Stephen Harold Riggins (Newbury Park, CA: Sage Publications, 1992).

6   Nordenstreng and Schiller, *National Sovereignty* ; Nancy Morris and Silvio R. Waisbord, eds., *Media and Globalization: Why the State Matters* (Lanham, MD: Rowman and Littlefield, 2001).

7   Meyrowitz as cited in Appadurai, *Modernity at Large*, 29.

8   Morris and Waisbord, eds., *Media and Globalization*, 12.

9   James Faris, "Anthropological Transparency: Film, Representation and Politics," in *Film as Ethnography*, ed. Peter Ian Crawford and David Turton, 171–182 (Manchester: Manchester University Press, 1992).

10   Ginsburg, "Screen Memories."

11   Prins, "Visual Media and the Primitivist Perplex."

12   Faye D. Ginsburg, "From Little Things Big Things Grow: Indigenous Media and Cultural Activism," in *Between Resistance and Revolution: Cultural Politics and Social Protest*, ed. Richard G. Fox and Orin Starn, 118-144 (New Brunswick, NJ: Rutgers University Press, 1997)

13   Faye D. Ginsburg, "Indigenous Media: Faustian Contract or Global Village," *Cultural Anthropology* 6, 1 (1991): 92. See also Ruud Koopmans, "Movements and Media: Selection Processes and Evolutionary Dynamics in the Public Sphere," *Theory and Society* 33 (2004) 367–391.

14   Ginsburg, "From Little Things Big Things Grow,"122.

15   John Hartley, "Television, Nation, and Indigenous Media," *Television and New Media* 5, 1 (2004): 7.

16   Timothy Asch et al., "The Story We Now Want to Hear Is Not Ours to Tell: Relinquishing Control over Representation: Toward Sharing Visual Communication Skills with the Yanomami," *Visual Anthropology Review* 7, 2 (1991): 102–106; Eric Michaels, *The Aboriginal Invention of Television in Central Australia 1982–1986* (Canberra: Australian Institute of Aboriginal Studies, 1986).

17   Lorna Roth, "The Delicate Act of 'Colour Balancing': Multiculturalism and Canadian Broadcasting Policies and Practices," *Canadian Journal of Communication* 23, 4 (1998): 487–505; Jay Ruby, *Picturing Culture: Explorations of Film & Anthropology* (Chicago: University of Chicago Press, 2000).

18   Shane Greene, "Indigenous People Incorporated? Culture as Politics, Culture as Property in Pharmaceutical Bioprospecting," *Current Anthropology* 24, 2 (2004): 211–37; Helen Molnar and Michael Meadows, *Songlines to Satellites: Indigenous Communication in Australia, the South Pacific and Canada* (Annandale, Austr.:

Pluto Press, 2001); Philipsen and Markussen, eds., *Advocacy and Indigenous Film-Making*; Terence Turner, "Representation, Politics, and Cultural Imagination in Indigenous Video: General Points and Kayapo Examples," in *Media Worlds*, 75–89; Stephen Turner, "Sovereignty, or the Art of Being Native," *Cultural Critique* 51 (2002): 74–100.

19 Nelson H.H. Graburn, "Television and the Canadian Inuit," *Etudes Inuit Studies* 6, 1 (1982): 7–19.

20 Gary Granzberg and Jack Steinbring, *Television and the Canadian Indian: Impact and Meaning among Algonkians of Central Canada* (Winnipeg: University of Winnipeg, 1980). Sol Worth and John Adair's 1970 participatory study of film production with the Navajo and Eric Michaels' 1986 video project with the Warlpiri in Central Australia make implicit use of a similar model of culture in their examination of the introduction of film, video, and television technologies to communities with little prior exposure to these media. A more detailed analysis of anthropological notions of culture employed in these three studies, including evaluation of their relative ability to account for aboriginal cultures as dynamic or emergent and to recognize ethnographic knowledge as "co-produced" by both anthropologist and informant, is carried out in Marian Bredin, "Ethnography and Communication: Approaches to Aboriginal Media," *Canadian Journal of Communication* 18, 3 (1993): 297–313.

21 Gary Granzberg, Jack Steinbring, and John Hamer, "New Magic for Old: TV in Cree Culture." *Journal of Communication* 27, 4 (1977): 154–157.

22 Gail Valaskakis, "Communication and Control in the Canadian North: The Potential of Interactive Satellites." *Etudes Inuit Studies* 6, 1 (1982): 19–28; Gail Valaskakis, "Restructuring the Canadian Broadcasting System: Aboriginal Broadcasting in the North," in *Canadian Broadcasting, the Challenge of Change*, ed. Colin Hoskins and Stuart McFadyen (Edmonton: University of Alberta and ACCESS, 1985).

23 Heather Hudson, "The Role of Radio in the Canadian North," *Journal of Communication* 27, 4 (1977): 130–139.

24 Wilbur Lang Schramm and Daniel Lerner, eds., *Communication and Change in the Developing Countries* (Honolulu: University of Hawaii Press, East-West Center, 1972).

25 Valerie Alia, *Un/Covering the North*; Lorna Roth, *Something New in the Air: The Story of First Peoples' Television Broadcasting in Canada* (Montreal: McGill Queen's University Press, 2005).

26 Sol Worth, *Through Navajo Eyes; an Exploration in Film Communication and Anthropology* (Bloomington: Indiana University Press, 1972); Eric Michaels, *The Aboriginal Invention of Television in Central Australia 1982–1986*.

27 Kate Madden, "Video and Cultural Identity: The Inuit Broadcasting Corporation Experience," in *Mass Media Effects across Cultures*, ed. Felipe Korzenny, Stella Ting-Toomey, and Elizabeth Schiff (Newbury Park, CA: Sage Publications, 1992) 130–49.

28 Avi Santo, "Inuit Television and Cultural Citizenship," *International Journal of Cultural Studies* 7, 4 (2004): 379.

29 Michael Robert Evans, *Isuma: Inuit Video Art*, (Montreal: McGill-Queen's University Press, 2008); Michael Robert Evans, "Sometimes in Anger: The Struggle of Inuit Video," *Fuse Magazine* 22, 4 (2000): 13–17.

30 Lisa Philips Valentine, *Making It Their Own: Severn Ojibwe Communicative Practices* (Toronto: University of Toronto Press, 1994).

31 Kathleen Buddle, "Aboriginal Cultural Capital Creation and Radio Production in Urban Ontario," *Canadian Journal of Communication* 30, 1 (2005): 7–40.

32 Ibid., 8.

CHAPTER 1

First Peoples' Television in Canada: Origins of the Aboriginal Peoples Television Network[1]

LORNA ROTH

Of all the First Peoples around the world, those in Canada have led the way in establishing legislatively based, nationwide television services reflecting their cultural perspectives and languages. The negotiation of an infrastructure for First Peoples' television in Canada occurred between 1970 and 1999. During that time, the federal government shifted from attempting to assimilate First Peoples (in 1969) to recognizing First Peoples as a national constituency group with collective broadcasting rights and a special status.

For most of this period, federally funded broadcasting undertakings were located north of the 55th parallel. This region includes one third of Canada's land mass and encompasses the Northwest Territories, Nunavut, the Yukon Territories, Labrador, and the northern parts of all of the central and western provinces. After consistent successes with pilot experiments and more permanent undertakings, northern broadcasters sought to integrate southern First Peoples into their established services and convinced the federal government of the viability of a national indigenous service. They subsequently gained federal, territorial, provincial, and a broad range of institutional support through legislation, regulation, and financial assistance to operate an Aboriginal Peoples Television Network (APTN).

In 1991, the federal government passed the current *Broadcasting Act*, which enshrined multiculturalism, multiracialism, and Aboriginal broadcasting. It reads: "Through its programming and the employment op-portunities arising out of its operation, [the Canadian broadcasting system should] serve the needs and interests, and reflect the circumstances and aspirations of Canadian men, women and children, including equal rights, the linguistic duality and multicultural and multiracial nature of Canadian society and the special place of aboriginal Peoples within that society."[2]

An Historical Overview of Aboriginal Television History Development

The history of Northern television can be divided into six phases distinguished by shifts in representational practices, improved technological infrastructures, and corresponding expansions of target audiences.[3]

Phases I and II:
Pre-Northern Television Context, (De)Romancing First Peoples

Phase I (1900s–1970) is well documented in the literature[4] and covers the period in which southern-produced imagery of First Peoples, when they were presented at all, consisted of stereotypical representations. This period preceded the entry of television into the Canadian North, but provides important background information. When television was parachuted into the North, its initial impact was to underscore this absence of First Peoples from media texts.

This was followed by Phase II (1968–1981), in which First Peoples became aware of the potential of televisual media to record themselves and their concerns. This phase coincided with the late 1960s, when Parliament debated the *Telesat Act* (1968), whose purpose was to introduce the second domestic satellite in the world (the first being the Russian Sputnik, launched in 1968). Concurrent with the passing of the *Telesat Act* in 1969, discussions around Aboriginal northern television commenced. At the time, federal policy strongly advocated the assimilation of First Peoples.[5] In response to the threat to their desired "special status," First Peoples began to realize the power of the media, on the one hand, to erode their cultures, and, on the other hand, to serve as a tool for self-development/empowerment in their efforts to resist conformity to the mainstream values of Canadian society, and to serve as a vehicle for mediating and repairing historical tensions in their social and race relations.

By 1975, in conformity with the Accelerated Coverage Package Program (1974), all northern communities with populations over 500 were equipped with television receiving dishes. From First Peoples' perspectives, the main activity of this period was the use of television as an experimental medium through which to explore interactive communications and community development practices. Simultaneously, the federal government wanted First Peoples to "modernize" and to become familiar with new technologies as a possible substitute for travel, especially in relation to education and health matters. Expenses related to such travel were very prohibitive at the time. The government also wanted First Peoples' feedback on alternative uses of satellite technology for community development, and on viable forms of inter-community communications. In other words, various interests and objectives converged in such a way that it became worthwhile for the government to invest in field tests and for First Peoples to undertake experimental project work.

Phase III (1978–1991): Policy-ing the North

Consequently, between 1978 and 1981 the Department of Communications established a competition among field groups in Nunavut (formerly the central and eastern lands of the Northwest Territories) and Nunavik (northern Quebec) for access to the Anik B satellite. Several groups received monies as part of the competition, but the most prominent was the Inuit Tapirisat of Canada (the Eskimo Brotherhood), which was given over $1 million to conduct interactive experiments in exchange for collecting and evaluating relevant data. As a result of two successful projects—"Inukshuk" in the Northwest Territories and "Naalakvik" in Northern Quebec—the Inuit were able to negotiate the licensing of the Inuit Broadcasting Corporation in 1981. At the same time, the CRTC (Canadian Radio-television and Telecommunications Commission) licensed Cancom (Canadian Satellite Telecommunications Company) to deliver southern programming to northern and remote communities and to carry northern-produced broadcasts. The CBC was "expected" to carry Native-language programming as part of its public service mandate.

In an overall sense, the time between 1981 and 1991 was a period in which *broadcasting policy* was reshaped. During this period, experiments in the field were carefully monitored and used as evidence to support the granting of access rights to constituency groups and the provision of fairer and more equitable distribution services for the North. Eventually, the work of lobbyists from the North and the South, academics, and historians resulted in the amended *Broadcasting Act* of 1991. The path that led to this parliamentary decision was rough and winding.

Phase IV (1983–1992): Consolidation and Expansion of Broadcasting Infrastructure

1983 was a key year for northern broadcasting. By this time, thirteen regional Native communications societies had developed "North of 60" and had organized a lobby campaign directed toward the establishment of a distinct Native broadcasting policy. On 10 March 1983, the Government of Canada responded by announcing a Northern Broadcasting Policy that recognized the importance of Native participation in both media programming and the regulatory process.[6] The Northern Broadcasting Policy consisted of the following five principles:

1. Northern residents should be offered access to an increasing range of programming choices through the exploitation of technological opportunities.
2. Northern native peoples should have the opportunity to participate actively in the determination by the CRTC of the character, quantity, and priority of programming broadcast in predominantly native communities.
3. Northern native peoples should have fair access to northern broadcasting distribution systems to maintain and develop their cultures and languages.
4. Programming relevant to native concerns, including content originated by native peoples, should be produced for distribution on northern broadcasting services wherever native peoples form a significant proportion of the population in the service area.
5. Northern native representatives should be consulted regularly by government agencies engaged in establishing broadcasting policies which would affect their cultures.[7]

An accompanying program called the Northern Native Broadcast Access Program (NNBAP) was also established, and $40.3 million was earmarked for the long-term goal of producing twenty hours per week of Native-language radio programming and five hours per week of Native-perspective television. The initial funding was for four years, but the program has continued to exist, albeit under considerable financial strain.

In 1983, therefore, there was initial cause for celebration of this recognition, but problems soon became apparent. For example, while both the CBC and Cancom did effectively deliver indigenous programming as part of their licensing conditions, they did so at rather unpopular hours. Hence, while the CBC Northern Service carried Inuit Broadcasting Corporation (IBC) programming for five hours per week, the programs were often broadcast around 3:00 a.m. Furthermore, national programming often pre-empted Native programming on the CBC. First Peoples came to believe, therefore, that the demand for carriage of their programming could not be left merely to the good-will of other agencies.

In 1985, interested parties began to discuss the establishment of a dedicated northern transponder to avoid the above-mentioned problems. In January 1987, Aboriginal and northern broadcasters formed a consortium with the goal of establishing a pan-northern distribution service. In 1988, the Federal Department of Communications approved monies to explore the feasibility of a separate northern channel. In 1990, $10 million was approved to prepare an application for a pan-northern distribution service. Meanwhile, there were severe budgetary cutbacks in NNBAP program funding as the federal government responded to pressures to privatize the cultural industries. This led to a bizarre problem. On the one hand, First Peoples were getting distribution money; on the other, they could not afford to produce programs to distribute. There was subsequently a scramble to find ways to diversify their funding sources. Some hired fundraisers; others increased efforts to find a stronger advertising base.

Phase V (1986–1999): Crossing Cultural, Racial, and Territorial Borderlines

Beginning around 1990, several Native communication societies (Inuit Broadcasting Corporation; Northern Native Broadcasting, Yukon [NNBY]; WaWaTay Native Communication Societies) initiated contracts to produce programming for southern viewers. This was partly in response to the cutbacks, partly as an effort to reach a broader audience and to assess how they might be perceived, and partly to overcome the historical dependency of First Peoples on the federal government. In the case of NNBY, a weekly program, *Nedaa (Your Eye on the Yukon)*, was negotiated with CBC Newsworld. This was the first ongoing national channel commitment to broadcasting First Peoples programming to a countrywide audience, and it caused both celebration and minor criticism around the issue of regional versus national audiences. But no one stopped the initiative.

In programming for a national audience, NNBY had to develop a culturally hybrid approach targeting at least two distinct audiences (Native and non-Native) that were already highly diverse. Given that federal funding was disseminated for the purpose of developing regional media, the secondary, non-Native audience was considered somewhat outside the criteria of the Northern Native Broadcast Access Program. Nonetheless,

NNBY's contractual arrangement was significant because it crossed social, racial, territorial, and cultural borders and opened a space—albeit small—for Aboriginal broadcasting within the mainstream of Canadian media. NNBY programming acquired a loyal following in the South, which provoked some interesting discussions in the North about how to build cross-cultural align- ments for political ends. Though bold, NNBY's national project did little to solve the challenge of pan-northern distribution.

Phase VI (1992–1997): An International Turn

After the *Broadcasting Act* was amended in 1991, the CRTC approved the application for Television Northern Canada (TVNC), a Native television network licensed to serve Northern Canada "for the purpose of broadcast- ing cultural, social, political and educational programming for the primary benefit of aboriginal Peoples in the North."[8] By granting the TVNC licence, the commission recognized the importance of Northern self-determination of the distribution of Native and northern programming. TVNC was to be- come the vehicle through which First Peoples would represent themselves and their concerns to the entire North. They would no longer be restricted by geography or technology to local or regional self-representation and identity-building. In this sense, TVNC constituted a *de facto* recognition of the communication rights of First Peoples in the North.

TVNC began broadcasting on 21 January 1992. Spanning 5 time zones and more than 4.3 million kilometres, TVNC broadcast approximately 100 hours per week to 96 communities (in English and multiple Native lan- guages).[9] TVNC was not a programmer, but a distributor of its members' programming, which consisted of:

- 38 hours per week of Aboriginal language and cultural programming
- 23 hours per week of formal and informal educational programming
- 12 hours per week of produced and acquired children's program- ming, over half of which was in Aboriginal languages. [10]

The rest consisted of wrap-around programming from Broadcast News and Environment Canada, and reruns.

TVNC was the only Aboriginal television network in the world to broad- cast such a high volume of programming from indigenous sources. At the time, the Central Australian Aboriginal Media Association (CAAMA) had a remote commercial television service license, awarded in 1987. Its "Imparja" service broadcast mostly to non-Aboriginal viewers; its programming tended to be more European-oriented.[11] TVNC and CAAMA programming had little in common besides being Aboriginal-controlled.[12]

As a pan-northern distribution undertaking, TVNC was theoretically able to forge connections (via program exchanges and uplink/downlink satellite arrangements) with Inuit and Aboriginal groups in other countries, such as Greenland, the United States, Finland, and Siberia, as well as Australia, New Zealand, Brazil, and Bolivia (among others). In reality, technical and financial barriers prevented it from doing much of this. What TVNC did offer to northern viewers was limited access to programming about the "activities of indigenous Peoples from around the globe," when this was feasible.[13] For example, the network aired a half-hour weekly current affairs program called *Heartbeat Alaska*, which originated in Anchorage, Alaska, and was supplied for the cost of one-way shipping.

TVNC's ambition to be picked up by southern cable operators on a voluntary basis did not work out well. The CRTC permitted TVNC to be listed for carriage by cable companies, but very few availed themselves of the opportunity. Furthermore, piecemeal distribution of the TVNC signal would not have been an appropriate form of extension into the south. The challenge was to become a Canada-wide network. This, however, posed further unanticipated cross-cultural questions. For example, what kinds of programming would meet the information and entertainment needs of both Native and non-Native northerners *and* Native and non-Native southerners? What considerations and constraints would be imposed upon or voluntarily assumed by programmers in order to please a hybrid audience?

Of even greater concern were program subjects that might generate controversy when they were removed from their original context. Consider the programs that stem from the eastern Arctic, in which details of animal killings are central to the visual presentation. The culturally sensitive issue of the hunt might stir protest from members of animal rights organizations.

Finally, the cost of acquiring broadcasting rights in the South would increase because the target audience would be larger. Northern rights were extremely inexpensive at the time because TVNC was a non-profit, public broadcasting distribution organization. Indeed, program distributors, who recognized TVNC's special financial conditions, virtually subsidized the rights. These were just a few of the programming considerations that TVNC would have to address if and when it negotiated a broadcasting arrangement with the South.

The Aboriginal Peoples Television Network—Going National

There are some 600 First Nations. We are always fighting for
this right or that right. But we are one People. This [channel] would
bring us together.

—Focus group participant

I am very excited by the opportunity the aboriginal Peoples of
Canada have been given. This historic decision will be a major step
in building bridges of understanding between aboriginal and non-
aboriginal Peoples in Canada.

—Abraham Tagalik,
former APTN chairman[14]

As of June 1997, TVNC undertook to become a nationwide network.[15]
With support in this endeavour from the Assembly of First Nations (AFN),
it began to make regular submissions to national Aboriginal organizations
and to the CRTC.

In January 1998, TVNC hired Angus Reid (a public-opinion consulting firm) to conduct a survey regarding the desirability of establishing a
national Aboriginal network. Results indicated that 79 percent or "two out
of three Canadians supported the idea of a national aboriginal TV network,
even if it would mean displacing a currently offered service."[16] In February
1998, the CRTC called for a license application from TVNC, and in June 1998,
TVNC submitted one. To be economically viable, TVNC argued, it had to be
a mandatory service, available to the nearly 8 million households with cable
and to those with direct-to-home and wireless television service, including ExpressVu, Star Choice, and Look TV.[17] To assure consistent and secure
funding, TVNC requested that cable operators charge fifteen cents per month
per household, thereby generating an anticipated revenue stream of $15
million in the first years, although APTN expected the budget to increase
with rising advertising revenues.[18] In exchange for the small charge of fifteen cents, subscribers would receive a service aimed at both Aboriginal
and non-Aboriginal audiences with programming of interest to all viewers:
children's animation, youth shows, cultural and traditional programming,
music, drama, dance, and news and current affairs, as well as live coverage
of special events and interactive programming.[19] APTN promised 90 percent

Canadian content with the remaining 10 percent consisting of indigenous programming from around the world.[20] It has subsequently decreased its Canadian content percentage to 84 percent, due to the high production cost of Canadian original programming.

Prior to the hearing, the CRTC received approximately 300 letters of support from the general public. This was not a large number, but along with the Angus Reid results, it was enough to reinforce the political will of the CRTC commissioners to make a decision in TVNC/APTN's favour. Support for the network was fairly consistent among the existing Native communication societies in the North; however, there were some expected challenges around issues of the Board of Directors' organization and control during the transition from a Northern to a national network, which indicated a need for a period of negotiation, clarification, and resolution. Primary among these challenges was one raised by the NNBY group involving the question of guaranteed Northern representation on the board. NNBY was concerned with shifting power relations and the possible "systemic changes that might undermine the interests of the Aboriginal Peoples of the North" and demanded guarantees for the "unrestricted right of continued distribution of their programs to support their languages, dialects, and cultures."[21] There were other considerations of a more technical and administrative nature, but this one was of primary significance in terms of the discourse it generated. In response to NNBY's concerns, TVNC assured them in writing that these issues would be appropriately addressed and that it was planning a professional workshop focused on board structure and selection, as well as some administrative training.[22] Eventually, these issues were worked out, and a twenty-one-member Native Board of Directors was selected from all regions of Canada.

However, strong and organized resistance to APTN came from some cable operators and from several existing broadcasters to whom the idea of a *mandatory* national channel seemed antidemocratic. There were some exceptions (Cancom and WETV, among others), but most cable operators would have preferred APTN to be licensed "on the same optional distribution basis as all other fee-based Canadian services."[23] Underlying their concern was the view that TVNC/APTN was a specialty service targeted to a particular audience. TVNC/APTN's perspective was that it was *not* a specialty service, but one with a special status, based on First Peoples being one of the three founding nations of Canada. That APTN would be carried on a mandatory basis as a parallel service to CBC or Radio-Canada raised the political/historical stakes in Canada's national debate about confederation.

Randy McKenzie and Robert Smith setting up a video shoot in the Yukon.
Photographer, Robin Armour. Used with permission of Northern Native
Broadcasting, Yukon.

The Canadian Cable Television Association (CCTA) took a position in favour of greater customer choice, complaining that the signal would be forced upon subscribers if they had to pay fifteen cents for an unrequested service. This argument was framed in terms of economic competition and choice and grew out of the assumption that APTN *should* be a *specialty, pay-TV service*. Beyond the monthly subscriber fee, the CCTA also protested the "one time costs associated with forcing a service on basic. These included expenses related to informing customers of the change in the line-up through channel line-up stickers and explanatory letters, and in order to receive the signal, additions to headend equipment."[24] Finally, it would be expensive to shift channel allocations and, in some cases, an existing channel could no longer be offered or would be bumped from one of the basic tiers to a more expensive package.

The cable industry's basic preoccupation was cost recovery for its investments. Most cable operators resisted the argument that First Peoples, only 3 percent of the population, should have either a special status or a mandatory national channel. The CCTA said that it "supported the concept of the network but not the insistence that it be offered as part of the basic cable service."[25]

On 22 February 1999, the CRTC approved TVNC's application and granted mandatory carriage on basic cable and satellite services throughout Canada with a fifteen-cent cost per subscriber per month in the South—to be used as a Program Production Fund for APTN. In the North, residents of the ninety-six communities would continue to receive the service free of charge.[26] To provide continuity of service to northerners, a separate northern feed was established in order to ensure "that special northern programming, including legislative coverage and special events will be broadcast in the North on an on-going basis."[27]

The time between the date on which the license was granted and the actual launch was a mere six months and a few days. This was highly unusual but necessary because APTN wanted to launch on the same day as several other specialty services. This meant that APTN expenses could be included within the one-time costs for publicity and head-end equipment incurred by the other service launches.[28]

APTN began broadcasting, as planned, on 1 September 1999. Until programming surpluses could be created, there were three programming cycles per day; that is, each day programs were repeated three times—once every six hours. There are still repetitions on APTN, though as time passes these are fewer and fewer. APTN currently broadcasts approximately 56 percent of its programming in English, 16 percent in French, and 28 percent in a variety of Aboriginal languages, including Inuktitut, Cree, Inuinnaqtun, Ojibway, Inuvialuktun, Mohawk, Dene, Gwich'in, Miq ma'aq, Slavey, Dogrib, Chipeweyan, Tlingit, and Mechif.[29]

Initial Impact of APTN

First Peoples' television did not go through the hearing/licensing process and launch without some controversy within the Canadian press. For a few days after APTN was licensed, and for about a week before and after it actually went on the air, APTN generated a fair amount of editorial comment, mainly about it being "the first in the world" and about the political context for the CRTC decision. A sense of the conflict in Canadian public opinion concerning APTN can be captured by comparing editorial perspectives published in several representative newspapers.

On the day after the CRTC decision, the *National Post* published a single article on the subject, titled "COMING SOON TO YOUR LIVING ROOM: The CRTC is forcing a new aboriginal TV channel—and its cost—on most Canadian cable viewers."[30] Despite its attempt to *look* objective, the overall impression was that the *Post* supported the cable operators.

On the other hand, the *Globe and Mail* noted in its 24 February editorial how important it is for non-Native audiences to have access to television produced by indigenous Peoples:

Television is so confusing. At the same time that it isn't reality, it is authenticity. Just to be seen on TV makes people genuine in a way that almost nothing else in 20th-century culture does.... Not only will the Aboriginal Peoples Television Network be a place for native Peoples to present themselves to one another in English, French and 15 native languages, but it will be an electronic arena in which many Canadians will encounter aboriginals in ways they might never do otherwise.... That's why we support the CRTC's decision to make this channel a part of the basic cable package. Not only will it provide a secure source of funding for the APTN's programs, but it will make the network something people will chance upon as they click their way along the TV dial.... Their relation to other Canadians isn't tangential; it is inevitable.[31]

The *Globe and Mail* editorial raises a very important issue, the (in)visibility and (in)audibility of an important national community in Canada. It is easy to pretend liberal tolerance when a subject/person/community is absent from our visible and conscious world. What remains unseen can be faded out of our social relations. Moreover, it is relatively easy to circulate a discourse of tolerance and "multiculturalism" in an era of political correctness. On a deeper level, it becomes harder to mask intolerance when an "unpopular" constituency group gains a notable presence in a highly visible and audible media form. At the very least, if audiences take time to focus on the programming, it might stimulate them to recognize First Peoples as integral citizens of Canada and the airwaves.

The launch of the Aboriginal Peoples Television Network service took place at 8:00 p.m. on 1 September 1999. The live broadcast wove together commentators, members of Native communication societies that had been involved in television production since at least 1983, entertainers, clips of key events in First Peoples' history, and landscape imagery. It was a celebration of the opening-up of mainstream Canada to the lives of First Peoples. Since the launch, APTN's regularly scheduled programming has become a centre of information and entertainment for First Peoples and for those interested in Native perspectives on the world.

Not surprisingly, at the time of APTN's launch not all Canadians were in the same celebratory mood. In an editorial titled "Consumers Should Decide What They Want to Watch," the Vancouver Province said, "The CRTC decision was another in a long line of loopy broadcast regulations that amounts to political correctness disguised as social engineering. We wish APTN the best of luck. But, while Ottawa can make consumers pay for the new channel, it can't make them watch it. It's a good job APTN won't have to rely on Vancouver ratings to pay its way."[32] Writing in the Winnipeg Free Press, arts commentator Morley Walker evaluated the way other newspapers had been covering APTN: "The tenor of commentary in the white man's press surrounding the fledgling aboriginal cable TV channel" is "skeptical, if not outright hostile." He adds his own perspective: "Fifteen cents a month today is a small price to pay as a cable subscriber to support a voice that is both indigenous to our country and vital to offering role models for a dispossessed minority. It seems to me that a first nations TV channel is an excellent addition to the Canadian television landscape."[33] Disappointed with those elements of the press that framed APTN as a project of social engineering and that kept pointing out that "CRTC documents show that only 300 Canadians asked the CRTC for the channel," Walker also raises the issue of APTN's remote location on the channel grid.[34] This is a subject that symbolizes the issue of First Peoples' social placement—slightly outside of the centre of things—in a most concrete way.

APTN: On the Margins of Mainstream Television

APTN is competing with an expensive technological and broadcasting infrastructure put in place in the 1950s that has been consistently updated as new and more sophisticated technologies have emerged. Although it benefits from these technologies, APTN's underfunding, difficulties in finding sponsors, and lack of national experience do have consequences in terms of its need for a transitional period in which to build human resource capacity, program surpluses, financial stability, and broad public support.

To watch the network, one has first to find it on the channel grid, and that is sometimes a challenge for APTN audiences. First Peoples have supported its development and have seen the value of television for the building of the Aboriginal community in Canada, but, relatively speaking, not many non-Native constituency groups are consistent viewers simply because they are not aware of its existence.

To make public-relations matters worse, a key technical issue that relegates APTN to the equivalent of a "media reservation" is its usual location in the high end of the analog channel grid on most cable and satellite systems across the country. These channels are often less visited by grazers, whose customary remote-unit hops tend to end at about Channel 50. Committed viewers will not care where it is located, but recruiting new audiences is a bigger challenge. If APTN is located so far from the centre of most popular analog television programming, how many potential new viewers will even have heard of its presence on the airwaves or will bother exploring the high end of the grid? APTN has been negotiating with the CRTC about lowering its placement across the country, but so far it remains in the remote range of upper-channel choices in most places. As digital services will become mandatory by 2011, it is likely that a more diverse mediascape will surmount this challenge.

APTN as a Public Medium in Canada

The case of APTN is a prototype for other states in which diverse constituency groups compete for service access in order to address and construct alignments across racial, social, economic, and territorial lines. Over the years, First Peoples have been granted political opportunities to build a nationwide mediaspace to heal the historical communication ruptures within their societies and between their communities and other Canadians. These community-building opportunities have been the result of First Peoples' persistence in overcoming challenges and demonstrating skills to develop and manage new broadcasting infrastructures. With the convergence of a strong political will on the part of the federal cabinet and the CRTC, amiable negotiations among all key parties, and the policy savvy that First Peoples have demonstrated publicly, APTN has evolved from an idea to a fully operational television network. It is secure in terms of its distribution infrastructure and funding. It generates revenue through advertising sales, affiliate revenues, and strategic partnerships. However, like most recent constituency-based services, it has definitely faced financial challenges and still needs to build human resource capacity, program surpluses, and broader cross-cultural audience support. Significantly, though, its existence is enshrined in national legislation. This regulatory support is a highly important and symbolic demonstration of Canada's collective will to include First Peoples' media/voices/ images as integral parts of its national broadcasting system. Furthermore, it represents a consolidation of new power relationships among Canadian media institutions, policy bodies, and audiences.

Through its broadcasting and its interactive website, APTN has enabled indigenous messages to be heard by groups that might otherwise never have had access to a live person of Aboriginal descent. It has provided an opportunity to share news, indigenous imageries, historical perspectives, and contextualized histories, as well as to build bridges of understanding, and to make cultural barriers more porous. Equally significant, however, is that APTN has *a national presence*: it is out there "in the air," is one of many services competing for audience attention, and is potentially a powerful performer on the electronic grid. As a consequence, it has had the effect of expanding and transforming the roles that were anticipated for public media since its early days.

This effect is important to recognize. APTN currently provides access to ten million Class 1 and 2 cable receivers, direct-to-home satellite (DTH) subscribers, as well as fixed wireless service and telco-delivered television subscribers. Many small cable operators have also opted to carry APTN. It attracts niche rather than mass audiences and reaches over 3.1 million non-Aboriginal viewers every week.[35] Web access increases its impact and, through live streaming, makes the service available worldwide. As a broadcasting service, APTN is still not free. To assure secure funding over the long term, the CRTC introduced a social cost to cable operators for carriage of APTN. Current subscriber costs of twenty-five cents per month are paid to cable operators, who then transfer the money to APTN to be used for television production in communities that cannot sustain media economies through advertising revenues.[36] As already noted, this may be an interesting model by which states can assure the sponsorship and sustenance of public service programming that might be otherwise unaffordable.

APTN is a hybrid between what have traditionally been defined as public and private broadcasting. It does not receive government funding for operations; it carries advertising, collects subscriber fees, and builds strategic business alliances.[37] Yet, it mainly addresses public issues and models itself after public-service television. It is multilingual, multicultural, and multiracial in content, production staff, and management. It attempts to be both local and global. It does very little original production on its own, with the exception of news and current affairs; it distributes locally and regionally produced cultural programming to a national audience of over 10 million potential viewers (more than 80 percent of all Canadian households). The fact that APTN is already integrating international programming and is considering expanding its service to become an international First Peoples' television network, comparable to CNN and the BBC World Service, clearly indicates that it shares the global objective of international constituency-group building across national borders.

The look of some of APTN's national programming closely resembles that of United States public-access television or Canadian community television. Its content quality is uneven, although its technical standard is consistently good. APTN still replays some programs simply because of budgetary constraints. Indigenous programming that originates in the North is now complemented by an expanded range of programs derived from southern Canada and international sources (30 percent of which come from Australia, New Zealand, Central and South America, and the United States). These include documentaries, dramas, comedy shows, variety shows, talk shows, a cooking show, and children's programming. In 2000, APTN introduced live news and current affairs programming that provide an Aboriginal lens through which to view (inter)national news and public affairs, as discussed in Hafsteinsson's chapter in this book. Its *Bingo and a Movie (BAAM)* program, which began in 2002, was very popular. Shown on Friday nights, it consisted of film segments broken up by bingo games, as well as interviews with guests who would have something interesting to say about the film (although the conversation was not limited to the film content). The program provided a uniquely Aboriginal perspective on the film while at the same time mobilizing indigenous communities' interest in electronic bingo (a popular means of raising funds for Native community radio across the country). Although it no longer carries *BAAM*, APTN currently runs five films per week and continues to search for novel and creative programming forms and methods of presentation.

Despite its complex and challenging program mandate to serve all Aboriginal and non-Aboriginal Canadian communities, North and South, the network has engaged with its constituency groups well in that it has northernized and indigenized Canadian programming. In 2005, APTN's television network license was renewed for another cycle of seven years by the CRTC. By this renewal, the CRTC has shown confidence that APTN has met its central programming and audience objectives and obligations from both its own and the CRTC's perspectives.

From my point of view, APTN has indeed delivered distinct imagery from coast to coast to coast with perspectives that express what it is like to "live the difference." I believe that in our age of the 500-channel universe and Web 2.0, APTN offers a symbolic mediated space for indigenous and non-Native peoples to mingle and to communicate their common interests. If APTN can widely stimulate reflections, deliberations, and conversations about First Peoples' cultures and issues, then it will have succeeded in providing a starting point for very necessary cross-cultural and international dialogues.

NOTES

1   This chapter was adapted and updated from Lorna Roth, "First Peoples' Television in Canada's North: A Case Study of the Aboriginal Peoples Television Network," in *Mediascapes: New Patterns in Canadian Communication,* ed. Paul Attallah and Leslie Shade (Toronto: Nelson Thomson Learning, 2005). Portions have been (re)published with the permission of Nelson Thomson Learning Publications. Research for this chapter draws upon personal interviews at APTN in 2004 with the following:

• Patrick Tourigny, former director, Regulatory Affairs and Industry Relations
• Jennifer David, former director of communications

- Abe Tagalik, former chairman of the Board of Directors
- Gerry Giberson, former operations manager
- Dan David, former news and current affairs director
- Rita Shelton-Deverill, former news and current affairs director

2   Canada, *Broadcasting Act* (Ottawa: Queen's Printer for Canada, 1991), S.3 [d][iii].

3   Lorna Roth, *Something New in the Air: The Story of First Peoples Television in Canada* (Montreal: McGill-Queens University Press, 2005); Lorna Roth, "Television Broadcasting North of 60," in *Images of Canadianness: Visions on Canada's Politics, Culture, Economics,* ed. Leen d'Haenens (Ottawa: University of Ottawa Press, 1998), 147–166.

4   Lorna Roth, *Something New;* Valerie Alia, *Un/Covering the North: News, Media, and Aboriginal Peoples* (Vancouver: University of British Columbia Press, 1999).

5   Canada, Parliament, Statement of the Government of Canada on Indian Policy Presented to the First Session of the Twenty-eighth Parliament by the Honourable Jean Chrétien, Minister of Indian Affairs and Northern Development (Ottawa: 1969).

6   Canada, Federal Government, "The Northern Broadcasting Policy," News Release, 10 March 1983.

7   Ibid.

8   Canadian Radio-television and Telecommunications Commission, *Decision CRTC 91-826* (Ottawa: CRTC, 28 October 1991).

9   TVNC's network members consisted of the Inuit Broadcasting Corporation (Ottawa, Iqaluit); the Inuvialuit Communications Society (Inuvik); Northern Native Broadcasting, Yukon (Whitehorse); the OkalaKatiget Society (Labrador); Taqramiut Nipingat Incorporated (Northern Quebec); the Native Communications Society of the Western Northwest Territories (Yellowknife); the Government of the Northwest Territories; Yukon College; and the National Aboriginal Communications Society. Associate Members included CBC Northern Service; Kativik School Board (Quebec); Labrador Community College; Northern Native Broadcasting (Terrace); Telesat Canada; and Wawatay Native Communications Society (Sioux Lookout).

10   Television Northern Canada. *Response to CRTC Public Notice 1992–13* (Ottawa: TVNC, 10 March 1993), 4.

11   Donald R. Browne, *Electronic Media and Indigenous Peoples: A Voice of Our Own?* (Ames: Iowa State University Press, 1996), 38.

12   For further information on the history of the Australian Aboriginal broadcasting situation, see Michael Meadows, "Indigenous Media Responses to Racism" (paper delivered to Post Colonial Formations Conference, Griffith University, Nathan, Australia, July 1993); Michael Meadows, "Voice Blo Mipla All Ilan Man: Torres Strait Islanders' Struggle for Television Access," in *Public Voices, Private Interests: Australia's Media,* ed. J. Craik, J. James Bailey, and A. Moran (Sydney: Allen and Unwin, 1993); Faye D. Ginsburg, "Indigenous Media: Faustian Contract or Global Village," *Cultural Anthropology* 6, 1 (1991): 92–112; Faye D. Ginsberg, "Aboriginal Media and the Australian Imaginary," *Public Culture* 5 (1993): 20. For more current information on CAAMA, see their website at www.caama.com.au/.

13   Television Northern Canada, *Response to CRTC Public Notice 1992–13* (Ottawa: TVNC, 10 March 1993), 4.

14   Quoted in Television Northern Canada, *North Link* [TVNC Newsletter], March 1999, 1.

15   Aboriginal Peoples Television Network, *APTN Milestones*, 2003, http://www.aptn.ca/corporate/milestones.php (accessed 1 June 2004).

16   Ibid.

17   Aboriginal Peoples Television Network, *APTN Fact Sheet*, http://www.aptn.ca/corporate/facts.php (accessed 3 August 2007).

18   Ibid.

19   Ibid.

20   Ibid.

21   Northern Native Broadcasting, Yukon, *An Intervention of Conditional Support of Application 199804068 to the CRTC* (Whitehorse, YK: NNBY, 19 October 1998), 5–6.

22   Television Northern Canada, *Replies to Interventions Submitted with Respect to an Application by TVNC Inc. for a National Aboriginal Television Network Application #199804068* (Ottawa: TVNC, 30 October 1998), 11.

23   Canadian Broadcasting Corporation, "Intervention Letter to CRTC," Ottawa: CBC, 19 October 1998.

24   Canadian Cable Television Association, "Intervention Letter to CRTC," Ottawa: CCTA, 12 November 1998, 3.

25   Chris Cobb, "Aboriginal TV Goes Canada-wide," *Gazette*, 23 February 1999, F5; "Consumers Should Decide What They Want to Watch," *Vancouver Province*, 2 September 1999, A36.

26   Television Northern Canada, *North Link* [TVNC Newsletter], March 1999, 1.

27   Ibid., 1.

28   Personal Interviews.

29   Aboriginal Peoples Television Network, *APTN Fact Sheet*.

30   Luiza Chwialkowska, "Coming Soon to Your Living Room," *National Post*, 23 February 1999, A3.

31   "The Native Media," *Globe and Mail*, 24 February 1999, A16.

32   "Consumers Should Decide What They Want to Watch," *Vancouver Province*.

33   Morley Walker, "Aboriginal TV Deserves Better Spot on Dial," *Winnipeg Free Press*, 4 September 1999, B7.

34   Ibid, B7.

35   Aboriginal Peoples Television Network, *APTN Fact Sheet*.

36   Fees for reception of APTN increased from ten to twenty-five cents monthly as part of its seven-year license renewal issued by the CRTC on 1 September 2005. As part of the social benefits package offered in exchange for taking over CTV, a national private network, Bell Canada Enterprises has agreed to give $3 million to APTN to establish several news offices across the country. These bureaus are currently located in Yellowknife, Montreal, Vancouver, Edmonton, Winnipeg, and Iqaluit.

37   Aboriginal Peoples Television Network, *APTN Fact Sheet*.

CHAPTER 2

Clear Signals: Learning and Maintaining Aboriginal Languages through Television[1]

JENNIFER DAVID

Television has played a seminal role in shaping and creating attitudes since it was first introduced in Canada in the early 1950s. Just as families used to gather around oversized radios set up in living rooms, so too Canadian families would gather around the television to watch American shows like the *Ed Sullivan Show* or early CBC broadcasts. Broadcasting became a unifying force, bringing together people across a vast nation, in a way that was similar to what the Canadian Pacific Railway had done several generations before. Although some Canadians purchased TV sets in the late 1940s to tune in to American stations, when the CBC began broadcasting Canadian programming in 1952, Canadians were quick to embrace the new technology. By 1954, more than a million TV sets had been sold. At first, it was a novelty, a kind of "radio with pictures," but TV soon became so popular that people realized its tremendous potential for information dissemination as well as for shaping and changing attitudes and viewpoints. Early on, it was obvious that television had the potential to be highly addictive. Since then, countless articles and reports have been written about the role television plays in such things as a predilection for violent behaviour, shortened attention spans, increased consumer spending, and altered perceptions of reality. Aboriginal people across Canada have not been immune to the effects of television, but the extent of these effects continues to have a devastating impact on the health and well-being of Aboriginal communities, particularly those still holding on to traditional ways and languages.

Aboriginal Languages in Canada

The precise number of Aboriginal languages in Canada depends on whose definition of "language" is used. Most authorities agree that there are between 53 and 70 Aboriginal languages in Canada. At a conference on Aboriginal languages in 2006, Phil Fontaine, Grand Chief of the Assembly of First Nations, was quoted as saying there are "55 indigenous languages spoken in Canada. Fifty-three are in various stages of disappearing."[2] In the 1996 census, just over 25 percent of the Aboriginal population reported that their mother tongue was an Aboriginal language. Respondents included Inuit, First Nation (on and off reserve), and Métis. However, only 15 percent of the entire Aboriginal population reported that they actually spoke an Aboriginal language at home.[3] In the more recent Aboriginal Peoples Survey (APS), 32 percent of respondents (off reserve) said they could speak or understand an Aboriginal language. Fifty-nine percent of non-reserve Aboriginal adults stated that keeping, learning, or relearning an Aboriginal language was very or somewhat important. There was broad agreement that language is a vital component of cultural survival.

Both the 1996 census and the 2001 APS suggest a measure of revitalization is occurring within some Aboriginal languages. While 12 percent of 2001 APS respondents said they had an Aboriginal mother tongue, 15 percent said they could converse in an Aboriginal language. This suggests that a number of individuals may be learning to speak an Aboriginal language later in life, despite not having spoken it at home. The likelihood of a language's survival is a function of the number of its speakers. Cree, Ojibway, and Inuktitut are the three strongest Aboriginal languages in Canada, and they are spoken fluently by the greatest number of individuals. Many other languages are in a critical state.

The Royal Commission on Aboriginal Peoples report noted that more than 92 percent of the Aboriginal people surveyed in 1991 with an Aboriginal language as their mother tongue came from the three strongest language groups.[4] The small remaining percentage of speakers is divided among more than a dozen other languages, many of which are endangered or threatened. The strongest enclaves of Aboriginal language speakers are in the North, which includes the northernmost parts of Quebec, Labrador, and the three territories, particularly Nunavut, as well as on reserves in both northern and southern parts of Canada. As statistics show more Aboriginal people, particularly youth, leaving reserves, this trend is not encouraging.[5] Many factors are contributing to the decline in Aboriginal languages: the proliferation of mainstream (mainly English-language) media, increased urbanization and often isolation from other language speakers, extensive and mostly exclusive use of English-language (or French-language) curricula in schools, difficulty for traditional languages to adopt and create new ideas and modern concepts, and the accelerating loss of Elders who speak the languages and who could have passed on language skills to a younger generation.

Aboriginal People and the Media

If you write a nation's stories, you needn't worry about who makes its

laws. Today, television tells most of the stories to most of the people,

most of the time.

—George Gerbner,
Montreal Gazette, 1990[6]

In his book *Understanding Media*, Marshall McLuhan outlines his famous assertion that "the medium is the message," a concept that is relevant to the discussion of Aboriginal language broadcasting. He says, "any medium has the power of imposing its own assumption on the unwary."[7] The medium of television has imposed a number of assumptions on its viewers, and many of these assumptions conflict with Aboriginal culture and language. A look at the penetration of television sets the stage. Nearly every household in Canada (98.8 percent) owns at least one television, 65.3 per cent have cable television and 23.7 per cent have satellite TV.[8] The amount of television that Canadians watch has remained fairly consistent for the past ten years, fluctuating between twenty and twenty-five hours per week.[9] Francophones in Quebec watch the most television, while residents of Alberta watch the least. Extensive research has confirmed the influence of the media in all areas of life, including children and advertising, media violence, hate crimes and the Internet, and media stereotyping. Many studies have shown that the media is a central factor in the formation of culture, identity, and community.[10]

Given the fragility of Aboriginal language, the effect of media on Aboriginal people is of critical concern. Most research suggests that, for Aboriginal people, mainstream media have been a major agent in the loss of culture, identity, and community. As Gail Valaskakis points out in her report to the Royal Commission on Aboriginal Peoples, "for Aboriginal Canadians, the experience forged through media is too often one of exclusion, stereotypical

Florent Vollant (from Kashtin, right) with unknown performer in studio. Used with permission of Mushkeg Media.

inclusion or appropriation."[11] Stereotypes of the alcoholic on welfare, the wise Elder, the squaw, the princess, the noble savage, and the warrior are just a few of the images that the media perpetuate through advertising, typecasting, and exclusion of contemporary portrayals of Aboriginal people. Aside from the CTV television hit *Corner Gas*, in which Lorne Cardinal plays a police officer, there are very few programs in which Aboriginal people are not cast in stereotypical roles. This continues despite decades of recommendations and policy statements from the CRTC, the federal government, and other agencies who point out the dangers inherent in dishonest and inappropriate characterization of Aboriginal people.

Appropriation is also a common issue for Aboriginal people in the media. Well-intentioned non-Aboriginal people are often asked to comment upon or categorize Aboriginal people or situations, leaving Aboriginal people without a voice and creating a void in the media. Aboriginal people are being seen and discussed, but not consulted or asked to contribute in a significant way. Finally, Aboriginal artists—performers, writers, producers, directors—are often excluded from mainstream television altogether, and have had to find access to media through Aboriginal-specific venues such as the Aboriginal Peoples Television Network (APTN). Much-touted programs such as *North of 60* and *The Rez*, while employing Aboriginal people and telling Aboriginal stories, are still a product of a mainstream network, subject to higher-management decisions and editorial control based on audience preferences and network policies. Decisions are made without consultation with Aboriginal people; mainstream television thus provides no consistent window on Aboriginal reality.

All these considerations have had serious consequences for Aboriginal people, and particularly for youth. A recent article by the Media Awareness

Network stated, "Anyone who understands or studies the social development of children and young people knows that attitudes, values and self-esteem are well developed by the mid-teen years, or even earlier. What young people see and hear in the media helps them to figure out how the world works and who and what is valued in our society."[12]

Mainstream images and coverage have a clear impact on how Canadians see Aboriginal people. In 2003, the Centre for Research and Information on Canada released its annual survey. One of the most surprising statistics showed that 51 percent of Canadians surveyed thought that Aboriginal people had a standard of living equal to or better than the average Canadian. In light of reports from the Auditor General and Statistics Canada about shortages of adequate housing, lack of access to safe drinking water, and health and education inadequacies, particularly on reserve and in remote and northern regions, this finding is disturbing. In this same survey, 57 percent of Canadians said that poverty should be blamed on circumstances beyond a poor person's control. That number drops to 48 percent in the case of a poor Aboriginal person.[13] The influence of media in shaping opinions and defining community identity cannot be overstated. This is why it is imperative, not only that Aboriginal people gain greater access to the mainstream media, but also that Aboriginal people control the media that they and their children are exposed to.

Aboriginal Broadcasting and Aboriginal Languages

From the early 1970s to the early 1980s, serious and substantial initiatives were put in place to provide Aboriginal people with the opportunity to develop their own radio and television networks. These were intended, in part, to counterbalance the sudden and overwhelming influx of foreign, English-language, culturally irrelevant programming flooding previously isolated northern, rural, and remote Aboriginal communities. The most pertinent elements of this history are surveyed in Lorna Roth's chapter in this book.

Despite four decades of Aboriginal media development, there has been no statistical or quantitative research done on the impact of television and radio on the preservation and revitalization of Aboriginal languages in Canada. At the same time, the influence of broadcasting is not easily separated from other influences. In surveys and interviews with Aboriginal radio and TV producers done in 2003, most respondents assert with some confidence that their programming has a positive impact on language use; this is one of their core values and reasons for existence. Yet very little objective, quantifiable information about this impact exists. One very interesting audience survey, completed for APTN in 2006, shows a dichotomy between respondents with an idealized view of the importance of language broadcasting and the number of respondents who were actually watching the programming.[14] Audience surveys are one way to establish the connection between broadcasting and language use. Surveys carried out by groups funded under the Northern Native Broadcast Access Program (NNBAP) in the 1980s included questions about acquisition of vocabulary, quality of on-air language, and the effect of these media on languages spoken at home. Findings all suggested that language programming is important, and that it does have a positive influence on the retention of language. However, no funding has been available to verify this through audience research conducted among NNBAP groups for more than a decade.

The APTN Audience Survey, completed in 2006 and focused on the North, includes some statistics on Aboriginal language programming. Language programming is on the list of the top ten types of programming that people watch, but it is at the bottom of that list, with only 8 percent watching daily and 62 percent never or rarely watching. For those who rarely or never watch, 78 percent are non-Aboriginal and 49 percent are Aboriginal. The highest percentage of people who watch Aboriginal language programming are those in Nunavik and Nunavut; Inuit are overall more likely to watch language programming than other Aboriginal groups.[15] In a report for the federal government's Task Force on Aboriginal Languages, I undertook limited research into the state of Aboriginal language broadcasting. This consisted of a survey of the following media outlets: NNBAP-funded radio and television production, local community radio stations (predominantly in southern Canada), and independent film and video producers who create language material for APTN. This does not encompass the entire spectrum of "Aboriginal language" broadcasting. More comprehensive research can and should be done in this area, taking into consideration northern community radio stations, CBC radio (particularly CBC North), Aboriginal language programming on mainstream radio, and television programming originally produced in other languages and dubbed in an Aboriginal language.

There is a great discrepancy between radio broadcasters who receive funding through the NNBAP program, located above the Hamelin line, and those who receive no core government funding, based mostly in southern Canada. It must be noted that these two separate groups of radio broadcasters have different needs and objectives, and also play different roles in the retention and revitalization of Aboriginal languages. Tables 1 and 2 summarize my findings, distinguishing between those northern groups who receive federal funding and those groups who do not.

Table 1: Aboriginal Language Programming by Broadcasters Funded by NNBAP

Organization	Region/number of communities served *	Total hours per week	Aboriginal language programs	Change in language programming since 1999
CFWE radio (Aboriginal Multimedia Society of Alberta)	Lethbridge and 55 communities in central and northern Alberta	Radio: 168 hours	15 percent	Fewer hours of Chipewyan programming: few speakers. Policy to add more languages but lack of funding
Inuit Broadcasting Corporation	Nunavut, 26 communities	TV: 3.5 hours, plus special programs, ICSL	100 percent	Down from 5.5 hours. Some shows down from 1 hour to 1/2 hour
Missinipi Broadcasting Corporation	Saskatchewan, 50+ northern communities, plus major southern cities	Radio: 112 hours / TV: 1 hour	Radio: 20 percent / TV: 90 percent	More language on radio: from 1 hour Cree, 1 hour Dene to 2 hours Cree (and Michif), 2 hours Dene
Inuvialuit Communications Society	Inuvialuit Settlement region in western NWT, 6 communities	TV: 1 hour	50 percent	Same hours, one 1 hour show became two 1/2 hour shows.
James Bay Cree Communications Society	Cree of eastern James Bay, 9 communities	Radio: 20 hours	80 percent	Same hours, programs aimed at hunters/trappers now aimed at community audience
Native Communications Inc.	Manitoba, 49 transmitters reach 96 percent of province	Radio: 159 hours / TV: 6.5 hours	Radio: 30 percent / TV: 30 percent	Mostly the same, lost some shows, gained others—lack of youth speakers
Northern Native Broadcasting, Yukon	All Yukon communities	Radio: 168 hours / TV: 1.5 hours	Radio: 20 percent / TV: 50 percent	Same programs and hours but policy level needs to increase
OkalaKatiget Society	Northern Labrador, 7 communities	Radio: 21 hours / TV: 1 hour	Radio: 30 percent / TV: 50 percent	No change in TV, more time on radio for Inuktitut-only program
Société de communication Atikamekw-Montagnais	5 regions in Quebec and southern Labrador, 12 communities	Radio: 25 hours	95 percent	Down from 27 to 25 hours. Increased use of news reviews in French. Reduced staff, smaller office space.
Taqramiut Nipingat Inc.	Nunavik, 15 communities	Radio: 15 hours / TV: ½ hour	Radio: 100 percent / TV: 100 percent	Radio increased from 10 to 15 hours per week. TV reduced from 26 to 13 episodes per season
Wawatay Native Communications Society	Northwestern Ontario, 39 communities	Radio: 40 hours / TV: 1 hour	Radio: 90 percent / TV: 20 percent	Radio: same shows but increased use of language TV: decrease from 100 percent language to 20 percent.

* *Organizations working in television have national distribution of programming through* APTN.

Community radio stations are small, independent, and isolated local operations across Canada. There is no association for Aboriginal community radio, virtually no support, scant acknowledgement of their work, and little opportunity for stations to network and learn from one another. Each station develops its own mandate and programming priorities. Many struggle to continue broadcasting and are sometimes kept on the air through the dedication of a small number of people, often volunteers. While the NNBAP-funded groups are sometimes given the opportunity to meet at a program-sponsored, government-funded event, there are no comparable opportunities for smaller, community-based Aboriginal radio stations to meet and network. Most community Aboriginal radio stations, however, see the value and potential of radio, and have developed policies that enable their station to play a role in language revitalization. A large number of them were set up specifically to enhance and revive languages, as Charles Fairchild points out in his article about CRKZ and other southern stations: "The emergence of a growing number of community radio stations on reserves throughout Southern Ontario and Quebec has been in large part a reaction to the erosion of Aboriginal languages and cultures all across Southern Canada which has accelerated dramatically over the last two decades."[16]

Table 2: Aboriginal Language Programming on Non-NNBAP Community Radio

Organization	Region/number of communities served *	Total hours per week	Aboriginal language programming	Change in language programming since 1999
CKRZ, Six Nations	Six Nations and outlying area for 80 km, southern Ontario	Radio: 24 hours/ day with repeats and music	10 percent	Increased number of shows in Mohawk and Cayuga. More acceptance.
CHFN, Cape Croker	Cape Croker and surrounding towns, 500 on reserve, central Ontario	Radio: 80 hours	5 percent. One show every day that teaches Ojibway	Decrease from two shows to one show. No volunteer to coordinate the show.
CKON, Akwasasne	Reserve straddles U.S., Ontario, and Quebec	Radio: 150 hours	10 percent. 10 minute "Word of the Day," 6 hour block in language	Increase. Added the "Word of the Day" program, very popular.
Muskwachees Radio, "The Hawk"	Hobbema, Alberta (4 communities)	Radio: 105 hours	Varies: approx. 40 percent. "Word of the Day," weather, talk between music	Concerted effort by DJs to speak more Cree on air. Language classes offered to DJs. Goal to make station 100 percent spoken Cree.
Kispiox Radio, CFNCR	Gitskan Nation, community of 700	Radio: 25 hours	0 percent	New station has translated stories and conversations and needs to record them for radio

*   *Organizations working in television have national distribution of programming through APTN.*

Television

Since the launch of APTN in 1999, Aboriginal film and television producers have had access to the network as a means of distribution for their productions and have been able to showcase work that other networks were unwilling or unable to broadcast. This opportunity has been particularly important for producers of Aboriginal language programming. Northern producers and communications societies had been broadcasting their programs on Television Northern Canada since 1992: APTN has now taken over that role. APTN is committed to broadcasting 25 percent of its programming in a variety of Aboriginal languages. This has enabled many producers to work in a language other than English or French, and to reach target audiences who may have had very little access to language programming.

In a recent audience survey, APTN discovered that its viewers are decidedly split on the issue of language programming. Some felt it was important for communities to see and hear programming in their own language, but many others had no patience for languages they did not understand. It seems many viewers welcome Aboriginal language programming, but only if it is in their own language.[17] Advertising is a major factor in scheduling Aboriginal language programming. Unless programs are dubbed, captioned, or subtitled, advertisers are not interested in placing ads within these programs; they realize the market for unilingual programs is very small. APTN would also like to see more original-language programming genres. Currently, the majority of Aboriginal language shows are documentary or news shows. It is difficult to find language speakers who can work in other genres, such as drama or comedy. These formats are very expensive, and there are very few funding sources available to produce such shows. APTN discovered this in 2010 when it broadcast ten hours per day for two weeks of Olympic coverage in English, French, and eight Aboriginal languages. The network had to find, then train, individuals who were fluent language speakers and who also had a background in broadcasting, never mind an understanding of sports terminology and commentating. It was a very complex undertaking.

In order to expand the reach of its Aboriginal language programming, APTN is developing various partnerships and vigorously promoting the use of broadcasting as a language-learning tool. The network has partnered with ExpressVu and Telesat to provide broadcasting services to SchoolNet, a Canadian educational website that encourages educators to use Internet technology to support learning. In Ontario and Quebec, every school with technology from ExpressVu and Telesat was given satellite dishes and decoders to receive APTN free of charge. These schools are able to tape, listen to, or watch any show on APTN for use in the classroom. APTN intends to partner

Paul Rickard and Paul Chaput taping interview. Used with permission of Mushkeg Media.

with other schools and is considering additional initiatives to make the network more widely available in the classroom. APTN is also considering partnerships with other broadcasters. An agreement with OMNI 1, an ethnic channel, sees OMNI providing APTN with production funding to create new programs in Aboriginal languages that can then be translated into languages other than English or French. This allows Canada's immigrant communities to hear Aboriginal stories and programs in their own languages.

Independent Aboriginal producers have raised a number of their own issues regarding language programming, particularly the need for more language programming funding. The Aboriginal language envelope in the Canadian Television Fund is inadequate to the demands placed on it. Producers also acknowledge the added cost of producing in various languages. Paul Rickard, a Cree producer, developed *Finding My Talk*, a series that profiled various Aboriginal language initiatives across Canada. Versions of the series were done in English, French, Cree, and Mohawk. It was most difficult to produce the Mohawk language version due to the limited number of speakers and difficulty in translating the concepts, as well as matching the text with the corresponding video. Producers want to provide their programming in various languages, Aboriginal audiences are eager for such programs, and APTN has its CRTC commitment to meet, but there is simply not enough financial assistance for the production of multiple language versions, and no compensation available to producers who cover the costs themselves.

Impact of Aboriginal Language Broadcasting on Language Use, Acquisition, Retention, and Quality

As noted previously, there have been no studies to determine the quantitative link between Aboriginal language broadcasting and the use, acquisition, retention, and quality of Aboriginal language among its audiences. There are a number of strong and valid indications, however, that broadcasting is having a vital and positive impact. The Aboriginal Peoples Survey reported in 2001 that the more sources an Aboriginal child could rely on for help in learning an Aboriginal language, the more likely the child was to achieve fluency in understanding and speaking the language. This assistance could come from parents, grandparents, other relatives, teachers, friends, Elders, the community in general, or the media. For example, only 15 percent of Aboriginal children living in non-reserve areas who could count on a single source of assistance for learning an Aboriginal language were able to speak and understand the language very well or relatively well. On the other hand, 38 percent of children who could rely on three sources of assistance to help them learn an Aboriginal language were able to better speak and understand the language.[18] Broadcasting is one of these "sources of assistance" that can strengthen language acquisition and retention.

In an audience survey conducted in 2004 by Taqramiut Nipingat Incorporated (TNI), 71 percent of the respondents reported learning new Inuttitut words from listening to TNI radio, and 72 percent learned new words from television. A large majority of respondents wish to see more programs on Inuit culture and to hear traditional stories told in Inuttitut. A large majority of the respondents also requested additional programming on Inuit culture. Inuit in Nunavik are very supportive of TNI's programs; 83 percent of respondents were familiar with TNI's radio programs and 73 percent were familiar with TNI's television programming.

Missinipi Broadcasting Corporation (MBC) also conducted an audience survey in 2004, and reported a slight decline in Cree language speakers but an increase in "other" language speakers, which includes Michif and Saulteaux, both languages in which MBC began to offer more programming. While respondents said the quality of the programming and of the announcing had declined slightly since the previous survey, in 1998, respondents said the quality of the Aboriginal language on the radio had improved. Some causes for concern, however, are that more people wanted to hear less Aboriginal language on the radio, or even none at all. There is a significant decrease in the amount people would like to watch or hear, with many people only wanting less than an hour per day. There was also a decrease in the percentage of people who think that MBC "helps preserve language and culture."

Periodic evaluations of government programs shed some light on the impact of Aboriginal language broadcasting. In a recent evaluation of the NNBAP, it was pointed out that the NNBAP members were very successful in meeting the objectives of the federal government with regards to Canadian content, cultural participation, and strengthened connections between Canadians. The study confirmed that the programming provided by the NNBAP members is valuable not only to their regional stakeholders, but also to Canada as a whole. The evaluation also described the impact that NNDAP programming has had on viewers. These include:

- Increase in children's programming to teach language
- Creation of public forum programs to engage people in civic opportunities
- Recording of Elders and ability to preserve language and cultural knowledge
- Role of APTN in providing a vehicle to produce language programming

The long-term influences of NNBAP have led to more opportunities for language speakers to work in the field of broadcasting, have opened up opportunities for youth, and have encouraged them to maintain their language.

The Aboriginal Languages Initiative (ALI) at the Department of Canadian Heritage also completed an evaluation in 2004. A case study included in that evaluation described a specific project related to Aboriginal broadcasting, showcasing the impact that broadcasting can have on language retention and highlighting the importance of finding new and innovative ways to use broadcasting in language retention. In 2001, for example, The Labrador Inuit Association initiated a program called a "Language Nest." This Language Nest was reviewed as part of the ALI evaluation and is described as an opportunity "to promote, advance and conserve the Inutktitut language through an Infant Care Program that offers intellectual, emotional, social and cultural development offered unilingually in Inuktitut."[19] The program is open to infants between three months and two years. Inuktitut speakers care for the babies and speak only Inuktitut to them. They participate in a wide range of activities and programs, all presented in Inuktitut. One activity involves watching the Inuit Broadcasting Corporation's program Takuginai, which is an award-winning children's program produced in Inuktitut. This program is presented on videotape to the infants. It plays in the background during the day and the infants are encouraged to watch and learn. Participants, parents, and the community have responded enthusiastically to the Language Nest: the program has a long waiting list, more families in the community are making a concerted effort to speak to their children in Inuktitut, and valuable employment opportunities for childcare workers to speak their language have been created. The program was extremely successful because it linked various ways of learning in order to enhance language retention in the infants.

The Royal Commission on Aboriginal Peoples was the most in-depth and comprehensive government review of Canadian Aboriginal perspectives to date. Both the submissions to the Commission and the Commission's final report included several key statements on the impact of Aboriginal language programming, such as this statement on television's potential influence:

> Over 90 per cent of the homes in the northern communities have a television set. As a Native journalist, I know this can definitely be one way to maintain a strong sense of Aboriginal identity in our changing environment.
>
> *—Shirley Cook,*
> *Native Communications*
> *Society of the Western Arctic,*
> *Yellowknife[20]*

In discussing the history and influence of Aboriginal broadcasting, the report has this to say:

> Biennial audience surveys indicate that Aboriginal language programming is vitally important, especially for older people who often speak neither English nor French. As a result, the percentage of respondents who watch or listen to Aboriginal programming when it is available is very high.... The surveys also suggest that Aboriginal audiences have acquired new knowledge and skills related to their languages, traditions and contemporary environment through Aboriginal media. There is strong interest in extending Aboriginal-language programming and in providing programs for youth, who make up the majority of the population in most communities. By increasing the presence and legitimacy of Aboriginal languages, broadcasting reinforces the interest and language competence of younger Aboriginal community members and helps slow the growing linguistic and generation gap between them and older unilingual members.[21]

While empirical data on the effect of language broadcasting on the retention of Aboriginal languages is limited, there is ample anecdotal evidence that broadcasting plays a significant role in the preservation of Aboriginal languages. In a predominantly oral culture, anecdotal evidence is viewed as a valid and valuable source of data. In the absence of in-depth academic studies, the statements of viewers and community members become increasingly important. After three decades of phone-in programs, audience surveys, government-program evaluations, and community consultations on various issues, it is clear that Aboriginal viewers and broadcasters alike link access to Aboriginal language media services with retention and promotion of language, as the statements included here illustrate:

> It's nice to hear somebody talking in Inuvialuktun. It's your own language. You feel so much more. There are no translations for the feelings, emotions. There are words, things that you can't translate. It's nice to hear that.
>
> —*Mary Teddy*[22]

> I know a lot of people have been trying to get into the language because they are enjoying the programs so much that they want to be able to understand them. They get so interested that they try harder to learn the language, at least to understand it.
>
> —*Ann Kasook*[23]

> As the saying goes, "the children are our future leaders." Without them perpetuating the language and culture, it is obvious that it will pass into anonymity. The OkalaKatiget Society is helping to prevent this. Their productions and publications are a great asset to us educators. [They] are used in many of our courses throughout the various grades.
>
> —*Wilson Belbin, Principal,*
> *Jens Haven Memorial School,*
> *Nain, Labrador.*[24]

> Aside from the Cree school board, the [James Bay Cree Communications Society] is one of the only major players in helping to preserve the language. It's heard every day in people's households. Elders have told us that it is really important and they are very grateful to hear Cree on the radio. The leadership in our communities realize they need fluency in Cree because we are there putting microphones in their faces and asking them to respond in Cree ... of all the things, we've taken from the non-native society, the best has been radio ... it's a great tool to help us preserve our language.
>
> —*Luke MacLeod, James Bay*
> *Cree Communications*
> *Society*[25]

People are more aware, especially the kids, about their language. We emphasize its importance. People are using SOCAM as a platform where they can express themselves in their own languages; they are more comfortable and willing to talk. We are complimentary to learning the language at home ... by broadcasting every day, people tune in and SOCAM plays an active role in informing people about what's happening.

—Bernard Hervieux,
general manager, Societé
Communications Atikamek-
Montagnais[26]

Language broadcasting has been "music to the ears" of those who understand it. It helps people reawaken to their language and culture and the two are intrinsic ... seeing and hearing the language on TV and radio, you feel connected to the language ... it has also provided consistency—a place where you can always hear the language, even if there is nowhere else, they can always tune into radio and TV programming to help re-learn the language.

—Nap Gardiner[27]

Television has to be harnessed as a tool to help preserve the language, culture and identity of Inuit....The desire to keep Inuktitut healthy has found a fitting medium in film as a way to preserve, and expose, Inuit culture to Inuit and the outside world.

—Zebedee Nungak,
Commentator, CBC North,
#168: InuiTV

These comments are all from northern Aboriginal people involved in broadcasting. The experience of southern Aboriginal language broadcasters, in the absence of government support, has been very different:

[W]hen the government drew that invisible line across the country and said that these communities north of this line need communication societies to preserve their languages, to preserve their songs, they gave them money for satellite networks, radio, printers for the newspapers and in the south we didn't get that. So when we started our radio station at Six Nations, we used that against the CRTC and told them that it was a form of genocide because they didn't give us the opportunity in the south to access those kinds of money so we could preserve our languages as well.

—Elaine Bomberry [28]

Paul Rickard filming rock painting. Used with permission of Mushkeg Media.

Because there is very little empirical data to support the widely shared perception that there is a clear link between Aboriginal language broadcasting and language retention, this relationship requires further study. Media, and broadcasting in particular, are powerful tools in the creation and maintenance of culture, values, and language. Television and radio are the most pervasive and invasive form of media, and they have been used to indoctrinate, enlighten, and educate viewers and listeners for more than half a century. As Valaskakis points out, "The stories we tell in written and visual narratives have long been recognized as a window on who we are, what we experience and how we understand and enact ourselves and others."[29] But media in general, and broadcasting specifically, have also been used by Aboriginal people to maintain and strengthen their languages and cultures. Unfortunately, this has not been adequately documented or acknowledged.

Broadcasting and other forms of communication, including the Internet, podcasts, and broadband technology, for example, must be considered more seriously in any discussion about the revitalization of Aboriginal languages, along with home, school, and community initiatives. As statistics show, the more influences that an Aboriginal person has, the more likely he or she is to succeed in learning and retaining Aboriginal language. Broadcasting should be one of the key pillars in language learning. The decline of so many indigenous languages in Canada makes this not only a viable option but also a vital tool in the struggle to maintain and sustain Aboriginal languages.

NOTES

1   Much of the research in this essay was originally compiled and submitted to the Aboriginal Peoples Television Network as part of a study for the Task Force on Aboriginal Language and Culture in 2003. It is adapted and presented here with permission from APTN.

2   Canadian Broadcasting Corporation, "Saving Native Languages up to First Nations: Chief," 14 November 2006, http://www.cbc.ca/canada/manitoba/story/2006/11/14/language-conference.html (accessed 24 November 2006).

3   Canada, Statistics Canada, *The Daily*, 13 January 1998, 1.

4   Canada, Indian and Northern Affairs, *Report of the Royal Commission on Aboriginal Peoples, Volume 3: Gathering Strength*, (Ottawa: Indian and Northern Affairs Canada, 1996), 604.

5   Consilium, *Evaluation of the Urban Multipurpose Aboriginal Youth Centres* (Ottawa: Consilium Consulting Group, 2004), 12.

6   Gail Valaskakis, "The Role, Development and Future of Aboriginal Communications," Research Report for the Royal Commission on Aboriginal Peoples (Ottawa, Government of Canada, 1995).

7   Marshall McLuhan, *Understanding Media* (Toronto: McGraw-Hill, 1964).

8   Canada, Statistics Canada, *Selected Dwelling Characteristics and Household Equipment*, 2008. Canada, Statistics Canada, *The Daily*, 18 December, 2009, 7.

9   Canada, Statistics Canada, *The Daily*, 21 November 2003, 3.

10   See Carlos E. Cortes, *The Children are Watching: How the Media Teaches About Diversity* (New York: Teachers College Press, 2000), as well as numerous articles and resources on media awareness websites including http://www.media-awareness.ca, in Canada, http://www.medialit.org, and http://www.mediaed.org, to name a few.

11   Valaskakis, "The Role, Development and Future of Aboriginal Communications."

12   Media Awareness Network, "The Impact of Stereotyping on Young People," http://www.media-awareness.ca/english/issues/stereotyping/aboriginal_people/aboriginal_impact.cfm (accessed 26 November 2003).

13   Centre for Research and Information on Canada, "Canadians Want Strong Aboriginal Cultures But Are Divided on Aboriginal Rights," press release, 26 November 2003.

14   Environics Research Group, *North of 60° and Remote Community Monitor 2006: APTN Omnibus Report* (September 2006), 30.

15   Ibid., 31.

16   Charles Fairchild, "Below the Hamelin Line: CKRZ and Aboriginal Cultural Survival," *Canadian Journal of Communications* 23, 2 (1998).

17   Strategic Inc, *APTN: Brand Equity Measure Programming and Promotional Test* (Winnipeg: APTN, 2002), 12.

18   Canada, Statistics Canada, *The Daily*, 9 July 2004, 3.

19   Consilium, *Aboriginal Languages Initiative Program Evaluation*, 2004, 63.

20   Canada, Indian and Northern Affairs, *Report of the Royal Commission on Aboriginal Peoples, Vol. 3*, 52.

21 Ibid., 56.

22 U. Koebberling. *Communication and Culture in the Western Arctic—A Case Study on the Growth of Inuvialuit-Controlled Broadcasts* (Inuvik: Inuvialuit Communications Society, 1986).

23 Ibid.

24 Wilson Belbin, Letter to OkalaKatiget Society, April 1990

25 Interview by Jennifer David, October 2004.

26 Ibid.

27 Ibid.

28 Canada, Indian and Northern Affairs, *Report of the Royal Commission on Aboriginal Peoples, Vol. 3*, 58.

29 Valaskakis, "The Role, Development and Future of Aboriginal Communications."

CHAPTER 3

Aboriginal Journalism Practices as Deep Democracy: APTN National News

SIGURJÓN BALDUR HAFSTEINSSON

In this chapter, I argue that the journalism practices of the Aboriginal Peoples Television Network (APTN) *National News* are an exercise in "deep democracy"[1]; they foster practices that are deeply local but simultaneously transnational. As such, APTN is already transgressive in that it gives voice to groups that assert their sovereignty within the boundaries of Canada. Moreover, APTN suggests an institutional model for the representation of difference that rejects mainstream news-media practices fraught with sensationalism and stereotyping. The individuals who founded and work at APTN have attempted to implement practices of deep democracy at the network. At the same time, these practices help to distribute democratic values through international institutions, thus forcing "national governments to recognize universal democratic principles within their own jurisdiction."[2] This argument diverges from writings about indigenous media that argue that media technologies have played a dynamic and revitalizing role in helping indigenous peoples[3] around the world to pursue social change through politics of identity and representation.[4] Faye Ginsburg, for instance, believes that media technologies serve as a self-conscious means of cultural preservation and production and as a form of political mobilization, which she calls "cultural activism." She sees media in the hands of indigenous peoples and communities as promoting difference rather than assimilation. Peoples who have previously found themselves misrepresented by the instruments of the dominant culture are now talking back to structures of power with a range of media technologies, including television. Indigenous media like APTN *National News* has, on the other hand, much broader scope to consider, because its endeavour is to introduce and revive Aboriginal democratic principles in ways that suggest "roots, anchors, intimacy, proximity, and locality."[5]

As described in Lorna Roth's chapter in this book, the creation of APTN accorded national recognition to Aboriginal issues.[6] On 22 February 1999, the Canadian Radio and Television Commission (CRTC) issued the not-for-profit APTN a broadcasting license for five years. Six months after the CRTC granted the license, APTN broadcast its signal across Canada. According to the CRTC decision, APTN was made available "on all large and mid-size cable, satellite, direct-to-home, and wireless TV service providers."[7] This assured APTN an immediate national distribution as well as a secure financial base from the subscription fees of about 8 million viewers. As Roth suggests in her chapter, cable companies vociferously opposed the CRTC mandate that obliges them to carry APTN signals as part of their basic cable service. After its first seven successful years of broadcasting, APTN began its second term of operation in the fall of 2005. Today, around 10 million people subscribe to a service that carries the APTN signal and are, as a consequence, potential viewers.

The mandate of the CRTC is to ensure that content in the Canadian broadcasting system reflects Canada's ethnic diversity and the special place of Aboriginal peoples within Canadian society.[8] CRTC policy emerges from a larger framework of multiculturalism that was formulated in the early 1970s. Since 8 October 1971, multiculturalism has been an official policy of the Canadian government. The policy asserts that despite two official state languages, English and French, no culture or ethnic group in Canada should take precedence over another. Beginning in 1973, multiculturalism policy has been implemented by several federal departments and is currently part of the Department of Canadian Heritage portfolio. All provincial governments have since formed their own multicultural policies, and many municipalities across Canada have done so as well. Though the federal policy is celebrated internationally for its progressive stance,[9] some scholars have argued that it is a political mechanism created to manage and control diversity for the sake of preserving power in the hands of the dominant group, of reinforcing political stability, and of strengthening national unity.[10] Can Aboriginal peoples use media technologies as the instruments of change if official multiculturalism amounts to little more than a legislative ruse? Roth, for example, points out that APTN sits so high on the spectrum of available channel numbers that one might ask whether a new form of reservation—a "media reservation"—has not been created.[11] If this is the case—that the legislation of official multiculturalism was undertaken to regulate and contain challenges to the hegemony of the dominant culture—how can media like APTN, created amidst this official drive for multicultural representation, talk back to the structures of power that brought it into being?

APTN National News

APTN headquarters are located in Winnipeg, a city of 700,000 inhabitants in the geographical center of Canada. Winnipeg has the largest urban population of Aboriginal peoples in Canada. Six stories high, grey, white, and blue, the APTN building stands in the heart of a busy downtown neighbourhood, flanked by regional headquarters for major corporations like the telecommunication giant Rogers and Air Canada. The founding of APTN gave Aboriginal peoples in Canada their own national television network, which aimed to share Aboriginal cultures and languages with other non-Native Canadians and, as stated by APTN CEO Jean LaRose, "to serve as a cultural bridge of understanding between Aboriginal peoples and non-Aboriginal communities."[12] Charged with reflecting the diversity of Aboriginal Canada, APTN attempts to represent numerous First Nations, the Métis, and the Inuit. In addition to this considerable range of cultural and linguistic groups, the network also tries to target audiences that are further differentiated by gender, age, and economic status. Thus, in order to provide programming addressing issues pertinent across these vast Aboriginal demographics, APTN purchases and commissions film productions with Aboriginal content from a variety of sources.

Given this landscape, Roth has argued that APTN provides "innovative perspectives that implicitly challenge those offered on other Canadian television channels."[13] Their innovation begins with the simple fact that Aboriginal peoples are now broadcasting their stories, images, and concerns in a Canadian mediascape that has been dominated by their colonizers since the advent of mass media. These innovative perspectives can be seen in daily national news programming that *explicitly* challenges other television stations across Canada. The news department's very existence is based on its explicit confrontation with the reality of Aboriginal peoples across Canada and the many forces that influence their lives, politics, experiences, and beliefs.

The news department's first show, *Contact*, launched in March 2000, was a call-in show about national Aboriginal current affairs.[14] One month later, in April, APTN mounted *In Vision* (now APTN *National News*), the world's first national television news program from an Aboriginal perspective. Dan David, a Mohawk with extensive experience as a journalist, was hired as the news director. He outlined his goals:

> I had a plan to start a national news television network, not exclusively with Aboriginal journalists, but mostly. I wanted to start telling stories with phrases that you are used to hearing—"Our stories," "Our voices," "Our perspectives,"—but more than anything else, I wanted it to be independent and brave. To take chances and maybe shock some people. But more than anything else, it had to set a standard, a journalistic standard that would stand up anywhere with anybody. It could not be soft-selling a story because it is an Aboriginal story. As far as I was concerned, there was no sense in doing this unless we made a very strong commitment in doing a free and independent democratic journalism. And if that meant breaking down walls that existed in a lot of communities, getting into the communities, get past the Band offices or the local government offices, then that was we had to do. As far as I was concerned, to do democratic journalism, you do not talk to the leaders, you talk primarily to the people who are affected by the decisions of their leaders.[15]

David described the state of Aboriginal news reporting at the time of the establishment of the APTN news room:

> I felt that it was really important having a kind of independent voice, free from political manipulation. In a lot of cases, Aboriginal newspapers that were out there had [on] their board of directors their Chiefs in the communities that they served. And similar with a lot of their broadcasting communities, the leaders of the communities would sit on these boards, so the politicians were not only making policy but very often interfering, micro-managing, with the production of the product, whether it was a radio program or whether it was a newspaper, weekly or monthly coming out. They could spike stories. They could fire editors, they could get rid of reporters if they touched on issues they felt they did not want to get exposed and sometimes that could be corruption, political corruption at the band office, financial corruption in programs that they served or it might be a touchy subject like religion or perhaps sexual habits of people.[16]

At first, *In Vision* was broadcast twice a week on weekdays. From October 2005 until 6 October 2008, the show was broadcast live twice a day (mid-day and evenings) on weekdays and in addition was made available online on APTN's website. On 6 October 2008, APTN *National News* moved from a half-hour format to a full one hour and added a second anchor. APTN *National News Daytime* (the mid-day newscast) was retired so that all of the news resources could be concentrated on delivering the primetime newscast. In the fall of 2009, a new investigative news series, APTN *Investigates,* was launched under the direction of a newly created executive producer of investigative news. The producer coordinates an investigative news unit within the department. The newsroom adheres to the principles of democratic journalism and public service that Dan David envisioned.

The station later implemented policies intended to ensure Aboriginal training and participation in APTN. After a term of two years, David left the newsroom, and APTN hired Rita Deverell as director of news and current affairs. An African-American born in the southern United States, Deverell brought with her considerable experience in journalism and television. Deverell's tenure lasted three years, and during that time she was charged with helping to put the station in Aboriginal hands by mentoring her Aboriginal successor. Other non-Aboriginal members of the senior management team who were hired at the same time as Deverell, such as the director of marketing and the chief financial officer, were similarly hired on a temporary basis with the expectation that they would mentor their Aboriginal successors. Today, over thirty-five people work for the news and current affairs department. All but five self-identify as Aboriginal, including the video journalists, reporters, camera operators, editors, researchers, host/producers, producers, assignment editor, line producer, executive producers, and the director of the department.

The APTN staff feels that a strong Aboriginal presence in the APTN newsroom is essential. Vera Houle, an Ojibway, succeeded Deverell in October 2005. All three news directors tell similar stories about the mainstream media's treatment of Aboriginal stories, underscoring the importance of APTN *National News.* Houle's perspective is informed by her own experiences working in mainstream media:

> I have spent nearly ten years [before coming to APTN] working in television and mainstream media in the non-Aboriginal component at CTV.... I feel such a big difference in how stories are told [about] our people, about our situation, and about everything that is happening all around us. It was never accurate or never of importance [at CTV]. It was always downplayed. When there was

something wrong and our people took any action, it was always negative. When I was trying to pitch those stories within the mainstream media to my employer at the time, the first reactions were always, "Who is going to care in our audience?"[17]

In contrast, APTN *National News* directly addresses Aboriginal history, covering Aboriginal stories that have been badly neglected by mainstream Canadian media. For example, reportage on the odious history of residential schooling highlights the need for a specifically Aboriginal news outlet. Between the early 1880s and mid 1980s, a church-state partnership funded and operated a school system for Aboriginal children that enacted a significant piece of the Canadian government's longstanding policy of assimilation.[18] In recent years, scholars, curators, journalists, and former wards of the residential school system have documented certain aspects of its operation, which included forced migration, separation from families of origin, and high incidences of physical and sexual abuse.

The residential system also contributed significantly to the attenuation of Aboriginal languages. Today, there are fifty individual Aboriginal languages in Canada that belong to eleven language families.[19] Many, if not the majority, of Aboriginal peoples in Canada speak English and/or French with an accent, a trait that further underscores their status as distinct from the mainstream. APTN's mandate is to address this diversity in their programming. APTN has a language policy that requires 60 percent of its programming to be in English, 15 percent in French, and 25 percent in Aboriginal languages. APTN also actively surveys the film and television production market for more Aboriginal productions. To this end, the network has taken an interest in commissioning documentary projects and children's programs with a built-in Aboriginal language component. The newsroom plays a vital but subtle part in this overall programming strategy. APTN's news broadcasting is predominantly in English and occasionally in French, particularly when reports come in from Quebec. The French reports are subtitled in English. APTN's 2004 journalistic policy outlines the relationship between representation and language:

> APTN News and Current Affairs will reflect the many Aboriginal languages in Canada whenever we have the opportunity to do so. However, News and Current Affairs is primarily broadcast in English with some French. In the spirit of keeping the entire audience informed, Aboriginal languages and French will use subtitles and/ or captioning whenever necessary. In addition to using Aboriginal languages in our broadcast, we are also mindful of the issues surrounding the preservation and enhancement of Aboriginal lan-

guages and will deal with language issues in our programs locally, nationally and internationally.[20]

APTN journalists are sensitive to the politics of language and the particular linguistic demands of Aboriginal peoples, as the journalists themselves reflect the range of linguistic practices among Aboriginal Canadians. Some journalists at APTN speak their native languages, while others understand occasional words and phrases, and some do not speak any language other than English and/or French. Vera Houle speaks Ojibway and is very conscious about the importance of the presence of Aboriginal languages in the news:

> Whenever I do a story as a reporter, I will always try to find people that speak the language, and then I will translate. Our reporters who speak their own language are encouraged to speak their language while they are working on stories and then translate. If we have someone coming in to APTN who speaks a language, and we are maybe not able to, then we will go out in the community and have someone to translate for us. There is a lot of working together with the community or the people. I have no problem with it if people are interviewed and they respond in their own language—in Cree, for example. We just translate it. I do not think that we will ever do news in Aboriginal language because we will not reach enough people. It is also a question of which language to pick. There are so many Aboriginal languages and dialects in Canada. There are ways that language can be preserved, but I think that it is not going to be preserved through our news. I do not think that is our place. We can definitely highlight the people who are doing it or try to do it. We do language stories all the time, especially language in the schools.... When it comes to preserving a language, a community has to do it.[21]

Thus, given the national reach of APTN, the news cannot promote one Aboriginal language, though APTN *National News* does include Aboriginal voices and languages in the national debate to an extent unparalleled by other news outlets.

The Practice of Deep Democratic Journalism

The mission statement of the APTN news division provides guidelines for fieldwork that set it apart from other news-gathering agencies in Canada: "The Aboriginal Peoples Television Network is dedicated to the ideal that the airwaves belong to the people and that the free exchange of information, entertainment, ideas and opinions is both the cornerstone of our democracy and the basis of our freedoms. APTN has the honor to serve the Aboriginal Peoples in Canada. While we are a unique, and, we believe, valuable window to the Aboriginal world for other Canadians, our primary mandate is to tell the stories of Canada's more than 2,000,000 Aboriginal Peoples to each other and all Canadians."[22] The policy specifies that the news and current affairs content must be chosen according to its relevance to Aboriginal People: the news is "told for, by and about Aboriginal Peoples reflecting [their] cultural values."[23] On the one hand, the mission statement and the corresponding newsroom programming and fieldwork clearly seek to provide an alternative to the usual mainstream media coverage of Aboriginal issues, which APTN staffers characterize as neglectful and negative. On the other hand, the policy explicitly states that the newsroom should not see itself as an advocate for Aboriginal issues: "We do not take on the role of public relations facilitator for Aboriginal issues, leaders, organizations, governments, individuals and communities. APTN is not government funded. We are an independent news service. We do, however, strive to reflect a real and balanced picture of the Aboriginal reality."[24]

The newsroom's emphasis on issues of interest to Aboriginal people emerges from a grave scepticism regarding the representations of these issues in the mainstream media. This scepticism has its root in the notion that—unlike mainstream newsrooms—APTN's newsroom is staffed by journalists that have individual experiences in and relationships to Aboriginal communities. As a result, APTN National News relies very little on other news agencies for their programs. In the course of our conversations, Vera Houle suggested that the dominant culture's seeming indifference to Aboriginal preoccupations and, perhaps more significantly, its ignorance of Aboriginal ways of knowing make an independent approach necessary, and that this approach extends to what some might consider unorthodox journalistic practices, including the foregrounding of narrative, feeling, and intimacy:

> There is still a big gulf between Aboriginal peoples and the rest of Canada in just understanding Aboriginal peoples, what they think, what is important to them, and why we feel that we have a different relationship in this country to the rest of everybody else. Reports on "this is what happened" and "this is what happened" and "this is who did what" without asking why this happened and without emotions! That is not us. Our storytelling is different. It is more from the heart and I think it is because we are actually telling our stories. We relate and share it with a ton of emotions.[25]

The newsroom maintains, on the other hand, a wide network of contacts with indigenous people around the world and frequently tells news stories regarding different indigenous groups. This does not, however, constitute explicit advocacy. One former APTN journalist, Greg Taylor (Métis), had this to say about the potential criticism that APTN *National News* serves only Aboriginal peoples:

> There are a lot of people that kind of insult you without realizing it. Some people have this perception that because we are Aboriginal journalists, we are biased towards Aboriginal Peoples all the time and that kind of thing. They forget the principles of journalism when they think that. Such criticism is ridiculous, especially if you look at some of the mainstream coverage. We are so much more critical of Aboriginal leaders than any mainstream reporter ever will be.... Our leaders can softball mainstream reporters, as they often do not know what they are talking about. When they talk to us, we do know what they are talking about. And we can challenge them. Often the leaders really do not like to be challenged.[26]

Indeed, APTN's journalistic policy focuses to a great extent on conventional journalistic codes of conduct that dictate how APTN's journalists should gather the news, request interviews, protect their sources, and report on protests, demonstrations, and riots. There is, however, a component of the policy that makes it distinct in terms of APTN reporters' approach to subjects. In particular, a section of the policy called "Cultural Consideration" dictates how APTN journalists should approach Elders. Aboriginal communities, both on and off reserves, identify Elders differently. Elders are not necessarily just older people; they are usually considered to have a symbolic connection to the past and are therefore respected for their traditional knowledge of Aboriginal ways, teachings, stories, and ceremonies. Elders are sought for spiritual and cultural leadership.[27] Children are taught respect for Elders in many ways, such as through tobacco gift-giving rituals. APTN's code of cultural consideration not only distinguishes it from other forms of journalism but also provides a model for the representation of cultural difference.

Representing Ceremonial Conduct

APTN's journalistic policy also guides journalists in the coverage of Aboriginal ceremony and ritual. APTN journalists believe that the mainstream media's approach to Aboriginal culture has tended to undermine Aboriginal values and way of life and has typically not treated Aboriginal peoples as worthy subjects. APTN's current news director, Vera Houle, feels that APTN's news practices, in contrast, promote respect for and understanding of Aboriginal cultures and issues. For Houle, it is important not merely to cover the issues, but also to cover them in a way that fosters comprehension of the distinct cultural significance of the people and practices represented.[28] An examination of the station's approach to Aboriginal ceremonies affords the opportunity to explore the important differences—of both content and style—in the coverage that APTN delivers. The journalistic policy establishes the guidelines for cultural consideration: "We will take care to respect and acknowledge ceremonial conduct and customs of a Nation. Certain ceremonies should not be named or shown for broadcast. For example, the 'Sundance' is not recorded and it should be referred to it as a 'sacred ceremony' or a 'ceremony' in the story. In respect for certain Inuit culture, when a person dies every effort will be made not to say the name of the person or show their image in a news story or program for at least one year."[29] Aboriginal ceremonies are not considered mere spectacles undertaken for the purpose of entertainment, or traditions that are void of contemporary significance. Houle explains that "We are looking at stories with eyes that ask, 'Why?' We are not telling our stories the mainstream way, which is just right to the point of what is there without any explanation of why things happened the way they did."[30] This approach goes across the board, from reporting on Aboriginal ceremonies to coverage of social issues like suicide.

Despite the general guidelines provided by the journalistic policy, individual journalists on the news team interpret the policy differently. These differences may have their origins in varied attitudes towards ceremonies within the many nations and Aboriginal groups that are to be found in Canada. For example, Ken Williams (Cree), a former journalist who worked for many years at APTN, outlines one possible source of different cultural approaches to representation: "Out in Eastern Canada they tend to have a different sense of what is allowable (and what is not) to film. In the West, people tend to have video cameras and are taking pictures all the time. There are some cultural differences among First Nations in what is allowed to shoot [on video]."[31] In order to respect these different cultural practices, Williams takes his cue from individual communities: "I do not shoot video unless I am invited to do so. That leads to a different question: what is sacred and what is not. Some people, for instance, look at Powwows as sacred. I do not. Powwow is just a gathering. Especially if competition is involved. I do not shoot prayers or a medium, unless it is totally relevant to the story. I have only shot one prayer that was relevant to the story. It was an instance involving several prayers, not only Aboriginal prayers."[32]

Unlike many mainstream journalists, who feel they must "get the shot," Greg Taylor accepts the fact that some groups might resist the filming of sacred ceremonies altogether:

> In Manitoba I have had people say that it is OK to shoot a sacred fire. In Ontario I have been told not to. It is just a matter of asking. And I find that, at least for news, that there is really no need to shoot these things. There is no need to shoot a sweat lodge ceremony. There is no need to shoot a sacred fire. It is just a visual. And I can find other ways to tell a story without having to show it. The only other thing that I would never shoot is a prayer. Not everybody feels the same way about prayers, but I was grown up that way. Someone is offering a prayer and you do not do anything else. Out of respect I turn off my camera. I have never lost a shot. I have never been able to not to tell a story because I did that. It is a common courtesy and people will recognize that. And they will really appreciate it. It just helps you, as they are then more willing to help you.[33]

Thus, in terms of its representation of individuals and groups, APTN has extended and altered the ethical imperatives of the journalistic code to respect both individual and group rights.

Internal Diversity of Nations

This recognition of group rights reflects the specific situation of First Nations of Canada. APTN does not serve a homogenous group of people in terms of race, nation, culture, or language. This fact challenges its journalists. Taylor, for instance, explains, "There is little education about Aboriginal peoples and Aboriginal cultures. We are just treated as 'the natives' and not as distinct people. There is little understanding of, let's say, how Mohawk is different from Ojibway in the Prairies or from the Mi'kmaq or the Métis."[34] APTN's journalistic policy addresses this internal diversity among Aboriginal Peoples: "When referring to a specific Nation we will—as much as possible—apply the term that Nation uses. For example the Ojibway may prefer Anishinabe."[35] In addition, Rosanna Deerchild, a Cree and former executive producer at APTN National News, told me that it might be misleading to have the word Aboriginal in the name of APTN because it implies that the network subscribes to the view that there are separate and discrete peoples and cultures within Canada.[36] For Deerchild, the very term Aboriginal implies a colonial frame of reference that Aboriginal people want to problematize and perhaps cure of its "primitivist perplex."[37] Against this habitual frame of reference, APTN's journalistic policy recognizes and underscores the diversity of social and political forms practiced by Aboriginal peoples. Moreover, by emphasizing the distinctiveness of Aboriginal nations, APTN's journalistic ethos provides a more rigorous understanding of the contemporary and future positions occupied by Aboriginal peoples within and against Canadian political structures.

APTN places correspondents, or "video journalists," as they are often called, in every part of the country in order to ensure faithful and in-depth reporting on issues affecting all First Nations. In the fall of 2008, there were video journalists in Ottawa, Halifax, Toronto, Montreal, Saskatoon, Alberta, Vancouver, Whitehorse, Yellowknife, and Iqaluit. This outreach program is very important to the mission of serving Aboriginal peoples in a democratic way. For Taylor, this program, perhaps more than any other aspect of the station's practices, shows how APTN does things differently from the mainstream media:

> We reach out to communities for stories. I know mainstream media reporters who have never, ever gone on overnight trips. It is just basic. If you have to travel more than one day, mainstream media reporters are not doing the story. While we have to. There is just no way to get around it. If we were to cover stories that happened only in urban centers, we would be failing our people. We have to go out there. And we do not do it enough because we still have the reality that we have to put out a new show every day.... When you are going into Northern Ontario, you cannot drive up there. You have to fly. It is going to take two or three days to get the story, but it is important because nobody else will do that. We are the last resort. If we do not do it, nobody will. If you are a for-profit, private broadcaster, they will not do that at all. They will not even think about going to Northern Ontario or any place North. Or even six or seven hours out of the city. It is just too costly. When you are more worried about profit, your story is not going to get done.[38]

In 2008 the news department restructured its editorial management by creating new posts in order to strengthen regional representation in the newscast. Instead of having one executive producer of news and current affairs there is now one eastern executive producer (based in Ottawa), one northern executive producer (based in Yellowknife), and one western executive producer (based in Winnipeg). In addition, there is now an official assignment editor and a line producer, where previously the senior news producer and the executive producer did all the assignment editor and line producer's duties. [39] By insisting upon gathering news from areas considered too small or too remote by mainstream stations, APTN reporters have changed the dynamics between media and Aboriginal politics, both on reserves and in urban areas such as Ottawa, the political and bureaucratic centre of government in Canada. Ken Williams describes how his presence and practice as an Aboriginal journalist is challenging conventions within Aboriginal politics in a way that may also set precedents for the fieldwork of mainstream journalists as they investigate Aboriginal issues:

> I will talk to anybody who wants to talk to me. I will go up and ask Aboriginal peoples questions. For my mainstream colleagues, that is the total opposite. For instance, I have had situations where my colleagues have been sitting outside a reserve because they were told by the Band office that they were not allowed onto the reserve. I then just told them "Hey guys, I'll see you later!" I left and talked to whomever wanted to talk to me on that reserve. I tend not to put much authority into voices of politicians. The [politicians] are not comfortable with that. We have a free press, a free media that can challenge the Chief's authority.[40]

Taylor, who resides in Ottawa, sees the importance of this changing dynamic and reflects upon the future of Aboriginal nations:

> It is absolutely vital for APTN to have a news department.... It is almost recognized everywhere that we as Aboriginal peoples have the right to self-government. We have been talking about and working on and developing our own system of government. And for any democracy, because most Aboriginal governments will take a democratic process, we need a well informed electorate, we need good people that know what is going on. And we cannot depend on the mainstream to do that for us. We cannot depend on Canada for taking care of us. We cannot depend on them to be our government. We have to take care of ourselves. And just as important, to inform ourselves. We have to run our own media. How can you have an election in Canada without news, without TV news, without newspapers? I know that the Métis National Council, within the next ten years, will have a national election for its president and our own Cabinet. The only way it will ever work and produce good results is if people know who they are voting for. And that they get an impartial and fair representation on issues and where our leaders stand, and how they perform. And it is just something that the

mainstream just cannot do. I do not think that they want to do it. For every reason I do not think that they are able to.[41]

Beyond the basic need for good information, Taylor's comments underscore the fact that news representation and coverage constitute the *sine qua non* of sovereignty and self-determination.

Conclusion

Aboriginal peoples in Canada live within national structures that have authoritatively shaped their lives for centuries. Therefore, to talk about difference as implying a world of separate peoples and cultures[42] begs for empirical studies of how difference is produced. A careful study of the construction of seemingly discrete groups must acknowledge a shared body of historical processes "that differentiates the world as it connects it."[43] APTN's *National News* and current-affairs programming are vital components of APTN's mandate and two of the strongest elements in restructuring the organizational logic of Canada and the nations within its borders.[44] As we have seen, the practice of the APTN newsroom is community based and penetrates areas that mainstream media in Canada do not consider areas of priority. In particular, the acknowledgement of the heterogeneity of discrete nations in programming decisions and reporting practices, as well as of the contingent and circumspect approach to the representation of ceremonies, resonates with the ethos of what we can call the practices of "deep democracy." These activities speak to structures of power and at the same time undermine the claim that multiculturalism is a political mechanism created to manage and control diversity. APTN's approach to ceremony respects the sacredness of both subjects and cultural traditions, with implications for the ways in which national media can and should approach Aboriginal people. In a similar vein, the emphasis on naming distinctive nations on the news, and on pointing out the existence of nations within the nation, is contributing to a redefinition of what constitutes a nation, and how citizens are imagined within their shifting boundaries.

Acknowledgements

I want to thank Arnar Árnason, Tinna Grétarsdóttir, Jay Ruby, Michael Antenbring, Marian Bredin, Lorna Roth, Cheryl McKenzie, and Taiaiake Alfred for their discussion and constructive criticism during the work on this essay. I also want to thank the people who have generously spent their time talking about their work for APTN *National News* and who have shared their aspirations for the network with me.

NOTES

1   Arjun Appadurai, "Deep Democracy: Urban Governmentality and the Horizon of Politics," *Public Culture* 14, 1 (2002): 21–47.

2   Ibid., 45.

3   In this chapter, I use "Aboriginal people" interchangeably with "indigenous people" (See Canada, Indian, and Northern Affairs, *Report of the Royal Commission on Aboriginal Peoples, Volume 1: Looking Forward, Looking Back* (Ottawa: Minister of Supply and Services, 1996).

4   Faye D. Ginsburg, "Screen Memories: Resignifying the Traditional in Indigenous Media," in *Media Worlds: Anthropology on New Terrain*, ed. Faye D. Ginsburg, Lila Abu-Lughod, and Brian Larkin (Berkeley: University of California Press, 2002), 39–57; Valerie Alia, *Un/Covering the North: News, Media, and Aboriginal People* (Vancouver: University of British Columbia Press, 1999); George Marcus, introduction to *Connected: Engagements with Media*, ed. George Marcus (Chicago: University of Chicago Press, 1996), 1–18.

5   Appadurai, "Deep Democracy," 45.

6   Doris Baltruschat, "Television and Canada's Aboriginal Communities: Seeking Opportunities Through Traditional Storytelling and Digital Technologies," *Canadian Journal of Communication* 29, 1 (2004): 47–59; Marian Bredin, "Aboriginal Peoples Television Network," in *Encyclopedia of Television, 2nd ed.*, ed. Horace Newcomb (New York: Routledge, 2004), 6–8; Lorna Roth, *Something New in the Air: The Story of First Peoples' Television Broadcasting in Canada* (Montreal: McGill-Queen's University Press, 2005).

7   Aboriginal Peoples Television Network, *APTN Promotional Brochure* (Winnipeg: APTN, n.d.).

8   Canadian Radio-television and Telecommunications Commission, *Mandate*, 1 November 2007, http://www.crtc.gc.ca/eng/cancon/mandate.htm.

9   UNESCO, Management of Social Transformation Programme, "Multiculturalism: A Policy Response to Diversity" (Paper presented at the 1995 Global Cultural Diversity Conference, Sydney, Australia, 26–28 April 1995).

10   Eva Mackey, *The House of Difference: Cultural Politics and National Identity in Canada* (Toronto: University of Toronto Press, 2002); Augie Fleras, "Racializing Culture/Culturizing Race: Multicultural Racism in a Multicultural Canada," in *Racism, Eh? A Critical Inter-disciplinary Anthology of Race and Racism in Canada*, ed. Camille A. Nelson and Charmaine A. Nelson (Concord, ON: Captus Press, 2004), 429–443.

11   Roth, this volume, 43.

12   Canada, Senate Committee on Transport and Communications, *Proceedings of the Standing Senate Committee on Transport and Communications. Issue 9–Evidence.* Winnipeg, 4 February 2005, http://www.parl.gc.ca/38/1/parlbus/commbus/senate/com-e/tran-e/09cv-e.htm?Lanugage=E&Parl=38&Ses=1&comm_id=19 (accessed 8 January 2006).

13   Roth, *Something New,* 215.

14   Since 2006 *Contact* has gone from a twenty-week production schedule to a twenty-five-week schedule.

15   Dan David, Personal communication, 25 November 2005.

16 Ibid.

17 Vera Houle, Personal communication, 2 August 2005.

18 John S. Milloy, "*A National Crime*": *The Canadian Government and the Residential School System, 1879–1986* (Winnipeg: University of Manitoba Press, 1999).

19 Mary Jane Norris and L. Jantzen, "Aboriginal Languages in Canada's Urban Areas: Characteristics, Considerations and Implications," in *Not Strangers in These Parts: Urban Aboriginal Peoples*, ed. David Newhouse and E. Peters (Ottawa: Policy Research Initiatives, 2003), 93–118.

20 Aboriginal Peoples Television Network, *APTN Journalistic Policy* (Winnipeg: APTN, 2004), 18.

21 Houle, Personal communication.

22 Aboriginal Peoples Television Network, *Journalistic Policy*, 5

23 Ibid., 5.

24 Ibid., 5.

25 Houle, Personal communication.

26 Greg Taylor, Personal communication, 9 September 2005.

27 Suzanne M. Stiegelbauer, "What is an Elder? What do Elders do? First Nation Elders as Teachers in Culture-Based Urban Organizations," *The Canadian Journal of Native Studies* 16, 1 (1996): 37–66.

28 Houle, Personal communication.

29 Aboriginal Peoples Television Network, *Journalistic Policy*, 17.

30 Houle, Personal communication.

31 Ken Williams, Personal communication, 6 September 2005.

32 Ibid.

33 Taylor, Personal communication.

34 Ibid.

35 Aboriginal Peoples Television Network, *Journalistic Policy*, 18.

36 Rosanna Deerchild, Personal communication, 24 November 2005.

37 Harald Prins, "Visual Media and the Primitivist Perplex: Colonial Fantasies, Indigenous Imagination, and Advocacy in North America," in *Media Worlds*, 58–74.

38 Taylor, Personal communication.

39 Cheryl McKenzie, Personal communication, 13 February 2009.

40 Williams, Personal communication.

41 Taylor, Personal communication.

42 Akhil Gupta and James Ferguson, "Beyond Culture: Space, Identity, and the Politics of Difference," in *Culture, Power, Place: Explorations in Critical Anthropology*, ed. Akhil Gupta and James Ferguson (Durham, NC: Duke University Press, 1997), 46.

43 Ibid., 46.

44 Stephen B.C. Wiley, "Rethinking Nationality in the Context of Globalization," *Communication Theory* 14, 1 (2004): 78–96.

CHAPTER 4

APTN and Its Audience

MARIAN BREDIN

During the process of applying for APTN's licence renewal in August 2005, APTN staff and management were able to take stock of the network's past accomplishments and consider the challenges that lie ahead. Since its launch in 1999, the network has built local, national, and international audiences within the highly competitive and fragmented universe of Canada's multi-channel specialty and digital television channels. This chapter examines the composition, location, and interactions of APTN's audience by considering three related research questions: how are the viewers of APTN imagined and positioned by the network's managers and producers; how are audiences located by their interaction with programming that actively encourages audience contact, and how are audiences measured by formal and informal, quantitative and qualitative tools of conventional media audience research?

A full understanding of the APTN audience lies in the answers to all three of these questions. The cultural, social, and demographic features of the network's audience can be determined by a triangulated analysis: first, of APTN producers' and hosts' conception of the "ideal viewer"; second, of the "active viewer," who provides informal feedback and dialogue through APTN's online forum and the call-in portion of its current affairs program; and finally, of the "actual viewer," as measured in qualitative and quantitative audience research conducted by both the network and commercial ratings services.

Before tracing these different potential conceptions of the APTN audience, this chapter begins with a brief overview of some theoretical models of media audiences that might usefully be extended to this analysis. This theoretical review is followed by a survey of methodological approaches to both Aboriginal and non-Aboriginal media audiences that can help more fully develop the categories of ideal, active, and actual audiences. The chapter then presents a summary of the contemporary APTN audience in the three modes described above. The chapter outlines the ideal APTN audience by drawing upon interviews with APTN board members, management, and staff in carried out 2003. The subsequent description of the active audience is based upon information from call-in programs, web forums, and focus group research at APTN. Finally, the chapter surveys existing research on APTN's actual viewership to provide a demographic picture of who is watching APTN from among Aboriginal people living on reserves and in northern communities, Aboriginal people in southern urban areas, and non-Aboriginal people across the country.

The APTN audience reflects the culturally, linguistically, and geographically diverse nature of Aboriginal communities in Canada. The broad mandate embodied in its Canadian Radio-television and Telecommunications Commission (CRTC) licence charges APTN to address urban and remote, northern and southern, Aboriginal and non-Aboriginal viewers. In the process of putting this mandate into practice, the network has begun to develop specific strategies for audience building to meet the varied and sometimes conflicting needs and expectations of its national viewership. This chapter concludes by looking at some of the potential conflicts between efforts to build audiences in each of the three main demographic groups identified above. While there is a certain degree of institutional and policy rhetoric around the network's ability to reach its "target audience," that target is both elusive and deeply fragmented.

Theoretical Perspectives on the Audience for Aboriginal Television

As S. Elizabeth Bird suggests, it has become somewhat commonplace in recent years to point to the "crisis of scholarship" in media audience studies.[1] Media scholars have described the "first generation" of audience research as limited to descriptions and analysis of the "mass" audience and the effects of media upon viewers. The second generation of audience studies might be characterized by a shift from this focus on a relatively homogeneous group of viewers, responding to a limited range of media content, to a sustained analysis of the modes of media reception and the production of meaning in media texts. As theories of audience move beyond these textually constrained methods of reception analysis to explore the media consumption habits and the practices of active audiences, studies are well into a third phase. This phase was triggered by the adoption of anthropological models of cultural interaction and of ethnographic methods by media researchers like Ien Ang, James Lull, David Morley, and Janice Radway. Scholars in media studies recognized the value of seeing individuals not merely as members of audiences but also as members of larger pre-existing social and subcultural groups. Like researchers in other social sciences disciplines, they looked to anthropology and ethnography for a more fully developed approach to understanding media consumption and reception as part of everyday life. These researchers shared a common desire for a more culturally comprehensive qualitative approach to understanding audiences, though the term *ethnography* is often imprecisely invoked to refer to even the most minimal forms of dialogue between researchers and their subjects. Debates concerning the validity of ethnographic methods used outside anthropology are complex and wide ranging, but Bird's assessment is that "we are now seeing a 'third generation' of reception studies, building on the models represented by Stuart Hall's encoding/decoding approach and the now-classic qualitative audience studies ... this third-generation approach acknowledges the very real problems associated with trying to separate text/audience from the culture in which they are embedded, yet also accepts that it may be perfectly valid to enter the discussion through a particular genre or medium."[2]

A theoretically informed model of APTN's audience thus needs to recognize the multiple ways in which television viewers and television viewing are embedded in various lived cultures in Canada. As Nick Couldry suggests, models of a "dispersed" or "extended" audience correspond to the need to account for the media saturation of contemporary societies.[3] As he puts it, "the contemporary audience is a dispersed phenomenon extending far beyond the act of sitting down to watch a particular programme. The dispersed audience allows us to think about the spatial location of audiences, while the notion of the diffused audience raises different questions about the social and power relationships between producers and consumers."[4] Converging technologies and multi-platform circulation of media content have made the boundaries between media production and media consumption more porous. While power, like audiences, may be dispersed within these new technological configurations (which are directly responsible for the multiplication of new channels like APTN), Couldry argues that the "symbolic power" of the media has not been reduced. Within contemporary media culture, the concept of the extended audience requires that all facets of audience activity, along with the audience's social constitution, technological formations, and spatial locations, must be examined.

Ella Shohat and Robert Stam extend third-generation audience theories to analyses of minority and marginal audiences by arguing that viewers or specta- tors are historically located and always constituted within networks of power beyond the media text itself: "Media spectatorship forms a trialog between texts, readers, and communities existing in clear discursive and social relation to one another. It is thus a negotiable site of interaction and struggle, seen, for example in the possibility of 'aberrant' or resistant readings, as the conscious- ness or experience of a particular audience generates a counter-pressure to dominant representations."[5] This idea of a "trialog" is particularly relevant to an understanding of the APTN audience because the network itself, along with its viewers, is clearly engaged in generating counter-pressures to domi- nant representations of Aboriginal peoples, thus shifting relations within and among the three elements of text, reader, and community.

In their coherently ordered and dynamic theoretical paradigm for produc- ing an ethnography of spectatorship, Shohat and Stam outline five registers to be considered,[6] each of which might be applied to an analysis of the APTN audience. First, the spectator or viewer is fashioned by the *text* itself. In the case of APTN, the cultural perspectives, languages, and narrative structures of APTN programs are encoded and decoded by viewers who must rely to varying degrees upon shared cultural knowledge and traditions. Second, the authors suggest that the spectator is shaped by the diverse and evolving *technical* apparatuses of media. In APTN's case, these technical factors include the con- straints and possibilities of a national TV network, including cable distribution, channel location, and an emerging Aboriginal production industry. The third element determining the audience is the *institutional* context of spectatorship. This includes the habits and practices of everyday television viewing—both in APTN's northern, root communities and in its new southern and urban areas—and the choices viewers make about APTN programs. This dimension also includes the public perception of APTN as a network: the way the network is viewed by politicians, policy analysts, media critics, and even by academic researchers. Fourth, the spectator is constituted by ambient *discourses* and ide- ologies including, in the case of APTN, dominant colonial and racist discourses about Aboriginal people in Canada as well as postcolonial and anti-racist dis- courses that circulate alongside them. The final dimension of the audience is what Shohat and Stam call the *actual* spectator. Individuals who watch APTN are each distinctively "embodied," historically situated by race and gender—or, in my definition of the actual viewer, demographically defined and described.

A comprehensive study of the APTN audience must look at the interplay among all five of these elements, and explore contradictions and congruencies among them. The viewer is constructed by each element, yet simultaneously shapes the media encounter herself at the level of reception and consumption of APTN programs. As Shohat and Stam warn, audience ethnography cannot easily assume a perfect match between the minority or Aboriginal spectator and the minority or Aboriginal television text. Researchers must be careful to avoid essentialist descriptions of the "politically correct" and "socially aware" APTN viewer, who may in fact be shaped by multiple identities and identifications, or be "crossed by contradictory discourses and codes."[7] Those individuals momentarily located as members of the APTN audience do not necessarily share common cultural, social, or political positions, whether they are Aboriginal or not.

Methodological Approaches to Audience

The three categories of the APTN audience that are outlined here incorporate and recombine the five elements listed by Shohat and Stam. Each category requires a specific methodological approach that can be described with reference to (the relatively few) existing studies of the audience for Aboriginal media in Canada and elsewhere.

The *ideal viewer* is both textually and institutionally produced. In Stuart Hall's terms, this might be a preferred reader, interpellated and ideologically positioned by the text.[8] This category can, however, also include an analysis of the ideal viewer as imagined by media producers, especially within minority or marginal media. To whom do managers and producers at APTN think the network programming is addressed? We can raise this question without automatically assuming that the producers' imaginary interlocutor is always or even usually successfully engaged by the media text. This is a somewhat neglected area of audience study, and one that is best explored with the methodological tools of participant observation and semi-structured interviews with producers and managers. The key research models in this area are studies undertaken by Faye Ginsburg, Eric Michaels, and Michael Meadows on Aboriginal media in Australia, and by Lorna Roth and Kathleen Buddle on Aboriginal media in Canada.[9] These studies document interviews with and observations of Aboriginal media activists and producers, and through this we learn about the imagined audience for Aboriginal media—although these imagined viewers vary widely according to the cultural and social contexts of the indigenous media undertaking. One of the most relevant methodological models for grasping the nature of the ideal viewer is Barry Dornfeld's idea of the "prefigured audience." In his detailed ethnographic study of the production of a documentary series at a United States Public Broadcasting System (PBS) affiliate, Dornfeld observes that: "Producers' projections about their audiences have a strong effect on the selection, encoding and structuring of the media forms these institutions disseminate, be they mainstream television programmes, commercials, feature films, or educational documentaries. The multiplicity of audiences' interpretive positions, the various things people do in consuming these texts through dominant, contested or oppositional readings ... are therefore constrained from the start by the way producers prefigure those acts of consumption."[10] Dornfeld goes on to demonstrate through his observation and interviews just how the PBS producers prefigure their ideal audience, based on their participation in similar social and cultural milieux and their own experience as viewers themselves. This model can be extended to an analysis of how APTN producers prefigure their own Aboriginal and non-Aboriginal audiences, as will be explored below.

The *active viewer* is institutionally, technically, and discursively produced and might be described as a negotiating or resisting reader. The active viewer is engaged in the production of meaning from media texts in ways that sometimes, though not always, challenge dominant racist and colonial discourses. In the case of APTN, the active viewer seeks out or discovers the network because it permits her to engage in oppositional readings of mainstream media representations of Aboriginal people. Methodologically, we can locate the active viewer through focussed ethnographic study, using focus groups, interviews, or observations of domestic viewing situations, such as those employed in studies by Janice Radway, David Morley, Marie Gillespie, and S. Elizabeth Bird.[11] The active viewer can be located in an equally useful way through a documentation of the conscious and critical interaction with media texts and producers that occurs on fan sites, discussion boards, and online forums associated with specific programs. There is very little existing academic research on viewers of Aboriginal media that might fall into this category. The active viewer must be traced through anecdotal evidence compiled from responses to specific programs on the network, or in more formal statements made to the CRTC during various policy processes.

Finally, the actual viewer is that much larger, amorphous, socially and historically situated group. This is the embodied viewer, defined by gender, age, race, class, culture, and region. These viewers are the members of both Aboriginal and non-Aboriginal audiences of APTN whose viewing practices can be measured. In the case of Aboriginal media, the actual viewer can be traced by consumer research conducted by the media industry and by related government statistical research using quantitative measures, surveys, metres, and diaries. In the case of APTN, even this research is relatively hard to find and, for various reasons I will explain, does not give us an accurate picture of the APTN audience.

APTN's Ideal Audience

To begin by outlining APTN's ideal audience, I will rely heavily on data collected from interviews at APTN in the summer of 2003. These interviews were carried out with ten people working out of the Winnipeg headquarters, including representatives from the board of directors, management, marketing, communications, and news production. Because interview respondents were ensured anonymity and confidentiality, they are not identified by name or job title. Each of the participants was asked whom they hoped was viewing APTN, whom they had in mind when producing particular programs, what they felt viewers wanted from APTN programs, and what kind of formal and informal feedback they had received from viewers.

The responses might be summed up as prefiguring an ideal audience that is engaged in communicating amongst First Nations, hearing Aboriginal stories, and experiencing pride and self-reflection. Almost everyone mentioned that they hoped APTN was reaching Aboriginal people everywhere, and that their ideal viewer was someone who wanted to know more about Aboriginal culture, who wanted to share their perspective and stories with members of other nations, and who took pride in APTN as a vehicle for Aboriginal self-reflection. One person, responding to the potential impact of APTN on viewers, said that he felt the most important impact on the viewer, whether Aboriginal or non-Aboriginal, was "just the act of seeing an Aboriginal person be the author of their own story."

The ideal viewer at APTN is dispersed amongst the diversity of Indian, Inuit, and Métis audiences, each shaped by historical, geographical, and cultural differences. Many staff members discussed the difficulty of imagining one homogeneous Aboriginal audience. While the ideal viewer was open to stories and perspectives of Aboriginal people across the country, respondents admitted that designing programming that "had something for everyone" was almost an impossible task. When discussing the potential APTN viewer and describing feedback from viewers, several people pointed to the overwhelming diversity of Aboriginal audiences. As the very first communications channel that was supposed to serve First Nations, Inuit, and Métis, several interview subjects mentioned diverging historical and colonial experiences and geographical and cultural differences as characteristics of a target audience with as many differences as similarities. Speaking about APTN's mandate to serve three distinct Aboriginal groups, as well as a secondary non-Aboriginal audience, one person admitted to a certain degree of cynicism and frustration in trying to meet the conflicting needs of these groups:

> I can't help think that this is somewhat of an experiment on the part of policy makers, by Indian Affairs, by the department of Canadian Heritage, by CRTC, and I'm not necessarily saying it's a bad experiment. But if they're going to experiment, what they should be aware of are the real political and social areas that they've asked us to take on. Regional and historical events, length of initial contact with European peoples, all this has a bearing on what we've been asked to do in terms of APTN's mandate. We've been asked to build bridges of understanding between the larger society, but also within our three Aboriginal groups [Indian, Inuit, and Métis, as defined by the Canadian Constitution]. Yet the political constructs are still there defining us. How can we, just as people, philosophically and through language, how can we understand that, that there are no borders, that we are really brothers and sisters, philosophically?

One other person echoed this sentiment and extended it to a larger challenge of representation for the network. The distinct histories of the three different groups coincide with different linguistic and cultural contexts and unique programming needs. The difficulty of imagining and conceiving of a common audience resulted in what this individual described as "a continual challenge in terms of Board resolve for direction for the network. Because they do come from different programming interests, different issues, different kinds of humour, different languages." So it seems that on one level the ideal APTN audience is also an impossible audience. The diverse and fragmented viewership of the network is reflected in the wider social fragmentation within and beyond television. APTN's ideal audience may not be so nearly contained and culturally homogenous as was documented by Dornfeld in his research at PBS.

When asked what kind of feedback APTN staff had received from viewers, most referred to various informal mechanisms of contact, including visits to communities, word of mouth, telephone calls, and e-mail. This gave them a sense of how programming was being received and how different groups within the audience were responding to APTN. Respondents mentioned various comments from family members, Elders in communities, and people encountered through activities and responsibilities beyond APTN. In each case, this face-to-face feedback reassured them that APTN programming was having an impact. As one participant said, "I get so many comments from word of mouth. And because I'm in so many different situations as not only a filmmaker, but because I'm ... involved in so many national organizations, where ever I go I meet our people, I meet Aboriginal filmmakers, I meet non-Aboriginal, I meet people in the industry and they're all very positive about our station. So I think we've done something, and we've filled a need." These responses further honed APTN staff's sense of whom they were trying to reach. At that point, in 2003, the network was just beginning to establish a separate function for viewer relations, which was being designed to deal with letters, faxes, phone calls, and e-mails. With over 1,000 letters or e-mails per quarter, the communications staff was beginning to build profiles of viewers with a sense of common programming interests and preferences.

When I asked people to talk about some of the challenges they faced in reaching their ideal viewer, many referred to obstacles created by the technical apparatus of national network television, such as promotion of the network, lower production values, reception quality in some areas, channel location in larger urban centres, and other barriers to access. The problems inherent in starting a national network from scratch with less than seven months between licensing and launch, in the remote channel location given to APTN at the high end of most cable line-ups, in the lack of training and technological and production constraints faced by Aboriginal program producers, and in audience expectations shaped by high-priced commercial television formats and genres, were all mentioned as barriers to reaching the ideal APTN viewer. As one person put it, "unless they watch only certain shows, some people will look at the network and just not connect with it. Because of low quality.... Once you get used to a certain kind of broadcast, everything else has to measure up. It has to be as slick, it has to be as professional, it has to be as current. We're still in that phase of 'Thank God, there's something.'" Clearly, APTN producers are aware that viewers bring the expectations of mainstream commercial TV to their assessment of non-profit Aboriginal television, and they are concerned about being measured against a standard that may not be appropriate to the emerging cultural codes and narrative structures of indigenous content. In this context, the network's increasing reliance on more commercial popular genres like reality TV, drama, comedy, and the weekly Hollywood movies are part of a long-term goal to attract viewers to the network in the hope that they will choose from among the wide variety of other programs available.

Several respondents identified cultural obstacles to reaching their ideal audience. These barriers related to the use of indigenous languages in programs. Producers and staff at APTN recognized that the Aboriginal language programming was addressed to a relatively limited and culturally specific audience. While almost everyone spoke to the centrality of APTN's mandate to provide television content in Aboriginal languages, several individuals remarked on the extent to which language programming excluded non-speakers due to lack of subtitles. There was some discussion of the need for subtitles to build the audience for all APTN programs. Yet not everyone agreed that subtitles were the solution, since they have the negative effect of diluting the role of language programming as a teaching tool for young Aboriginal speakers. Cultural barriers that emerged when redesigning a national television network to serve the needs of indigenous language speakers in remote and isolated communities have created some very real contradictions for APTN.

Several of the people I spoke to addressed the desire to use APTN programming to reach Aboriginal youth. As one person put it, young Aboriginal people, like young people across North America, have grown up immersed in a global popular culture sustained largely by television and popular music. Influenced by consumer-driven trends in TV drama, music video, and entertainment programming, young viewers are looking for that kind of content on APTN. While one person pointed out that it was good marketing strategy to try to reach the youth segment, she also admitted that it was "tough to do programs that keep their attention, when there's so much to see and do and be." Another person felt that youth wanted programs similar to those available on mainstream networks, but they wanted them with a cultural awareness that supports their own identity: "They want this kind of edgier cultural expression while living in their own Nation." These examples reflect the technical and institutional formation of young APTN viewers as a mobile and dispersed audience. Moving easily between majority and minority cultures, between the global and the local, they will require specific audience-building strategies to keep them engaged in APTN programs.

When imagining the ideal potential viewer for APTN, several of my interview subjects did mention the non-Aboriginal viewer. When asked to describe the ideal APTN viewer, one respondent gave a description of someone who was willing to listen, to learn, and to participate in changing majority attitudes about social and political conditions of Aboriginal people. This viewer was implicitly positioned as non-Aboriginal, someone who came to APTN because "they want to hear, they want to learn about us and in that learning, we begin to make some kind of change in the attitudes and the racism that exists in this country.... The kind of viewer who wants to share what they've learned with someone else. We need more viewers in order to get more people understanding where we come from." These viewers might be educators or bureaucrats who turn to APTN for reliable information about Aboriginal issues, or they might be ordinary people who are happy to find the unique cultural contrast APTN provides to commercial television offerings.

Finally, in their construction of the ideal viewer, one or two people addressed the conflicting audience needs for information or awareness and for entertainment. One participant dismissed the now-cancelled Friday night program *Bingo and a Movie* as a commercial ploy to attract eyeballs: "it's a game to get people to watch, it's not really what APTN is all about. It's like a stunt to get people to tune in so you can redirect them to other programming." She contrasted the movie nights and cooking shows to the genres of documentary, news, and current affairs, which she felt were of more genuine interest to viewers because "it gets inside our head, it's from our perspective." Yet another respondent suggested that while APTN was a not-for-profit network, this was not the same as "not-for-revenue," and so the commercial movies were an important element of the network's business plan and audience-building strategy. This apparent contradiction between entertaining audiences and informing them is not easily resolved. As an element of audience production, APTN's need for revenue generation further complicates the technical and institutional production of the spectator. Dornfeld notes a similar conflict at PBS when producers work to imagine a viewing community who, by being attracted to specific programs, will not only affirm the legitimate place of public broadcasting in the American system, but more importantly will buy memberships in local affiliates. In this manner, the imagined ideal audience is "institutionally enabling."[12]

APTN's Active Audience

As suggested earlier, the active viewer seeks out or discovers the network because it permits her to engage in oppositional readings of mainstream media representations of Aboriginal people. A fully developed portrait of the active audience is clearly beyond the scope of this chapter, but it seems to me that the active viewer can be located in the forms of regular interaction and engagement with APTN programs and practices.

In 2003, viewers could call in to the current affairs program *Contact* to respond to that day's topic and ask questions of the various guests. As was pointed out to me while I was at APTN, the "call ratio" for *Contact*—representing the ratio of total number of calls received to calls actually broadcast—is quite high. This indicates that people were not only watching the program but also engaged enough in the topic to attempt to call in. My impression, supported by anecdotal evidence from newsroom staff, is that *Contact* viewers are predominantly Aboriginal. However, when I was at APTN the topic of the program was the question of whether or not non-Aboriginal people should participate in Aboriginal ceremonies. This topic generated a few calls from non-Aboriginal viewers and many more responses on the web forum.

APTN's web forum has been relatively lively since it was first launched in 2001. The discussion topics were threaded according to present and past news stories and *Contact* topics. While it is not always possible to identify people posting to the APTN boards as Aboriginal or non-Aboriginal, most users self-identify and explicitly locate themselves culturally and politically. The forums would in themselves make an excellent source for ethnographic study. The discussions range far and wide along the political spectrum and posts indicate a healthy degree of contestation and debate within the APTN viewing community. Furthermore, some of the independently produced programs on APTN have their own websites and discussions boards. Both *Mocassin Flats* and *RenegadePress.com* had parallel online postings, used mostly by young fans to share personal responses to social and cultural issues raised by these shows. In the spring of 2007, APTN announced that it would be redesigning and outsourcing its forums. With the assistance of Canadian Culture Online, in 2008 the network launched a new website dedicated to Aboriginal cultural expression, *DigitalDrum.ca,* to "encourage on-line and real-world interactivity for youth, Elders, and others by providing access to a User Forum. Tools will also allow user generated creations such as video and audio clips, images and other online community building functionality to aid in storytelling, media literacy, community traditions, activism and music."[13] The active APTN viewer will need to migrate to this independent media platform, though at this point it is too early to determine how much the broadcast and online content will coincide.

Another interesting way of looking at the active APTN viewer is to look more broadly at the political, economic, and cultural stakeholders in the network—those people who come to APTN programming not only with an interest in its success or failure, but also with considerable influence over public perceptions of the network. These seven key groups of stakeholders were outlined to me by a member of the APTN staff. We might think of them as the "meta-audience" because they are not only viewers of but also players in the Canadian television industry as a whole. They help fashion the technical, institutional, and discursive contexts within which other APTN viewers are constructed. As my respondent described these stakeholders:

First are the *viewers*, the potential viewers that APTN is trying reach.

Second is the BDU, Broadcast Distribution Undertaking, that is the satellite and cable *affiliates*, that distribute the programming to the subscribers.

Third are the *media buyers*, that is the people you are trying to sell commercial air time to.

Fourth would be *media writers*, both industry writers and entertainment writers, who write about programs and shows you might have in entertainment guides or columns.

Fifth is the CRTC, the "VIP list" in government and industrial relations. You are communicating with them on a regular basis, so that come licence renewal time, you're prepared and they have a thorough understanding of what you've tried to do, and what you might need in the next phase of your licence.

Sixth are *independent producers*. There's a real need to keep communicating with up-and-coming Aboriginal "above-the-line" producers, directors, writers to get the kind of content we need.

Seventh is the *staff* of the network, who have their own unique stake in the development of APTN as an institution.

Clearly members of each of these groups watch APTN for different purposes and are, to varying degrees, active and critical viewers. These stakeholders do not all easily share the same ideological and discursive positions with respect to the kind of programming carried on APTN, but in Shohat and Stam's trialog, these groups form an integral part of the APTN community.

APTN's Actual Audience

What do we really know, as APTN enters its second decade, about who is watching the network, when, where, and why? There are now a few reliable sources of quantitative measurements that can be drawn upon to paint a picture of the actual audience. Some of this data is proprietary research and thus difficult to obtain, so I have relied on summaries of it provided by the APTN marketing team and sales staff. These sources include weekly Bureau of Broadcast Measurement (BBM) and Nielsen measures of Canadian television viewership, a focus-group study of viewers and non-viewers commissioned by APTN in 2002, a 2004 Print Measurement Bureau (PMB) study of urban Aboriginal media use, Environics and Pollara surveys commissioned by

APTN in communities north of the 60th parallel, and a 2003 Indian and Northern Affairs Canada (INAC) study of on-reserve residents' response to APTN.

APTN has been hampered in its measurement of actual viewers by a severe lack of industry-standard measures and under-reporting in the markets it reaches. The network spent most of the first five years of its operation with no reliable means of tracking its target Aboriginal audience, and it continues to struggle to obtain good demographic information about its viewers. The BBM and Nielsen ratings surveys do not ask respondents to identify as Aboriginal, and they are not even conducted in the Northern Territories or on reserves. There is no single reason for this situation, except that these ratings services are purchased by major media conglomerates as a means of pricing media advertising time. For the most part, neither Aboriginal people nor reserve communities have been considered a desirable market for the advertising of consumer goods and services. As far as commercial ratings systems go, APTN, like other ethnic minority media, faces a "media measurement under-reporting challenge" that limits its ability to raise ad revenue.[14]

Despite the under-reporting challenges arising from instruments that do not even track Aboriginal viewers, APTN's viewing audiences in Canadian cities can be seen to have experienced substantial growth. According to BBM, APTN's average weekly reach has climbed steadily from 560,000 in 1999, to 1.5 million in the fall of 2003, to over 3 million in November 2005. The vast majority of these viewers are non-Aboriginal. These figures compare favourably with those from many of the specialty digital channels in the Canadian market.

APTN had its first reliable measure of its northern and on-reserve audience in 2002 when it undertook focus-group studies in the North and on reserves. The focus groups were designed to test public awareness of the network and to analyze early responses of viewers to specific programs and formats. More than 80 percent of the on-reserve sample reported watching APTN, which was still a relatively new operation at that time. Further northern polls conducted in 2003 showed a substantial level of satisfaction with APTN programs. Respondents had mixed responses to Aboriginal language programming, as suggested earlier, but were especially positive about children's programming on APTN.[15] An INAC study in 2004 included specific questions about APTN and found that 24 percent of on-reserve viewers who receive APTN watched it as often as possible, while 43 percent watched sometimes. Older Aboriginal speakers are the most dedicated audience members in these communities. It is also important to note that the same study showed that 88 percent of respondents felt it was very or somewhat important to have a station giving access to a range of Aboriginal languages. Also, the study found, "people who see this role for APTN as important are more apt to report that they are satisfied with the programming and that they watch the station often."[16]

In 2003 to 2004, PMB included questions on APTN in its media-use survey and for the first time was able to identify Aboriginal viewers in southern media markets. According to this survey, urban APTN viewers are 75 percent white, 7.4 percent Aboriginal people, 5 percent black, and 12.6 percent from "other ethnic backgrounds." The consumer indicators for this audience (measures of other tastes, interests, and purchasing habits) show that these urban viewers spend money on cultural activities, entertainment, computer equipment, and sporting events.[17] Southern and urban Aboriginal viewers are clearly aware of APTN, and it has an average weekly reach of 31 percent of these viewers. This rises to 46 percent in the all-important eighteen to twenty-four year-old segment, and is slightly higher for men than for women.[18] Most importantly, among urban Aboriginal viewers APTN is ranked as the third most watched network, behind only Discovery Channel and MuchMusic.[19] Finally, Aboriginal APTN viewers watch more hours of television overall and watch more day-time television than the total population. From this data it is apparent that APTN is reaching a broad audience in urban areas and is clearly attracting young Aboriginal viewers to its programs.

Senior management and marketing and sales staff at APTN have been quite happy to exploit the newly described APTN "audience commodity." In their advertising sales information, APTN has made key arguments to media buyers about APTN's broad viewership across the country, and about the youthful, growing Aboriginal population with substantial disposable income that is watching the network. At the same time, the sales staff has worked to dispel myths that APTN is a government-supported entity that only attracts a marginal, niche audience. Using weekly ratings figures for prime-time movies, APTN can present itself as a very viable choice for advertisers.

With these audience-building (and selling) strategies, is APTN at risk of neglecting its cultural community? APTN is still of key significance as a primary service in the North and is the only source of television programming in Aboriginal languages. But APTN is not exploiting prime-time slots to show popular Hollywood movies simply to improve its ratings. In effect, ad revenue from weekend movies can be used to subsidize the network's other, less "marketable" programs, especially those in Aboriginal languages with much smaller reach. APTN has also entered into a number of partnerships that will build audiences across a broader spectrum and are more likely to increase the number of active viewers. For example, APTN is promoting the network as a language-learning tool in schools, and with ExpressVu and Telesat it has ensured that the network is available in every school in Ontario and Quebec. APTN also has entered into a partnership with the Rogers channel OMNI that allows the network to version some of its Aboriginal language programs for the multicultural network and to co-produce other programs.[20]

Conclusion

APTN has entered its second seven-year licence term with a much more coherent sense of its audience and some clear strategies for developing program formats that are both entertaining and informative. The network is still constrained by its status as the only medium to reach such a diverse Aboriginal population and it will, under these conditions, never really be able to satisfy the very different needs of its northern/southern, reserve/urban, and Aboriginal-speaking/English- or French-speaking viewers. The support for APTN in its licence renewal process was strong. Conflicts remain within the APTN community, stakeholders, and beyond concerning board structure, acquisitions policies, and programming strategies, but these sometimes-public disputes have not yet substantially undermined the legitimacy of the network. In its licence renewal brief to the CRTC, APTN proposed to create more regional offices, separate eastern and western feeds, and develop sideband audio technology so that viewers can choose to watch programming in multiple language versions; these measures will address some of the main constraints that APTN faces in meeting audience needs.

If we return to Shohat and Stam's model of the audience as a trialog between texts, readers, and communities in discursive and social relation to one another, we can see that APTN is a very productive site of interaction and struggle over what it is to be Aboriginal in Canada today. Ideal, active, and actual APTN viewers are constructed in this ongoing conversation about cultural difference and social and political possibilities.

NOTES

1.   S. Elizabeth Bird, *The Audience in Everyday Life* (New York: Routledge, 2003).
2.   Ibid., 4.
3.   Nick Couldry, "The Extended Audience: Scanning the Horizon," in *Media Audiences*, ed. Marie Gillespie (New York: Open University Press, 2005), 183–222.
4.   Ibid., 186.
5.   Ella Shohat and Robert Stam, *Unthinking Eurocentrism: Multiculturalism and the Media* (London: Routledge, 1994), 347.
6.   Ibid., 350.

7. Ibid., 350.

8. Stuart Hall, "Encoding/Decoding," in *Popular Culture: Production and Consumption*, ed. C. Lee Harrington and Denise D. Bielby (Oxford: Blackwell, 2001), 123–132.

9. Faye D. Ginsburg, "Embedded Aesthetics: Creating a Discursive Space for Indigenous Media," in *Internationalizing Cultural Studies: An Anthology*, ed. M.A. Abbas and John Nguyet Erni (Malden, MA: Blackwell, 2005), 277–294; Eric Michaels, *For a Cultural Future: Francis Jupurrurla Makes TV at Yuendumu* (Sydney: Art and Text Publications, 1989); Michael Meadows, "Broadcasting in Aboriginal Australia: One Mob, One Voice, One Land," in *Ethnic Minority Media*, ed. Harold Stephen Riggins (Newbury Park, CA: Sage Publications, 1992), 82–101; Lorna Roth, *Something New in the Air: The Story of First Peoples' Television Broadcasting in Canada* (Montreal: McGill Queen's University Press, 2005); Kathleen Buddle, "Aboriginal Cultural Capital Creation and Radio Production in Urban Ontario," *Canadian Journal of Communication* 30, 1 (2005): 7–40.

10. Barry Dornfeld, "Envisioning Reception," in *The Construction of the Viewer*, ed. Peter Ian Crawford and Sigurjon Baldur Hafsteinsson (Højbjerg, Denmark: Intervention Press, Nordic Anthropological Film Association, 1996), 229.

11. S. Elizabeth Bird, *The Audience in Everyday Life*; Gillespie, Marie. *Television, Ethnicity, and Cultural Change*, (London & New York: Routledge, 1995); David Morley and Charlotte Brunsdon, *The Nationwide Television Studies*, (London & New York: Routledge, 1999); Janice A. Radway, *Reading the Romance: Women, Patriarchy, and Popular Literature*, (Chapel Hill: University of North Carolina Press, 1991).

12. Ibid., 229.

13. Aboriginal Peoples Television Network, *Board Offline*, 2007, http://www.aptn.ca/forums/ (accessed 22 June 2007).

14. Aboriginal Peoples Television Network, "APTN Viewing Audiences Continues to Grow," news release, 2004, http://www.aptn.ca/index.php?option=com_content&task=view&id=39&Itemid=39 (accessed 16 Feb. 2006).

15. Strategic Inc., *APTN: Brand Equity Measure, Programming and Promotional Test* (Winnipeg: APTN, 2002).

16. Canada, Indian and Northern Affairs, *Survey of First Nations People Living on-Reserve, Integrated Final Report* (Ottawa: Ekos Research Associates Inc, 2003).

17. Aboriginal Peoples Television Network, *APTN Fast Facts*, 2005, http:/www.aptncsr.com/fast_facts.php (accessed 16 Feb. 2006).

18. Aboriginal Peoples Television Network, *APTN Media Sales Package* (Toronto: APTN Media Sales, 2006).

19. Aboriginal Peoples Television Network, *Aboriginal Urban Population and APTN* (Source: PMB 2005) (Winnipeg: Brave Strategy, 2005).

20. Jennifer David, *Aboriginal Language Broadcasting in Canada: An Overview and Recommendations to the Task Force on Aboriginal Languages and Cultures, Final Report* (Ottawa: Debwe Communications Inc and APTN, 2004), 23.

CHAPTER 5

Aboriginal Media on the Move: An Outside Perspective on APTN[1]

KERSTIN KNOPF

The recent emergence of global mediascapes has increased the influence of Western (mostly United States–American) film and television products worldwide and the dissemination of Western news media via the internet and satellites. In that context, Peter Lewis observes in his introduction to *Alternative Media: Linking Global and Local* that there are "communities and minorities whose access to information, and means of self-expression, are not guaranteed by mass channels, and that more sharply focused, customized and essentially smaller or local media are important, filling this gap."[2] The Aboriginal Peoples Television Network (APTN) is one media outlet in Canada that is filling this gap, not as a small or local channel, but as the world's first television channel created and operated by Aboriginal people that has a country-wide broadcast license. It is a great achievement that Aboriginal media makers themselves are finally able to control the images of Aboriginal people and the discourse on Aboriginal-related issues in one small section of the Canadian media. Aboriginal media makers now have a media outlet, where *they* can decide what the mainstream and Aboriginal people should know about Aboriginal culture, politics, languages, and traditions, and where they can determine how this information is relayed. Moreover, Aboriginal media makers have a platform from which to contest the ideological and imaginary Aboriginal constructed in Western media discourse.

In this chapter I will summarize APTN's programming and acquisition policy, discuss apparent Aboriginal discursive strategies, and also look critically at some of the network's programs. I will show how the production of Aboriginal media content at this television channel fosters new perspectives, in terms of politics and culture, by applying program policies that are shaped according to local Aboriginal cultural needs. My argument is that, on the one hand, the production and broadcast of self-controlled, anti-colonial media through APTN works toward a gradual decolonization of Canadian airwaves, and that, on the other hand, APTN's sometimes insensitive program choices endanger this decolonizing process. This chapter undertakes a critical reading of examples of advertising, news programming, children's animation, and entertainment programs that promote the decolonization of media and yet sometimes reintroduce negative stereotypes and tropes of the vanishing Indian. These ideological contradictions indicate some of the risks that APTN faces in reiterating dominant Western representations of indigenous people instead of countering them.

APTN's motto is "Sharing our stories with all Canadians as well as viewers around the world," and thus the website states that "APTN offers all Canadians a window into the remarkably diverse worlds of Indigenous peoples in Canada and throughout the world." The website states further that "APTN offers an unprecedented opportunity for Aboriginal producers, directors, actors, writers and media professionals to create innovative, reflective and relevant programming for Canadian viewers."[3] Although the primary audience of APTN is Aboriginal people on reserves, in Canada's North and in southern urban centers there is a growing audience among non-Aboriginal people as well. Nielsen Media meter-data reports have found that weekly viewing numbers have increased from 900,000 in 1999 to over 1,750,000 in 2003, though, as Bredin indicates in her chapter in this volume, these figures do not track Aboriginal viewers as a separate group. Studies conducted by Environics (north of the 60th parallel) and Statistics Canada (on reserve) found that there is "an emotional attachment between APTN and the Aboriginal viewing audience. Over 90 percent of respondents indicated that they watch APTN 'sometimes' or 'all the time.'"[4] This success of APTN among the Aboriginal population is due to the fact that for the first time Aboriginal people have a media outlet with which they identify and where they see their own concerns, politics, and cultures contextualized. Thus, the chief executive officer of APTN, Jean LaRose, says, "When Aboriginal Peoples finally see themselves portrayed as they actually live their lives and are involved in the communication of issues from their first-hand perspective, we create a powerful emotional attachment with our viewer—an envious and coveted position by any Broadcaster."[5]

APTN broadcasts almost twenty-two hours per day, and, except for the news shows and live coverage of nationwide events, all programs are acquired from independent Aboriginal producers, from sources such as the National Film Board of Canada, and from other Canadian and international sources. This means that there is less than 10 percent in-house production and more than 90 percent program acquisition.[6] 86 percent of APTN's programming has Canadian content, a number that exceeds the CRTC target of 70 percent.[7] APTN's program policy requires an all-Aboriginal program, meaning that its content has to be 100 percent Aboriginal-related. The channel is "by, for and about" Aboriginal people, a distinction that is easily confused when the "and" gets replaced by "or," as I will demonstrate later. APTN's mandate is to promote and buy the programs of independent Aboriginal media creators. To meet this mandate it is necessary to define what an "Aboriginal production" is. According to APTN's definition, an Aboriginal production company may be "a sole proprietorship, a limited company, a co-operative, a partnership, or a not-for-profit organization in which Aboriginal persons have at least 51 percent ownership and control," or "a joint venture consisting of two or more businesses, provided that the business(es) has at least 51 percent Aboriginal ownership and control of the joint venture."[8] As this definition reveals, APTN has a non-exclusionary approach to Aboriginal media making. It ensures that more than half of its production source is Aboriginal, but it does not exclude non-Aboriginal involvement in the production process. Yet the definition of an Aboriginal program as one produced, at least in part, by Aboriginal people does not apply to all of the content on APTN. It is in the non-Aboriginal content, especially in popular films and some animation programs in which Aboriginal control of production is not evident, that the major contradictions arise in evaluating the ideological and cultural impact of the network.

While APTN is financed by a twenty-five cent monthly cable subscriber fee, the network also depends on advertising revenue. APTN has to consider the fact that advertisers are not interested in Aboriginal language programs that are not dubbed, captioned, or subtitled, because the market for unilingual programs is small. When a program is dubbed, captioned, or subtitled, statistics confirm that viewer numbers grow, and consequently the advertising revenue for these programs grows.[9] Currently, APTN carries commercials for computers, cars, tools, insurance, etc., like any other commercial television channel. APTN's advertising policy forbids showing any commercials for alcohol and tobacco in order to avoid supporting the abuse of these substances.[10] There is, however, one questionable commercial seen currently on APTN (as well as on other Canadian networks), for Lakota pain killers and arthritis ointment that are supposedly produced according to traditional Lakota medicine. The commercialization of Aboriginal cultural knowledge (such as traditional herbal ingredients) is one thing to contest, but the character of the commercial is another. The well-known Native American actor Floyd Red Crow Westerman is dressed as and performing the role of a "traditional Indian" while suggesting that viewers might try traditional Lakota medicine. The ad reintroduces the romanticized wise and noble savage "who will share his medicine with all whites." When APTN uncritically carries this commercial, it risks endorsing the commercialization and appropriation of Aboriginal cultural knowledge and symbols that are so vehemently contested when they appear in other areas of popular culture, such as sports mascots and Hollywood westerns.[11] The network also undermines its potential to create media free of the stereotypes and clichés of Aboriginal people that are still rampant in Western discourses.

Aboriginal Discursive Strategies in APTN Programs

In her study of Aboriginal discourse in Canada's news media, Steffi Retzlaff describes several Aboriginal discursive models that are employed in order to project Aboriginal cultural values into contemporary discourses.[12] She observes that Aboriginal discourse is characterized by various properties derived from traditional discourses that are "used for projecting cultural values in contemporary contexts and for positively (re)affirming Aboriginal identities."[13] These properties include cultural address markers (opening and closing formulae in an Aboriginal language, such as "Aaniin/Ahnee," "Boozhoo," and "Meegwetch"), the concept of "family," and emphasis on past or future generations (signified by phrases such as "my parents, grandparents and extended family members," "individuals, families, communities, and Nations," "our ancestors as well as our living and our unborn" and "seven generations past and future"), and the appeal to authority of the Elders (signified by phrases such as "our Elders have always told us" and "the Elders have said"). Other discursive strategies include references to the Medicine Wheel as representing "traditional spirituality, philosophy, [social system,] and psychology"[14] and an engagement of Aboriginal humour with the indirect speech acts of irony and teasing. One key discursive strategy is the introduction of Aboriginal terminology in order to construct collective and national identities and to counter hegemonic discursive practices. According to

Retzlaff, this terminology includes the usage of "Native," "Aboriginal," "First Nations" (or "indigenous people"), the cultural term "Turtle Island," referring to a national territory and including "references to a land base, national resources and landscapes as well as to local and geographical borders," and the use of the first person plural pronoun "we" and its associated forms "our" and "us," "which induces the readership to conceptualize group identity, solidarity, and a national collective as members of an in-group."[15] These strategies and properties characterize the verbal and visual discourse of a variety of APTN's programs. For example, some programs, such as *Finding our Talk, Tamapta*, and *Suaangan*, contain cultural address markers, depending on the host. It seems that programs hosted in Aboriginal languages more readily include such cultural address markers, whereas programs hosted in English, like *Death at Ipperwash, Beyond Words*, and *Cooking with the Wolfman*, use the more common "Welcome" and "Hello."

Using examples from specific programs, I will now consider aspects that distinguish APTN from mainstream television, apart from the Aboriginal content, and will trace the discursive models outlined above as they shape these programs. The daily half-hour news show APTN *National News* covers Aboriginal-related local, national, and international news from Canada, the United States, Latin America, Australia, and New Zealand, to name a few locations that are frequently mentioned. APTN not only covers stories that do not make it into the news shows of other national broadcasters, or are at least underrepresented there, but also offers this news coverage from an Aboriginal perspective and with an Aboriginal focus that is not provided in other news programs. APTN states on its website that the news show "provide[s] balanced, accurate and provocative coverage of national issues" and "looks beyond the headlines and offers context and historical perspectives on issues."[16] The *National News* of 22 September 2004 covered the opening of the Smithsonian National Museum of the American Indian in Washington, DC, as well as the Indian Summit in Vancouver and the continuing land claim process in British Columbia. In the first example, the Aboriginal perspective comes to the fore through the terminology used. Former news anchor Nola Wuttunee says, "The Grand Opening festivities started with the procession of nations. Around 25,000 indigenous people from across Turtle Island marched through the US capital." She uses the terms "nations" and "indigenous people" instead of the misnomers "tribes" and "Indians," as well as the term "Turtle Island" instead of "North America" or "Canada and the United States." Thus, she introduces and sustains Aboriginal terminology in media discourse, establishes a national indigenous identity, and counters discursive practices of Western media discourse. The news

piece contains images of the procession of Aboriginal people and the as-
sembled people outside of the museum, and only a few outside shots of
the museum itself. It does not include speeches of the opening that would
feature non-Aboriginal officials, and thus the visual and verbal discourse
stresses the Aboriginal perspective of this event. In the second example,
Wuttunee presents the perspective of British Columbia chiefs rather than
that of Canadian government officials on this issue. She opens by quoting
one of the chiefs who describes the land claim processes as "disgraceful" and
also notes that Aboriginal chiefs disagree with the government claim that
there has been recent progress in treaty talks. This piece contains two clips
featuring the Aboriginal negotiators Ed John and Doug Kelly and only one
featuring Indian Affairs minister Andy Scott, giving more screen time to
the Aboriginal negotiators. As a result, the structure of this news piece also
sustains the Aboriginal perspective of the content.

Within the news show, APTN regularly features studio discussions on
various issues, such as the financial compensation for residential school survivors, Aboriginal youth gangs, and the recently stated government agenda
to decrease poverty in Aboriginal communities. National events that have an
impact on Aboriginal people are presented and discussed, such as Belinda
Stronach's switching from the Conservative Party to the Liberal Party and
the crucial budget vote on 19 May 2005. Studio guests discussed the consequences of the small Liberal majority for Aboriginal people and their
relations to and expectations of the Liberal government at the time. On 25
March 2005 the spiritual cultural counsellor and educator Sakoieta' Widrick
and University of Manitoba student April Seenie were invited to discuss the
high-school shooting at the Red Lake reservation in Minnesota. According
to APTN's mandate, this event is presented from the Aboriginal perspective,
through the news anchor and studio guests and also through a presentation
of an APTN clip from the location. Even more importantly, the program
structure gives Aboriginal studio guests a platform to comment on this issue,
to provide opinions and explanations and thus an Aboriginal point of reference for an event that greatly shocked Aboriginal North America. Widrick
explains that the reasons for incidents like this one are to be found in the
colonization of indigenous populations worldwide, where, in the process of
colonization, the indigenous spirit, identity, culture, language, and customs
are being destroyed. He says:

> Our main purpose here on the earth is to look after these gifts of
> these children. In our culture as Mohawks we even say "the seventh
> generation coming, we're preparing for them. And while they're

here we need to nurture them like a seed so that they can establish a good basis to begin growing and live life here on earth." And when that doesn't happen, and that's taken away, where a young man like this does not have the nurturing of the family, does not have the nurturing of the community, because the community is in chaos because of a lot of the colonialistic things that have been done, we're going to see this happen over and over and over again.

Widrick provides a historical and socio-political analysis of the state of indigenous North America that many APTN viewers might not have considered before, and that helps them to better understand existing social problems and identity crises as consequences of colonization and existing power relations in North America. His rhetoric also demonstrates Aboriginal discursive strategies: he focuses on the concepts of family, community, and the seventh generation and places forthcoming generations at the centre of Aboriginal social organization. In his talk he indirectly employs the philosophical concept of the Medicine Wheel in order to illustrate that the break in Aboriginal socio-cultural traditions is responsible for alienation and disruption in Aboriginal communities and eventually for the actions of this young man. Aboriginal philosophy as a discursive property also emerges in Widrick's usage of the phrase "here on [the] earth" instead of "world" or "country," revealing a stress on the importance of land for Aboriginal peoples.

Another key pillar of APTN's programming are ongoing dramatic series, such as *North of Sixty*, set in a northern community and aired previously on CBC; *Jackson's Wharf*, set in a New Zealand community; and *Moccasin Flats*, created and produced by two Aboriginal women, Jennifer Podemski and Laura Milliken, and their company Big Soul Productions. As is discussed in extensive detail in Christine Ramsay's chapter in this book, *Moccasin Flats* is a show about urban Aboriginal youth set in an Aboriginal ghetto in Regina. It explores such current issues as gang wars, alcohol and drug abuse, prostitution, family violence, and poverty of young single mothers. The series features the (former) drug-dealer and pimp Jonathon Bearclaw, who dominates the "flats," and a number of characters who are entangled in this urban scene and who succumb to substance addiction and ensuing crime and prostitution. But there are also characters like Candy Foster and Mathew Merasty, who find ways to get out of these situations. There have been both positive and negative responses to the show. Some Aboriginal viewers criticized it for presenting only a serious and negative side of Aboriginal life and upholding stereotypes that involve violence, women and child abuse, Aboriginal criminality, and substance abuse. The program reveals one aspect of Aboriginal reality, and it is made by young Aboriginal talent who will continue to create shows that reflect their view of society, which is, in essence, self-controlled media making.

A number of APTN programs introduce Aboriginal oral tradition into electronic media by recording Elders talking in their traditional language (often with subtitles) about cultural traditions, colonial history, and residential school experience, or telling other stories. Examples of such programs include *Tamapta, Haa Shagoon, Our Dene Elders,* and *Nunavimiut.* Often, only the Elders are filmed as they describe how they were raised, how they hunted, trapped, and fished and used to prepare food, what games they played, how they made arts and crafts, and how they were taught by their grandparents. In *Nunavimiut* the narratives are illustrated by drawings, animated cartoons, and archival photographs, complemented by images of the storyteller and a children's audience. In *Haa Shagoon* visuals of the Elder are accompanied by images of the settlement and surrounding environment, of people fishing and processing fish, and of arts and crafts work such as beaded moccasins and vests. The Elders often start by introducing themselves and their families and saying where they were born and raised, and thus the programs keep the narrative pattern of the oral tradition in which the storyteller first introduces him/herself and explains the origin of the story to be told. The intent of these programs is most likely to re-introduce younger generations to the tradition of oral storytelling that was suppressed by the Canadian government's assimilation program when young children were brought to residential schools and cut off from their families, language, and traditions. As more and more Elders pass away, electronic media proves to be a vehicle for transmitting these stories to younger generations and for preserving and teaching traditional languages. One needs to keep in mind that, while the recording reflects the content and character of the narration of the Elder, and the illustrative visuals root the relayed information in a visual cultural context, these are a limited replacement for the socio-geographic context. The recording process removes this cultural knowledge from its cultural and storytelling context, cuts off the interaction between storyteller and audience, and freezes one version of the tales. In the oral tradition this cultural knowledge would be subject to changes, and there would be different versions of the tales adapted to the audience and the respective storytelling context. In this sense, these programs cannot replace oral storytelling, but they do become electronic containers of cultural knowledge that otherwise would be seriously diminished.

In addition to these oral storytelling programs that focus on a younger audience, APTN has a variety of other programming for children. These include *Canadian Geographic for Kids*, the puppet shows *Tipi Tales* and *Longhouse Tales*, and the cartoon *Inuk*. In *Canadian Geographic for Kids* the young Aboriginal hosts, Jennifer and Jamie, visit various parts of the country, such as the Rocky Mountains, a Quebec island, the prairies, or the British Columbia rainforests. On these trips they usually meet young people who introduce them to their homeland, its geographic and cultural specifics, and their way of life. The young hosts are often not very knowledgeable themselves; they sometimes do silly things in the show and tease each other or the people they visit. Thus they do not present themselves as superior to their prospective audience but as part of it. Often, the young host Jay illustrates concepts like the origins of the Rocky Mountains or how avalanches develop with simple experiments in his "Gee! Ology" studio. Interspersed "triviography" questions and "geopops" facts are employed to help sustain the acquired knowledge. Colloquial youth-oriented English, unconventional framing, extreme mobile framing with fast zooms and pans, out-of-kilter shots, high and low camera angles, fast motion effects, faster cuts, and an accompanying funny sound track also contribute to making this show appealing to a young audience.

Programs like *Tipi Tales, Takuginai,* and *The Wondrous World of Greenthumb's Garden* contain traditional teachings but also hold lessons about how to achieve self-fulfilment and how to cope within mainstream society. The series *Longhouse Tales*, created by Tom Jackson, introduces Jackson as the storyteller Hector Longhouse, who tells stories brought to him by Coyote, which are then "enacted" by puppets. There is a framing sequence in which the storyteller talks with puppet characters, which gives him the idea for the central story. *Longhouse Tales* actually contextualizes oral storytelling in a modified way and adapts it to contemporary times. The stories are told by a modern-day storyteller, and cultural knowledge is presented in a mix of fantasy and traditional Aboriginal characters and mythology, but the show is still modelled on traditional stories as the way of teaching children how things came into being. In one example, Jackson tells the audience how little pepper became a lucky charm and how see-through stones are made. Within the framing sequence, the turkey rooster Tycon prepares to take part in the Turkey Toastmaster Speech-off competition but is a total failure. Here, the children's audience is taught by the example of Tycon that it is okay not to be a great speaker, it is okay not to be perfect, but that self-confidence is necessary to make one a whole and successful person. This teaching is particularly important, as many Aboriginal youth in Canada feel unable to cope within mainstream, contemporary society and to live up to its expectations. High-school drop-out and suicide rates among Aboriginal youth, which are much higher than the national average, bear witness to this general feeling of loss, incompleteness, and marginalization. Thus, the didactic function of such programs is of utmost importance. For Aboriginal children, such programs present a reference point for cultural support and identity construction, and they make the children feel good about themselves and their culture.

Contradictory Representations and Dominant Discourses in APTN Images

There are, however, two children's shows that rely on sometimes problematic representations of Aboriginal people. The cartoon *WesToons*, for example, is a German production with an American Indian consultant that is based on the German writer Karl May's Winnetou novels. May was an author of popular adventure fiction in the late nineteenth century and created the characters of the noble Indian Winnetou and his white blood brother Old Shatterhand, who roam the Wild West and fight for law and order and for the victory of White civilization.[17] The bourgeois values and escapist fantasies inherent in May's texts "were in tune with the dreams and fancies of the Kaiserreich which favoured maintaining the status quo," writes Hartmut Lutz.[18] May's texts, as those of authors like Fritz Steuben, who created the proud, courageous, stoic, and enduring Tecumseh,[19] were then appropriated for the German nationalist ideology in the Nazi era. By using May's characters, the program latently carries the nationalist ideologies of the Kaiserreich and the Third Reich. The cartoon also features the adventurous Winnetou/Old Shatterhand couple, the goofy Old Sam, Winnetou's beautiful sister Ntscho-tschi, and the young warrior Hakshiva[20] as the good guys fighting against the bad ones in the Wild West. Although the show is at times a satire of life in the old West, it also upholds clichés of the romanticized noble Indian by introducing these characters in immaculate beaded buckskin clothes and with stereotypical "Indian" gestures. For example, Winnetou raises one hand, palm facing Old Shatterhand and Sam, when he greets them with the words "It is good to see my blood brother and Sam." Winnetou is also fitted with a flowery and obscure "Indian" language that apparently knows no first-person pronoun, as in "Winnetou will find Ntscho-tschi." Winnetou, as an Apache dressed in Plains-style clothes, and living with Ntscho-tschi in an Anasazi-like cliff-dwelling, illustrates some of the homogenizing tendencies of this program. Ntscho-tschi's appearance and her conduct are reminiscent of Disney's Pocahontas, and the tall, strong, blue-eyed and blonde Shatterhand fits easily into the ideological Aryan model race constructed in fascist Germany. In one part, Winnetou gets caught by train robbers, and Shatterhand, together with the cavalry, rescues poor Winnetou along with the gold that the robbers have stolen. In two other episodes, Winnetou and Ntscho-tschi are caught in a blizzard and trapped in a cabin, where natural forces and a mountain lion threaten to kill them. They are, again, rescued by Shatterhand. The idea running through the show is that the Aboriginal people do not know how to take care of themselves in the country that they are indigenous to. Yet in another part, Winnetou and Shatterhand restore a cattle herd, stolen by rustlers, to farmers who assumed that the Indians had stolen the cattle. That done, they ride, as at the end of all other shows, peacefully into the marvellous sunset. The program is a strange mix of the stereotypical imaginary Indians of Western media discourses embedded in narratives that attempt to relate historical issues of frontier life and wars, interspersed with one-liners that correct historical and ideological misconceptions such as "the cowboys learned their skills from the Indians." Although the program usually portrays non-Aboriginal people as the bad guys, it is still a manifestation of the notion that "Indians" could not exist in the old West independently, were not able to fight frontier wars on their own, and could only survive with the help of their "white" brothers. It thus reiterates the theme of white colonialists with Indian sidekicks in Western discourse, such as the Lone Ranger and Tonto, and James Fenimore Cooper's Natty Bumppo/Hawkeye and Chingachgook, where the Indian is defined as the ward of his colonial guard and is clearly positioned as the inferior. This inferior/superior dichotomy, in turn, serves to uphold Eurocentric hegemonies and colonial discourses of superiority.

The cartoon *The Last Reservation* presents the A-tchoum tribe, which lives in an Indian world from the past recreated on top of a city skyscraper in a future world that is environmentally polluted. Only the chief, Trusting Bull, does not know that he lives in this zoo-like "Indian" environment. His family is concerned with upholding this illusion and have to prevent Pesos Bill, "owner" of the rooftop, and his helper from the lower world from destroying this illusion. The cartoon casts wolves, crocodiles, and buffalos as stereotypical noble Indians dressed in buckskin and feathers, living in tipis beside totem poles and engaging in all kinds of "Indian" activities, such as hunting buffalo, dancing around a fire, and making magic potions. This program reintroduces humiliating and romanticizing stereotypes, homogenizes various indigenous cultures, and clearly creates a burlesque of Plains cultures. In one episode, the characters manage, with the help of a magic stone, to restore their past world without environmental destruction. The environmentalist agenda of this cartoon does not excuse its ridicule of indigenous cultures as it freezes the imaginary Indian in the untouched, pure past while it denies cultural change and a contemporary Aboriginal experience.

A few additional examples illustrate the variety of programs on APTN, which often reflect and stress cultural change and negotiate the traditional and the modern. *Creative Native* is a program on Aboriginal arts and crafts that shows how various items, such as moccasins, shields, and totem poles, are made. The program not only features the materials used and the creation process, but also teaches about the traditional meanings of the materials and items. Similarly, *Qaujisaut* introduces traditional and modern tools, demonstrating how they are made and their purpose. *Qaggiq* also teaches traditional activities, like fishing, in Inuktitut. The cooking show *Cooking with the Wolfman* mixes traditional ingredients, such as moose and caribou meat, turnips, and squash with Western ingredients and styles of cooking. *Spirit Creations* presents Aboriginal clothing designers and their work, which is often a combination of modern and traditional materials and designs. *Profiles of Success* focuses on entrepreneurial success stories of Aboriginal people and presents role models and ways to battle poverty and welfare mentality. *Finding Our Talk* is a program that concentrates on survival of Aboriginal languages and features cultural events and community profiles in various languages.

Outside of these independent programs, APTN relies on mainstream feature films for the APTN *Movies* program. APTN's choice of feature films for this slot in their program sometimes lacks sensitivity to the implications and consequences of stereotypical Indian images in the media, while neglecting the potential to highlight non-stereotyped, decolonized programming. For some time, the feature film program was called *Reel Aboriginal Movies*. The program title itself was misleading, as the *reel* (as in film reel) sounds like *real*, and it poses the question, what are "real" Aboriginal movies supposed to be? Ideally the programming policy of APTN should give preference to movies that are made by an Aboriginal director or producer, or by an Aboriginal production company. However, according to human resources director Kent Brown, APTN's policy for choosing "Aboriginal" feature films is that they should be "by, for *or* about Aboriginal people."[21] At this point the replacement of the "and" by "or" comes into play. This policy means that either producer or director of the movie has to be Aboriginal, that it is produced by an Aboriginal company, that the content is Aboriginal, *or* that the movie stars Aboriginal actors. As a consequence, APTN shows movies by Aboriginal and Maori directors, such as Randy Redroad's *The Doe Boy*, Chris Eyre's *Skins*, and Lee Tamahori's *Once Were Warriors*. In these cases, there is a positive opportunity for indigenous filmmakers to find a major media outlet for their works. But APTN also screens movies like Bruce McDonald's *Dance Me Outside* and Bruce Beresford's *Black Robe*, which have Aboriginal content but are made by non-Aboriginal filmmakers and can also be criticized for reproducing clichés and conveying non-Aboriginal perspectives. Finally, there are often movies on APTN like *Mermaids* and *The Witches of Eastwick*, starring Cher; *Batman Forever*, starring Val Kilmer; *Point Break*, starring Keanu Reeves; and films starring Cameron Diaz, David Hasselhoff, and Elvis Presley, based on the fact that these actors are part Aboriginal. This was the only factor that qualified these movies for the *Reel Aboriginal Movies* program. In this way, the program title and the choice of movies rendered a misguided and detrimental concept of Aboriginal movies. The choice of these movies is not contested here, but rather the way they are promoted and contextualized as "Aboriginal" movies.

APTN changed the program title to APTN *Friday Movie*, giving the network the freedom to broadcast movies that deal only marginally, or not at all, with Aboriginal culture and come from non-Aboriginal sources. This is reasonable, given the small numbers of movies available that are made by Aboriginal filmmakers. But APTN still airs clichéd frontier romances that clearly perpetuate contested representations of Indian imagery and Western historiography, such as Kevin Costner's *Dances With Wolves* that polarizes the noble Lakota and the bloodthirsty, savage Pawnee. Donald Shebib's *The Pathfinder* and Michael Mann's *Last of the Mohicans* (these two latter are both based on James Fenimore Cooper's Leatherstocking novels) reiterate the trope of the vanishing Indian and legitimize Manifest Destiny. In Edward Zwick's *Legends of the Fall* Tristan Ludlow collects scalps of German soldiers on a revenge spree. Similarly, Danièle J. Suissa's *Pocahontas: The Legend* falsifies history, reproduces the discredited myth of the romance between Pocahontas and John Smith, introduces viewers to the "court" of Powhatan, "princess" Pocahontas, and "prince" Kocoum, and sells them the image of Powhatan's people wearing buckskin dresses and dancing powwow style. Moreover, frontier grotesques like *A Man Called Horse* and *The Silent Enemy* have been shown in the APTN Friday movie slot. *A Man Called Horse* is a ludicrous spectacle that animalizes the Sioux; they look like comic figures who make strange gestures and expressions, dance much too fast, and treat their elderly and hostages badly. The filmmakers do not provide subtitles for long stretches of Sioux dialogue spoken in the film, reducing the Sioux language to an unintelligible babble.[22] Apart from the distortion of Sioux culture, the film stages a Sun Vow ritual and a parody of a sweat lodge ceremony, both of which staged ceremonies are sacrilegious insults to Sioux spiritual culture. In the silent movie *The Silent Enemy*, viewers are not given information about the nation of the people staged, there is the dying chief Chetoga, his beautiful daughter, the scheming and mean medicine man Dagwan, who is in love with the chief's daughter, and the good guy Baluk, played by Chief Buffalo Child Long Lance, an Indian impostor who wrote the fake autobiography *Long Lance: A Self-portrait of the Last Indian*. Like *A Man Called Horse*, the film ridicules traditional ways of life, grotesquely distorts Aboriginal ceremonies, and introduces the polarized stereotypes of the bloodthirsty devil and the noble savage. The film is also reminiscent of Robert Flaherty's ethno-romantic *Nanook of the North* in its staging of "man's eternal fight against unrelenting natural forces." *On Deadly Ground*, a movie about an Alaskan oil magnate and an Inuit protest against a new refinery, has a Chinese actress playing the Inuit lead role and upholds the contested Hollywood practice of starring non-Aboriginal actors as Aboriginal characters. The horror movie *Wendigo* appropriates the spiritual concept of the Wendigo in order to explore the psychological horror of a New York City family's weekend trip and thus misuses Aboriginal spirituality as a dynamizing force for a narrative that has nothing to do with Aboriginal experience.

Such movies are presented without a critical or subversive context, and consequently APTN reiterates Western media practices of presenting Aboriginal culture instead of countering them. Early in its first licence term, APTN ran *Bingo and a Movie*, a program that provided just such a critical context for the various movies "with Indians" shown on the program. For each show, host Darrell Dennis had a prominent Aboriginal person from the realms of politics, media, or the arts as a guest in a studio that had the appearance of a living room. They would watch a movie in segments, have popcorn, and chat about the film between the segments, mostly joking about stereotypical elements and clichéd presentation, or simply commenting on cultural inaccuracies. The program also intermittently cut to a live televised bingo game, for which viewers could download the cards from the website.[23] Lorna Roth observes that *Bingo and a Movie* is "uniquely aboriginal in tone and approach. To recruit an audience, it exploits the popularity of bingo in aboriginal communities; it features a guest and covers an issue of social interest; and it entertains—all within the same three-hour time slot on a Friday night."[24] Since this program was cancelled and there is no similar replacement with subversive contextualization of certain feature films, APTN misses the chance to fully utilize a self-controlled lens to correct the colonial perspective that defined Aboriginal cultures as inferior and exotic. APTN has the unique potential to provide anti-colonial media, to counter Aboriginal clichés that have poisoned Aboriginal and Western views of Aboriginal cultures, but it does not always fulfill this potential. David states, "Stereotypes of the alcoholic on welfare, the wise Elder, the squaw, the princess, the noble savage, and the warrior are just a few of the images that the media perpetuates through advertising, typecasting, and exclusion of contemporary portrayals of Aboriginal people."[25] However, a closer look reveals that many of these stereotypical typecasts can also be found in programs carried by APTN.

Aboriginal Authority in an Electronic Medium

As has been seen, Aboriginal discursive strategies are found in a number of APTN programs and also partly inform APTN's overall schedule. The focus on programs featuring Elders as carriers of cultural knowledge and authority is one such strategy, and this helps position contemporary Aboriginal electronic media in the context of oral tradition. Also, a large part of APTN programming concentrates on Aboriginal children and youth as the target audience by creating entertainment and educational shows to help them locate themselves in their cultural traditions and in the contemporary world at the same time. Here APTN indirectly applies the traditional Medicine Wheel teaching to regard and cherish children as the centre and future of Aboriginal societies. One program is even entitled *The Seventh Generation*; it is hosted by Jennifer Podemski and created, directed, and produced by Big Soul Productions. It features young Aboriginal role models and their accomplishments in a variety of fields, such as arts, entertainment, music, business, politics, sports, medicine, science, and technology. By showcasing Aboriginal youth excellence, shows like this provide incentives to strive for personal achievement and help counter the feelings of hopelessness and lack of faith in the future that loom large among the younger Aboriginal generation.

In the network promotions between programs, APTN presents its logo alongside portrait shots of Aboriginal individuals of various cultures and generations dressed in both modern and traditional clothes. Some of these cameos feature individuals who explain the meaning of oral storytelling for themselves and their cultures, saying that Aboriginal stories have "the power to move and inspire," that they connect "young and old, friends and families," and that everyone can be a storyteller. One such segment holds that "Elders value telling stories to children, because children are the ones that will keep this tradition alive" before a voiceover states the APTN motto: "Sharing our stories with all generations, APTN." This cameo defines Elders as authorities of traditional culture, stresses the necessary connection between older and younger generations, and, even more importantly, assigns responsibility for survival of cultural knowledge to younger generations. With programs that contain traditional teachings and cultural knowledge · from Elders alongside more conventional educational programs that have young people as a target audience, APTN structurally underlines the message of these cameos. The emphasis on the importance of oral storytelling in the cameos, and the commitment to sharing Aboriginal stories with all generations, Canadians, and people around the world, reveal APTN's self-image as an electronic transmitter of Aboriginal experience in the fields of politics, economy, society, culture, tradition, drama, music, and dance. In this sense, APTN understands its programming as modernized Aboriginal storytelling in an electronic medium.

The Ambivalence of Indigenous Screens

In conclusion, APTN's programming content can be seen as ambivalent. On one hand, the network operates an Aboriginal television channel run by Aboriginal people that supports the production of independent Aboriginal media, presents contemporary society from an Aboriginal perspective, and offers a media discourse that Aboriginal people can identify with in the daily act of decolonizing the media. Many programs contribute to a self-controlled Aboriginal media discourse that teaches and entertains Aboriginal and non-Aboriginal Canadians and attempts to undo the effects of Aboriginal people's exposure to mainstream, colonial media discourse. APTN deserves great respect for this daily effort and its achievement cannot be appreciated enough. However, APTN program policy as reflected in some children's programs, commercials, and feature films is seriously flawed. These APTN programs risk reintroducing Eurocentric stereotypes and hegemonies into a purportedly self-controlled Aboriginal media discourse and could potentially reaffirm these clichés in both mainstream and Aboriginal discourses. The resulting message is that these Aboriginal images and portrayals are permissible because they are presented by an Aboriginal media outlet. In view of the examples discussed above, APTN's mandate "to share our stories with all Canadians and viewers around the world" appears misguided. To call these programs and movies Aboriginal and "sharing" them as such undermines the decolonizing efforts of the network and its objective to show what Aboriginal peoples and their cultures truly are and might become.

NOTES

1 This is a slightly revised and shortened version of a chapter in Pierre Anctil and Zilá Bernd, eds. *Canada from the Outside In: New Trends in Canadian Studies / Le Canada vu d'ailleurs: Nouvelles tendances en études canadiennes*. *Canadian Studies – Études canadiennes Vol. 7.* Bruxelles: Peter Lang AG, International Academic Publishers, 2006, 169-187. The empirical basis for the article is programs aired between May and October 2005.

2 Peter Lewis, preface to *Alternative Media: Linking Global and Local*, ed. Peter Lewis (Paris: UNESCO Publishing, 1993), 3.

3 Aboriginal Peoples Television Network, "About APTN," http://www.aptn.ca/corporate/about.php

4 Statistics Canada, *Aboriginal Peoples Survey Community Profiles*, 2001; Environics Research Group, *North of 60° and Remote Community Monitor 2006: APTN Omnibus Report*, (Ottawa: Environics, September 2006).

5 Aboriginal Peoples Television Network, "About APTN," http://www.aptn.ca (accessed 2 May 2005).

6 Kent Brown, human resources director of APTN, Personal communication, September 2004.

7 Whiteduck Resources Inc. and Consilium, *Northern Native Broadcast Access Program (NNBAP) and Northern Distribution Program (NDP) Evaluation. Final Report*, 25 June 2003, http://www.pch.gc.ca/pgm/em-cr/evaltn/2003/index-eng.cfm, 3.

8 Aboriginal Peoples Television Network, "Eligibility and Rating Criteria for Development and Licensing," http://www.aptn.ca/corporate/producers/eligibility.php.

9 Jennifer David, *Aboriginal Language Broadcasting in Canada. An Overview and Recommendations to the Task Force on Aboriginal Languages and Cultures, Final Report* (Ottawa: Debwe Communications Inc and APTN, 2004), 9.

10 Kent Brown, human resources director of APTN, Personal communication, September 2004.

11 Several instances of cultural appropriation and popular stereotypes of indigenous people are discussed in Peter C. Rollins and John E. O'Connor, eds. *Hollywood's Indian: The Portrayal of the Native American in Film* (Lexington: University Press of Kentucky, 1998).

12 Steffi Retzlaff, "'The Elders Have Said' – Projecting Aboriginal Cultural Values into Contemporary News Discourse," in *Aboriginal Canada Revisited*, ed. Kerstin Knopf (Ottawa: University of Ottawa Press, 2008), 330-359.

13 Ibid., 331.

14 Ibid., 331-338.

15 Ibid., 340-341, 349-350.

16 Aboriginal Peoples Television Network, "APTN Factsheet," http://www.aptn.ca/corporate/facts.php.

17 Hartmut Lutz, "Images of Indians in German Children's Books," in *Approaches: Essays in Native North American Studies and Literature*, Beiträge zur Kanadistik Bd. 11, ed. Hartmut Lutz (Augsburg: Wissner, 2002), 16. In this article Lutz theorizes the

"Karl May phenomenon" or "Indianthusiasm" as he terms it, Germans' romantic infatuation with "Indians" that is largely grounded in May's texts and the movies created thereof. Analyzing May's and Steuben's texts, he discusses their discursive exploitation of Aboriginal cultures and their construction of the noble, tough, and stoic Indian who embodies mental and physical ideals that served the idea of a pure model/master race: strength, endurance, fearlessness, and unwavering allegiance.

18   Ibid., 16-17.

19   Ibid., 17.

20   The author was unable to verify the spelling of this character.

21   Brown, Personal communication.

22   Providing subtitles elevates the spoken foreign language of a film to the same level as the written, thereby validating that it is actually spoken and that it has certain phonetic and grammatical structures, which are comparable to the written one. However, when subtitles are not given, there is the danger that the spoken (in this case Aboriginal) language is considered babbling that has no real meaning. Thus, this language is either defined as non-existent or subhuman.

23   I am indebted to Allan J. Ryan for this information.

24   Lorna Roth, *Something New in the Air: The Story of First Peoples Television Broadcasting in Canada* (Montreal: McGill-Queen's University Press, 2005), 211–218.

25   David, *Aboriginal Language Broadcasting.*

CHAPTER 6

Regina's *Moccasin Flats:* A Landmark in the Mapping of Urban Aboriginal Culture and Identity

CHRISTINE RAMSAY

Moccasin Flats is a landmark in Aboriginal Canadian screen culture. Not only is it the first dramatic television series in North America to be created, written, produced, and performed by Aboriginal people, it also has received national and international critical acclaim, and it has galvanized the energy, commitment, and creative potential of Regina's inner-city youth.

"Moccasin Flats" is the term that the young people of North Central Regina use to refer to their neighbourhood—which Jana G. Pruden describes as a "place of crisis and community, of serious social problems and great promise."[1] Trading on the global influence of American hip-hop culture on disaffected urban youth, *Moccasin Flats* portrays Regina in a gritty "'hood" style that explores the harsh realities of homelessness, sexual abuse, addiction, the sex trade, gang warfare, and the penal system for many Aboriginal kids living in the ghetto of North Central. Laura Milliken, the series producer, suggests that location is key to the story. "It's a special place," she says. "There is no place like North Central in Toronto.... Nobody in Canada knows that in a 17-block radius there are people dealing with these issues, that in their backyard there are people living in sometimes third-world conditions."[2] Life in North Central is an aspect of everyday life in Canada that most Canadians do not see—and do not want to see. Until now.

The series began in the summer of 2002 as one of the initiatives in the media empowerment project called "repREzentin,'" run by Milliken's Toronto-based Big Soul Productions to give voice and opportunity to at-risk Aboriginal youth. Based on interviews with North Central teenagers about their experiences, Milliken and Darrell Dennis shaped a short twenty-four minute neo-realist-meets-cinema-verité film, directed by Randy Redroad, in which most of the secondary actors used their own first names. The dramatic tension revolves around Dillon, played by Justin Toto, who wants to leave home to attend university, but his love for Sarah, played by Kristin Friday, a sex trade worker trying to escape a violent pimp, keeps him tied to the ghetto. Shot entirely on location with a cast and crew of forty, the production unexpectedly took on a life of its own, "like a volcano" about to explode, says Big Soul partner Jennifer Podemski. "I knew that the talent and the integrity and the foundations were so strong.... It was just something that felt way too big for the little shoes it was in at the time."[3]

A surprise hit at Sundance, *Moccasin Flats* went on to further acclaim at ImaginNATIVE and the Toronto International Film Festival, evolving into a six-part, scripted, character-driven series directed by Stacey Stewart Curtis that debuted on Aboriginal People's Television Network (APTN) in November 2003 and was then picked up by Showcase. A third and final season wrapped up production in summer of 2005, with the series growing to include stories about the humour, camaraderie, and hope of the neighbourhood as well as its challenges. In order to give the show some star power, Saskatchewan actor and singer Andrea Menard came on board as Constable Amanda Strongeagle, while veteran actors Gordon Tootoosis and Tantoo Cardinal took on the roles of Joe Redsky and Betty Merasty, respectively, and functioned as Elders and mentors to the relatively inexperienced cast and crew. In 2006, *Moccasin Flats* garnered three Gemini nominations, for Best Dramatic Series, Best Original Music, and Best Actress for Menard, and in 2008 it briefly returned to APTN as a movie of the week entitled *Moccasin Flats: Redemption*, directed by Rob King.

At last, says Milliken, Aboriginal people are "controlling our own voice in the media."[4] Moreover, the series is at the centre of what Tom Lyons reports is being called an "aboriginal youth explosion"[5] in the performing arts across Canada. It has thematized critical issues affecting our Aboriginal cultures, such as the experience of metropolitan dystopias in a global context; the clash between traditional and local culture and the colonizing potential of American hip hop; masculine posing, violence, and misogyny; and the impulse to escape problem environments versus the desire to stay and be a force of positive change. It has raised the profile of Aboriginal talent across

Jimmy Bighorse (Michael Leisen) stalks Amanda Strongeagle (Andrea Menard) in an episode of Moccasin Flats. *Photographer, Calvin Fehr. Stills from* Moccasin Flats. *used with permission of Big Soul Productions.*

Canada and North America, launching the career of Mathew Strongeagle (as Dillon Redsky's best friend, Mathew Merasty), who won a major role on Steven Spielberg's series *Into the West*. And, as Regina MP Ralph Goodale has suggested, it has played a key role in the burgeoning of Regina as a creative "model for the rest of the country in the way it deals with urban issues."[6]

Moccasin Flats and the Urban 'Hood Genre

This chapter will discuss *Moccasin Flats* and its important impact on urban Aboriginal Canadian culture and identity through a focus on its debt to the American 'hood film genre as it functions within the larger cultural specificities of place and space in a global context. As Paula J. Massood argues, the 'hood film is primarily concerned with the urbanscape of the inner city, setting up a dialogue between the city as a utopia—"a space promising freedom and economic mobility"—and a dystopia—"the ghetto's economic impoverishment and segregation."[7] Through an analysis focusing on Episode 1 of the first season, I will examine the way *Moccasin Flats* adapts the thematic and stylistic tropes of the genre, particularly its self-conscious examination of "the socioeconomic environment of the inner city" and "the family situated in an urban milieu,"[8] while giving a distinct voice to the particularities of the urban experiences of Regina's Aboriginal youth.

Regina's North Central: Space and Place in the National Imagination

As Milliken insists, location is the key to the story. The question of Regina, Saskatchewan, as a place is fundamental to understanding both the meaning and the cultural achievement of *Moccasin Flats*. In *Places on the Margin: Alternative Geographies of Modernity*, Rob Shields argues that we live in a signifying system of "overall spatialization: a modern geomancy" in which one's "spatiality" determines one's relation to the world, and "places or regions mean something only in relation to other places as a constellation of meanings." This social spatialization is a process of cultural production that has a "mediating effect," he writes, juxtaposing "social and economic forces, forms of social organization, and constraints of the natural world" to create "place-images" that are charged with emotional content, mythical meanings, community symbolism, and historical significance. Place-images are the myths and metaphors we live by in the various regions and cities of Canada. They emerge out of the modern system of spatial divisions and hierarchies that has grounded our national perception (centre/margins, near/far, civilized/natural) and, since they often come about by the oversimplification, stereotyping, and labelling that are part of everyday discourse, they can easily become what Shields calls "hypostatised" signifiers of the "essential character" of a place, despite obvious historical changes and developments in its nature.[9]

Thus, places are marked in and by broad cultural systems of social spatialization in which nation states fragment the real into parcels, creating margins, peripheries, regions, and hinterlands around a centre valued as superior. "The social 'Other' of the marginal and low cultures is despised and reviled in the official discourse of dominant culture and central power," Shields argues, "while at the same time being constitutive of the imaginary and emotional repertoires of that dominant culture."[10] Centre and margins are enabling conditions. In the spatial logic of inclusion and exclusion that has historically created the mythical meanings of Canada and its regions, "Saskatchewan" is both hinterland and heartland. The province is socially peripheral, construed as a cultural wasteland, the "Big Empty," or, to borrow a popular metaphor about the American Midwest, the "fly-over" between the important action in the East and West, in Toronto, Montreal, and Vancouver. Yet, at the same time, Saskatchewan is symbolically constitutive of official Canadian identity. It is embraced as foundational in terms of images of the hearty farmers of Canada's breadbasket who helped build the nation in the early decades of the twentieth century, toiling among the gently swaying fields of endless wheat and sun-drenched skies; the ubiquity of the RCMP, formed to police the West, inevitably polished and at attention at every official function on Parliament Hill; or the eternal interpellation in the national discourse of Saskatchewan as the birthplace of Canada's cooperative movements, social values, and national identity.[11]

Regina, as Saskatchewan's capital, is interesting in this context. Its place-image rightfully begins as Wascana, or Pile of Bones, named by the Cree who hunted buffalo in the area for thousands of years in pre-contact and contact times, and for whom the area is a sacred site. However, by the late 1800s the place had been thoroughly colonized as farmland by European immigrants, leading to its re-naming as the village of Regina, after Queen Victoria. With the arrival of the railroad and its modernizing promise in 1883, and the trial and execution of Métis leader Louis Riel in 1885, it became the official site of colonial rule as the capital of the Northwest Territories and the headquarters of the RCMP. Regina was incorporated as a city in 1903, becoming the capital of the new province of Saskatchewan two years later, as well as a site of class struggle and influential social agitation throughout the first half of the twentieth century. As Dave Margoshes reports, the Cooperative Commonwealth Federation (CCF, precursor to the NDP) was born there with the signing of the Regina Manifesto in 1933; the Regina Riot, an important event in the Canadian workers' movement, took place in the downtown core in 1935, not far from North Central; and national hero Tommy Douglas delivered many rousing speeches on Medicare and social justice from the Queen City.[12]

Nevertheless, in the 1960s, as people began migrating from reserves to urban centres across Canada, Regina's downtown became a site of racial and class division. The city became demographically bifurcated into North and South by Dewdney Avenue, which runs east-west through the downtown, just north of and parallel to the Canadian Pacific Railway tracks. As Aboriginal people came from a number of Assiniboine, Cree, Dakota, and Saulteaux reserves surrounding Regina to live mostly "north of the tracks," many working-class and upwardly mobile whites moved "south of Dewdney" and into the burgeoning middle-class eastern and western suburbs, leading to the increasing decay of the "North Central" neighbourhood and giving the lie to the colonizers' vision of Saskatchewan-style social justice and equality for all Canadians. Currently, Regina's reputation outside Saskatchewan is notorious, as racism, poverty, and violence have earned it the title of the crime capital of Canada—the hypostatized place-image of a dangerous backwater. This situation has been exacerbated by Jonathon Gatehouse's 2007 article in *Maclean's*, Canada's national magazine, which labelled Regina's North Central "Canada's worst neighbourhood": "How did the province where Medicare was born end up with a city this frightening?" he asks. Slum landlords, unemployment, poverty, depression, gangs, violent crime, assault, and children in the sex and drug trades are the key problems for the inner-city residents of North Central, 42 percent of whom are of First Nations ancestry, and many of whom compare it to living in a Third World country. Gatehouse quotes Kathy Donovan of the University of Regina's Social Policy Research Unit, who calls Regina, where the Aboriginal unemployment rate is "more than triple that of non-natives," the "most segregated community in Canada" and "a pigsty of repression." "Regina is the only place I've heard of where they steal the food out of people's freezers during break and enters," she jibes.[13] If, as Iain Chambers argues, the modern metropolis is "above all, a myth, a tale, an allegory of the crisis of modernity" spinning bleak urban portraits of exile, anguish, despair, and a "cheerless destiny,"[14] then Regina serves as Canada's locus of modern metropolitan crisis *par excellence*.[15]

However, the so-called Queen City's deposing and descent into a metropolitan dystopia cannot simplistically be laid at the feet of its North Central citizens, nor is the portrait of a cheerless destiny the complete picture. Rather, as *Moccasin Flats* makes clear, Regina and North Central must be understood in the context of the racist legacies of a colonial nationalist modernity; the forces of postmodern globalization; the culture of urban poverty; the tensions between American media imperialism, Aboriginal cultural traditions, and masculine identity; and the dignity, resilience, and hope of the individuals and families who call these places home—indigenous postcolonial urban people whose struggles are now premised, above all, on what Marian Bredin has called "the demand for a future."[16]

Bredin, who is particularly concerned with the important role of Aboriginal media in making that demand, insists that our approach to Aboriginal media analysis must involve "an effort to understand local cultures, local meanings, and symbolic processes, without losing sight of macro-processes of economic exploitation and historical change."[17] Brenda Longfellow agrees: Canadian cities and Canadian media representations are now shaped globally, as much by what Arjun Appadurai calls transnational "ethnoscapes," "mediascapes," "technoscapes," "financescapes," and "ideoscapes" as by the older modern "national determinations" based in centre-margin dichotomies.[18] International flows of money, cultures, people, and ideologies create struggles for identity across the regions and urban centres of the globe. Strict divisions between "the local" and "the cosmopolitan" no longer make sense, producing what James Clifford has called the world's "discrepant cosmopolitanisms."[19] Paul Rabinow offers a new definition of "the cosmopolitan" as "an ethos of macrodependencies, with an acute consciousness ... of the inescapabilities and particularities of places, characters,

Candy (Candace Fox, left) and Sarah (Kristin Friday, right) on the streets of the Flats. Photographer, Calvin Fehr. Stills from Moccasin Flats. *used with permission of Big Soul Productions.*

historical trajectories, and fates."[20] Appadurai, Longfellow, and Saskia Sassen applaud this critical attention to how globalization is actualized and located in particular places, with Longfellow calling for a focus on the "vivacity of regional and sub-national cultural identities in Canada," such as the Aboriginal youth of North Central—people "whose political sense of self and identities are not necessarily embedded in the nation or the national community"—as they struggle in their screen representations against "the backdrop of accelerated continental economic integration and American domination of mass media consumption."[21] This emphasis on the specificities of sites and texts that show how the effects of globalization enter people's everyday urban realities is important in helping to reveal "the contradictions of globalization" and the ways in which "locality," "difference," and "resistance"[22] can challenge postmodern American cultural imperialism and racist Canadian stereotypes in places like Regina and with texts like *Moccasin Flats*.

North Central Regina, to borrow a phrase from Renato Rosaldo, is a "cultural borderland"—a place with "multiple and often conflicting sources of individual and collective identification."[23] Such conflict is particularly acute for young people, as they struggle with various tensions, such as those created between wanting to preserve the local cultural traditions and community values of their Elders and the resonance that globalized youth culture inevitably has for them, including hip hop and the 'hood film; or those created between the imaginary (Massood's urban utopia, "the city that one wants") and the real (Massood's urban dystopia, "the city that one has").[24]

"Pile of Bones": City As Utopia/Dystopia

The opening episode of *Moccasin Flats*, entitled "Unearthed," offers a distinctive take on Regina and the 'hood of North Central, demonstrating how deftly the show contextualizes the various issues and conflicts of individual, collective, and urban Aboriginal identity that it aims to expose. The plot of this episode introduces a mystery on which the entire season hinges, much like mainstream versions of the 'hood genre: a skeleton has accidentally been unearthed on the lawn of the neighbourhood churchyard, a situation that is particularly upsetting to Elder Joe Redsky (Gordon Tootoosis) for reasons that become apparent as the season unfolds. The "pile of bones," however, is more than a mere plot point for the narrative. It is an obvious metaphor for the "skeletons in the closet" of the Aboriginal ghetto—for the debilitating effects of white European institutions (such as the legacy of residential schools), racism, and emotional and sexual abuse on generations of Aboriginal people. As in the 'hood genre, whose genealogy Massood traces back to the black action films of the early 1970s, the "primary conditions" for the narrative in *Moccasin Flats* are the "inner city impoverishment and crime"[25] that have resulted from the socioeconomic disenfranchisement and devastation of the First People of Wascana/Pile of Bones through colonization and the development of Regina as a modern provincial capital. Through this symbolic insertion of "Wascana"—the historical space of memories of economic autonomy and a centuries-old heritage of a dignified life on the land—into the troubled urban 'hood, *Moccasin Flats*, like films such as *Boyz N the Hood* (John Singleton, 1991) and *Menace II Society* (Allen and Albert Hughes, 1993),[26] examines the "duality" in which the city is experienced as both utopic and dystopic by its inner-city residents, and makes "visible the dynamics of power inherent in the city's self-imagery."[27] How? Through the process, Massood writes, of "placing on the screen those fragments of the city which have been previously made invisible or erased and by 'focus[ing] on space not defined by American [or Canadian] urban maps.'"[28]

In the case of the Los Angeles–based Singleton and Hughes films, this means placing 'hoods such as South Central and Watts, respectively, in full view in order to counter the forms of exclusion that Hollywood has practiced in helping LA to reify what Massood calls a particular set of utopic urban signs: "palm trees, sun, abundance, paradise."[29] In the case of the Regina-based *Moccasin Flats*, this means placing North Central at centre stage and "re-re-appropriating" the sign "Wascana" in the Aboriginal space of the 'hood in the interests of historical truth, and countering Aboriginal invisibility in the Queen City's (white) self-image. What I mean by this is that the name "Wascana" has been repeatedly appropriated by a litany of Regina business interests as they attempt to turn a profit, and by the City of Regina itself as it attempts to build an image as a prairie oasis in the middle of what is often assumed to have been an unhistoried desert until the arrival of European settlers. For example, a quick perusal of the Regina phonebook under "W" yields a litany of enterprises, from Wascana Animal Hospital, Wascana Archers Club, Wascana Auto Body, through Wascana Country Club, Wascana Daycare Co-Op, Wascana Dog Obedience Club Inc., Wascana Energy, Wascana Flower Shoppe, Wascana Manor Condo Corp, and Wascana Pistol Club, to Wascana Remedial Massage Centre. Moreover, Wascana Centre Authority is charged with managing Wascana Park and Wascana Lake, the downtown greenspace that is at the centre of the utopic self-promotional discourse that has emerged in the city in recent years, particularly with the current Mayor Pat Fiacco's "I Love Regina" campaign. Margoshes participates in that discourse, as well as in the ahistoricizing discourse that erases pre-settler Aboriginal culture from the place-image of Regina/Wascana, and I will quote him at length:

> In many ways, Regina is a dumb city. What a place to put it, in the middle of a flat stretch of treeless prairie, with only a small creek to provide water, no shelter from the baking heat, the bone-chilling cold, the incessant wind. But coming here from ... Vancouver-by-the-sea, as I did, it's hard not to think of the often repeated observation that Vancouver is the city that's done the least with the most, while Regina's done the most with the least. Lots of trees (some 250,000 of them, hand planted); the largest urban park in North America (bigger even than Stanley Park); a sparkling lake (hand dug by thousands of men during the depression) in the heart of the city; a green belt that winds its way through town (more green space than any Canadian city other than Ottawa), along with fabulous sunsets and an average annual total of 2,331 sunshine hours (it's one of the sunniest spots in the country). All go a long way to making a pretty plain place attractive.[30]

Why, then, does Regina get no respect? Margoshes quotes then-mayor Doug Archer, who says it comes down to two things, weather and landscape: "But what doesn't get taken into account is the quality of life—there's no question that ours is exceptional. And we have the time and the disposable income to enjoy it."[31] My point is that as big and green as it is, Wascana Park certainly does not wind its way to the inner city; most of the green space around the lake is also almost exclusively white space; most of the businesses named in its honour are owned by white people; and, as the *Maclean's* controversy attests, many of North Central's Aboriginal residents do not share the disposable income that would allow them to participate fully and equally in the city's increasingly celebrated "quality of life." Clearly, what is happening here is that the original history and meaning surrounding Wascana (the ongoing history of the home and lifeworld of the Assiniboine, Cree, Dakota, and Saulteaux people and the treaties they signed with the Canadian government in good faith, followed by their displacement from their traditional buffalo-hunting grounds onto reserves and, later, into the urban ghetto by white settlers and the government) is erased by the City of Regina as a colonizing force, then superficially re-appropriated in its flattering utopian self-portrait. But, as I will show, *Moccasin Flats* is interesting in the way it then manages to "re-re-appropriate" the sign to effectively reveal the truth about this subterfuge, not only through the layered imagery of the skeleton/pile of bones/Wascana, but also by borrowing aesthetic strategies common to the 'hood genre—strategies that self-consciously examine the dual Aboriginal experience of the city as utopia and dystopia by "making complex their representation of the cityscape."[32]

The establishing scene of "Unearthed" shows an image of the Regina skyline and the shiny glass towers of its downtown business district, but the use of an extreme long shot succeeds in "making Regina strange." As in *Boyz N the Hood*, camera work and cinematography are used critically to undermine the sense of a "homogeneous" and "unified" cityscape[33] typically created in mainstream representations of the modern urban environment. Here, Regina is made distant and small as the prairie metropolis is dwarfed by a teepee in the left foreground—unskinned but still standing and, most importantly, taking up space—a powerful symbol of the tenacity of Aboriginal cultures in the face of the ravages of modernization, colonization, and attempted cultural genocide. This aesthetic strategy thus uses space to shift the discourse of what Manthia Diawara has called "power and powerlessness," as the sign representing those who are usually marginalized (i.e., the teepee) takes centre stage, while the sign representing those who are usually empowered (i.e., the skyline) is relegated to the background and so diminished or metaphorically "put in its place."[34] Typical of the 'hood genre, the city centre and its economy are re-imagined from the perspective of the ghetto as a "structuring absence" that excludes it: "both there and not there but always central to the narrative."[35]

A low-angle cut from the teepee to traffic numbly flowing into the city, and another quick cut to the heart of North Central, brings us face to face with the problems of violence, drugs, and the sex trade for the Aboriginal youth who live there. Thus, the fragment of Regina that has previously been erased or made invisible in mainstream discourses like Margoshes's is brought starkly to our attention. Spatiality, as Edward Soja writes (specifically, here, the marginalized space of Regina's downtown ghetto) is revealed as simultaneously "a social product (or outcome) and a shaping force (or medium) in social life."[36] North Central, once a proud and tree-lined working-class neighbourhood whose inhabitants in past decades found employment in the factories, small industries, and rail yards of Regina's nearby Warehouse District, now finds itself disenfranchised. Housing is typically run down; storefronts sit empty; there is no grocery store; unemployment, crime, and the sex trade have skyrocketed as globalization and the information economy disappear jobs into Third World sweatshops; and the ensuing culture of poverty and under-education in the space of the ghetto (despite the inroads that have been made by the Regina-based First Nations University, Canada's first indigenous-run, degree-granting post-secondary institution) leads its disenfranchised people into desperate situations.

As bell hooks suggests, in a hyper-material globalized media culture in which your value is tied to what you have and what you buy, such desperation makes perfect sense. While mainstream culture stereotypes the poor as shiftless, mindless, lazy, dishonest, unworthy, and, above all, without values, any connections between poverty and personal integrity vanish. American popular culture, she observes, rarely portrays the poor as having dignity: "Television shows and films bring the message home that no one can truly feel good about themselves if they are poor. In television sitcoms the working poor are shown to have a healthy measure of self-contempt; they dish it out to one another with a wit and humour that we can all enjoy, irrespective of our class."[37] Thus, derided, shamed, and humiliated, the disenfranchised learn to be nihilistic and self-exploitative and, in the case of African American youth, or the Aboriginal youth of North Central, to turn to deflection, substance abuse, violent masculine posing, outlaw behaviour, and crime to relieve their psychological and emotional pain. "To change the devastating impact of poverty," hooks writes, "we must change the way resources and wealth are distributed. But we must also change the way the poor are represented."[38] As we have seen, Milliken concurs: we need texts that represent the poor and disenfranchised in their own voices, from their own perspective, and that show one can live with integrity and dignity in the midst of poverty. And that is exactly the achievement of *Moccasin Flats*.

While the first images we see of North Central are brutally frank in their dystopic depiction of mindless violence, petty crime, drug deals, and teenagers in the sex trade (in quick succession, a group of young teens chases down and kicks another youth to the ground, a back-alley drug deal goes down with jaded nonchalance, and a young woman hands off her infant to a friend while she picks up her next trick), the place is also portrayed as a neighbourhood like any other, with spaces where good things can happen. This combination of images sets up the dialogue between the dystopic and utopic impulses that Massood identifies as typical of the 'hood genre.

From the credit sequence of "Unearthed" we cut to the main character, Dillon Redsky (Justin Toto). He is comfortable in his space as he plays street basketball (we later learn that he has earned a university athletic scholarship) to the rap lyrics of Jonathan Garlow and TruRezCrew and exudes the hip hop attitude that pervades the series. As Liam Lacey reports, the cool hip hop styling of *Moccasin Flats* has rankled some as doubly inauthentic coming from Canadian Aboriginal culture, on the one hand, and in what is often dismissed as an isolated and decidedly "un-hip" backwater prairie town, on the other hand:

> There's a scene in *Moccasin Flats* when a teenaged girl, Kristin, wants to know if her boyfriend, Justin, is trying to start a fight with her: "You frontin' me?" she demands to know. The audience at the Sundance festival ... initially laughed at the rap slang in the context—spoken by a native Canadian girl from north-central Regina. Nor were they accustomed to the rap music of TruRezCrew from the Six Nations Reserve in Southern Ontario. The movie also shows native teens trash talking while playing basketball on a cement court. The 'hood in question, known as *Moccasin Flats*, is as mean as any ghetto ... and maybe—in a place where teenaged prostitution, incarceration, drug use, suicide and an overall mortality rate [are] 3 ½ times the national average for youth—the tough talk of the American ghetto fits in.[39]

However, as Randy Redroad, director of the pilot film and a Cherokee-American, says, "This is the way kids all over the place are speaking. I find it funny when I hear Dan Rather talking about someone being 'dissed,' but it's everywhere. People have this crazy notion that African-American language causes violence, but it's the other way around. The language applies to their experiences, it doesn't create them."[40] Moreover, the show's use of hip hop suggests that American pop culture might be more meaningful to Aboriginal

Red (Ron Harris). Photographer, Calvin Fehr. Stills from Moccasin Flats *used with permission of Big Soul Productions.*

youth than contemporary Aboriginal institutions in Regina like First Nations University, the Federation of Saskatchewan Indian Nations, and powwows, which are not a central part of the series.

As part of the American global-media complex, hip hop flows everywhere. But it is the contradictions of globalization as they play out in local circumstances that are interesting and productive, as Longfellow suggests and Massood would agree. On the one hand a disturbing sign of the ubiquity and colonizing potential of American cultural imperialism—white or black—hip hop represents, on the other hand, the power unleashed when the formerly disenfranchised gain access to the means of representation, and the experiences they represent have unforeseen global resonances. On the one hand an often highly conservative and incendiary discourse of masculine posing and misogyny, hip hop represents, on the other hand, a fluid discourse like any other that can be meaningfully used and adapted to different and new purposes. I am thinking of the rap lyrics that accompany Dillon as he plays, which are used critically and intelligently to suggest this young Aboriginal man's dignity, self-worth, and potential, rather than used stereotypically and simplistically to celebrate male ego run amok: "Destined for greatness. Great minds can do great things. Always remember that." The meaning is cinched as Dillon then dribbles a symbolic circle around two Elders (Joe Redsky and Betty Merasty [Tantoo Cardinal]) who happen to cross his path on their way to the neighbourhood picnic/powwow (and who are later revealed to be his grandfather and aunt, respectively) as the lyrics pound, "I'm gifted. I'm blessed.... To the very deepest depths." The suggestion is that while Dillon and his young friends may be poor and troubled and have many challenges, they are rich in spiritual heritage and in the love, support, and wisdom of their families, relations, and Elders–and these are foundational values in Aboriginal cultures. Thus the editing, character behaviour, and iconography of these opening scenes make it very clear that, like Dillon and his best friend Mathew, the young people of *Moccasin Flats* do have choices, but those choices are difficult and hard won, and making them requires personal commitment, as well as encouragement and mentoring from nurturing adults.

From images of Dillon's skill and prowess on the court we cut to two young toughs who work for Jonathan Bearclaw (Landon Montour), who is Sarah's former pimp, Dillon's childhood friend, and one of North Central's most notorious small-time "gangstas." They are cruising around the neighbourhood, giving attitude to anyone who crosses their path and obviously scouting new recruits as runners for their gang. The car, as Massood suggests, is a highly charged signifier in the 'hood genre. It is, for gangstas, the utopian space of urban mobility and success, the cherished "ride" that enables the dealing and conspicuous consumption that allows them to participate in the white consumer economy, which otherwise excludes them. However, the car is also a trap in the way it contains and limits these youths; it is symbolic of the internalized boundaries that life in the ghetto, and the inability to imagine something better, has placed on their existence. While Nate, Dillon's younger brother, is seduced by these young toughs' hypermasculine posing and seems ripe for the picking, Dillon and Mathew try to ignore their predictable, emasculating taunts about being "pussies" interested in "university" and "dancing powwow." Together, these friends show that the future of Aboriginal youth lies in solidarity, education, exposure to the world beyond the ghetto, and a questioning of globalized American screen stereotypes (such as gangsta behaviour), as well as in remembering and honouring cultural traditions and the sense of place and belonging that can come from family and community life. From the two gangstas we cut to a big blue Saskatchewan sky, pan down to a drummers' circle at full tilt, and join the crowd gathered to watch Mathew dance on a beautiful summer afternoon. With his characteristic gentle good humour and quiet self-confidence, Mathew mixes the traditional powwow steps with some hip-hop flourishes, again symbolizing the kinds of progressive creative syntheses that must occur, and are occurring, for Aboriginal youth in North Central. "I wanted to show the beauty, to show it with some lyricism, instead of the usual fast and jumpy camerawork they use on youth shows," Lacey quotes Redroad as saying, and clearly his vision in the pilot film has prevailed throughout the television series. Redroad continues, "The place isn't ugly. The streets are tree-lined and everything looks pretty, until you look a little closer or go inside. In that sense, it's not much different than life in the suburbs."[41]

The next sequence is important for the way that it deliberately and proud-ly names North Central Regina as a site where good things are happening in the midst of poverty and despair. We cut from the dance scene to a middle-aged, white, male official making a speech at a sod turning that is initiating the conversion of an old church into a theatre company for Aboriginal youth and a public day-care centre. Plans for such projects are actually emerging in the neighbourhood through a grassroots community movement that, with the participation of tri-level government funding and consultant Jeremy Parnes, has produced a strategy document on community development that sees the strength of North Central deriving "from the cultural diversity of its members working together and their emphasis on the value of family, seniors, children, and youth."[42] Mathew and the other characters in *Moccasin Flats* may be understandably sceptical about white officials and their mo-tives and methods, given the history of colonization, racism, and sexual abuse in the city and the province: "Politicians," Mathew smirks, "It takes him an hour to say he's going to dig a hole." However, the series nonetheless celebrates an opening-up to seeing people—all people—differently, and with tolerance, compassion, respect, and faith in our ability to change, grow, and challenge harmful stereotypes. The show's opening episode, after all, includes an Aboriginal lesbian cop, Constable Strongeagle (Andrea Menard), and a white detective who are called in to investigate the skeleton unearthed at the churchyard dedication ceremony. Through this turn of events, the detective is forced to ask himself hard questions about the racist and sexist stereo-types he has lived by. While his racist partners try to dismiss the case as the suicide of "just another drunk Indian," Strongeagle insists that the skeleton belonged to a person, Reginald Thundercloud, who deserves the same investigative care and dignified treatment that any non-Aboriginal victim would receive, and she intends to see that he gets it. As the premiere episode of *Moccasin Flats* closes, there are no easy resolutions: while Dillon is visited by a haunting dream, his grandfather, Joe Redsky, secretly visits the place where Thundercloud was unearthed with a symbolic offering of tobacco, and Sarah gets into the car of a suspicious-looking john, who, we have been cued to believe, may well be murdering girls from the 'hood. Viewers in western Canada will easily read the critical subtext here and be reminded of the Aboriginal men who have died at the hands of Saskatoon police in recent years, the victims of so-called starlight tours, and of the Aboriginal women who have disappeared from the streets of Edmonton, with little or no police follow-up.[43]

Spirits, Secrets, and Lies

As the first season progresses, we begin to see that several of the main characters in North Central Regina have skeletons in their closets, which are developed through a network of comparable and interconnected storylines. For example, parallels emerge between Joe and Betty, Dillon and Mathew, and Dillon and Jonathan around the question of loyalty and support between friends, and the devastating impact that sexual abuse and its repression can have on oneself, one's family, and one's entire community.

In the case of Elders Joe and Betty (the constant voices of wisdom and caring throughout the series), Betty is aware that her old friend Joe has simply not been himself since the unearthing of Reginald Thundercloud's body. As they sit on his porch discussing how it used to be different between the trio of childhood friends Dillon, Mathew, and the obviously troubled Jonathan, Betty suggests, "We got to bring the teachings back to them, Joe." "Kids won't sit down with the old folks now," he replies, and this leads her to challenge him on his own lack of openness about what is really going on with him. Dillon and Mathew's friendship is also challenged by Dillon's increasingly erratic behaviour, which is tied through editing to the secret that is haunting him and giving him nightmares—the same secret, it turns out, that is haunting both Joe and Jonathan. Like Betty, Mathew confronts his friend and demands to know the truth about the three hundred dollars that has gone missing from the profits on their summer landscaping business. "I started this business so you could go to university ... play ball ... live your dreams," says Mathew. "I didn't ask for your help," Dillon snaps. "You didn't have to ask me for help. Friends do shit for each other. They go out on a limb for each other. They don't fuckin' lie to each other."

This theme of the power of secrets and lies to erode and destroy relationships reaches its climax in the parallel the narrative draws between Dillon and Jonathan. They are, in fact, as Betty and Joe revealed, close childhood friends who used to dance powwow together and whose teenage lives have taken them in opposite directions, but whose paths cross again because of both a shared nightmare and Sarah. (Sarah is one of Jonathan's hookers who has given up drugs and is now trying to escape Jonathan and life on the streets, and she is also Dillon's love interest, the girl he is trying to help and protect.) As Amanda Strongeagle discovers through her investigation, the

Jonathon Bearclaw (Landon Montour, foreground), with (from left) gang member 1 (male extra), gang member 2 (James Donais), Sarah (Kristin Friday), and Candy Foster (Candace Fox). Photographer, Calvin Fehr. Stills from Moccasin Flats *used with permission of Big Soul Productions.*

nightmare the two share is tied directly to the skeleton in the churchyard, which, Joe finally reveals, turns out not to be the remains of Thundercloud at all but those of Kenny Bearclaw, Jonathan's uncle, who had stolen Thundercloud's wallet, hence the mistaken identity of the corpse. Through a series of flashbacks, Joe confesses on tape to Strongeagle and Betty what had happened to Dillon and Jonathan ten years earlier, and the role he himself played in the nightmare that haunts them all. It was "another drunken house party" at Jonathan's mother's place, he says, to which women would bring their johns, and from which Jonathan always wanted to escape. Jonathan was planning to stay at Dillon's for the night but was waylaid by his uncle Kenny, who had been sexually abusing him for years. Catching Kenny in the act of molesting his friend, Dillon grabbed a trophy and hit the man on the head. Panicking, the boys fled, turning to Joe for help, who proceeded to cover up the incident and rid the community of a "sick man"—a "broken spirit"—by dumping Kenny's body in a hole at the construction site at the churchyard: "I buried a part of myself in that hole that night.... A part I'll never get back as long as I live. I'm not proud of what I did, but I believe it was the right thing to do. Those boys shouldn't have had to deal with something like this. They were innocent. I'm not." However, as Joe offers his hands up to Strongeagle for arrest, she pauses, lost in thought, and instead of handcuffing him, decides to

Betty Merasty (Tantoo Cardinal, left) and Candy Foster (Candace Fox, right). Photographer, Calvin Fehr. Stills from Moccasin Flats *used with permission of Big Soul Productions.*

let sleeping dogs lie. "Yep. It's a shame Kenny got drunk and fell down that hole," she says, destroying the tape and, in effect, dropping the investigation in the interests of community justice.

As Joe and Constable Strongeagle attest, and as the two friends come to understand, spirits, secrets, and lies can haunt you. By recovering the bear claws that Joe had given the boys for protection years ago, but that they had long since discarded, Dillon and Jonathan symbolically mend their friendship to the extent that is possible, given the very different paths their lives have taken. "Do me one favour," says Dillon. "Leave my little brother alone." Jonathan nods in agreement. However, whereas Dillon will get his chance to escape the ghetto, due in large part to the support of his family, Jonathan is alone, caught in the downward spiral of the ghetto's dystopian energy. The gangstas he owes money to are on their way to collect, and, rather than bolting the door as he usually does, he takes out his bear claw and leaves the door open, cynically taunting his fate.

Thus, the first season of *Moccasin Flats* ends as it began, by representing the ongoing dialogue between the utopian and dystopian impulses at work in places like North Central through what still remains a highly complex cityscape. There is hope for some: Sarah, with help from the Sweet Grass Safe House, escapes Jonathan and boards a bus for Saskatoon; Nate gives up his fascination with Jonathan's gang and is back on the court playing ball with his old friends; Mathew and Dillon renew their bond as Dillon dances to Mathew's rap songs at the hip-hop competition in full powwow regalia (which symbolically establishes a productive synergy between the boys' attraction to contemporary youth culture and the wealth of their own cultural traditions); and Dillon eventually leaves the city for university, presumably in Vancouver. For others, hope seems entirely absent: Dana is found half beaten to death (we assume at the hands of Jonathan) by Candy, who has discovered she herself is pregnant and HIV positive. The message seems to be that, in the Flats, there are no easy answers. Yet one thing is certain: Aboriginal communities must no longer let racism and the skeletons in their closets haunt them and rob them of their dignity and choices in the present, or of the meaning and value of the traditional ways of the past. The final episode, entitled "Resting Place," closes with a repetition with difference of the opening moments of "Unearthed," once again shifting the discourse of power and powerlessness and signifying movement and new beginnings for the people in the 'hood. In the background, on screen left, the dwarfed Regina skyline has been replaced by the church (similarly put in its place, if you will), while in the foreground, on screen right, the battered and empty teepee has been replaced by Elders Betty and Joe—she proudly wrapped in a red ceremonial blanket, he slowly beating the drum—as they keep Joe's promise to finally "give Kenny a proper ceremony. Send him to the other side in a good way." The final image is of Dillon, who, having said goodbye to his family—"What can I say, Mom, I couldn't have done it without you"—drives past the church and away to university in a high-angle, sun-filled crane shot of North Central's tree-lined streets, a much different view than the dystopian one that introduced the 'hood in the series' opening moments.

In this way, *Moccasin Flats* succeeds in realistically portraying the complex "socioeconomic environment of the inner city" and its challenges, while not betraying the ability of "the family situated in an urban milieu" to live, as hooks and Bredin suggest, with integrity, dignity, and the sense of a future. The result is a landmark in Canadian television and Canadian identity achieved through regeneration, renewal, and obvious development of the place-image and sense of individual and collective identity of North Central Regina. Saskatchewan's Queen City, as a globalized site of discrepant cosmopolitanism and an increasingly forward-looking urban prairie environment, thus becomes a beacon for Aboriginal cultural production and the innovative screen treatment of urban Aboriginal issues.

NOTES

1. Jana G. Pruden, "Aboriginal TV Series Set in Regina Neighbourhood," *Saskatoon Star Phoenix*, 7 September 2004, C3.
2. Ibid., C3. See also Gabriel Yahyahkeekoot, "Problems behind Problems: A Young Person from 'The 'Hood' Endeavors to Stop the Ripple Effect of Cultural Genocide," *Briar Patch* 31, 6 (2002): 8. As a person who grew up in North Central, Yahyahkeekoot offers a first-hand perspective on life in the 'hood and is now forging his way as a writer, poet, and filmmaker.

3. Cheryl Petten, "All-Aboriginal Television Drama Set to Air," *Wind Speaker* 21, 8 (2003): 21.

4. Ibid., 21.

5. Tom Lyons, "Young Aboriginals Flock to Hip-hop, Acting Work," *Toronto Star*, 30 August 2003, H4. Conferences and symposia dedicated to Aboriginal arts and culture are also beginning to play a role in spurring interest in such activity among youth. For example, as Lyla Miller reports, in February 2004 Carleton University hosted its third annual conference on Aboriginal art. Organized by Allan Ryan, New Sun Chair Professor—"the only endowed university position in Canada dedicated to promoting aboriginal arts"—the conference profiled five emerging artists, including *Moccasin Flats'* Darrel Dennis and Tamara Podemski (Jennifer's sister), a singer and actress who has had a starring role in the musical *Rent* on Broadway. (See Miller, "First Nations' New Wave Taking Art to the Edge," *Ottawa Citizen*, 29 February 2004, A3). And, as Joanne Paulson suggests, a critical mass is being formed as "household names" emerging from Aboriginal culture—such as actors Gordon Tootoosis, Tantoo Cardinal, Alex Rice, and Lorne Cardinal, and playwrights Tomson Highway, Drew Hayden Taylor, and Molson Prize–winner Maria Campbell—converged in Saskatoon 27–29 May 2004 for the Saskatchewan Native Theatre Company's (SNTC) first performing arts symposium and "benefit extravaganza." The goal is to build a new state-of-the-art home for SNTC and to "create a social atmosphere for aboriginal youth to work on living a healthy, drug- and alcohol-free lifestyle ... and longer term a residence for aboriginal youth who are participating in our programs," says SNTC's general manager Donna Heinbecker. (See Paulson, "Top Native Talent in City for Symposium," *Saskatoon Star Phoenix*, 19 May 2004, A1). In the last couple of years, the work of Dr. Charity Marsh (Canada Research Chair in Interactive Media and Performance (IMP), Faculty of Fine Arts, University of Regina) has also been important in inspiring Regina's North Central youth. Her IMPLab and its focus on research and practice in hip hop culture has established strong ties to and cross-programming with North Central's Scott Collegiate (see http://www.interactivemediaandperfomance.com/).

6. Qtd. in Sheri Block, "North Central Gets $6M Federal Boost," *Regina Leader Post*, 31 January 2004, B1. Goodale, a Regina MP, was in town to announce $6 million in federal funding for inner city projects targeting such issues as homelessness, poverty, drug addiction, and the sex trade through educational programs such as Street Culture Kidz. In fact, Block reports, it was Goodale who approached Big Soul Productions back in 2002 and invited them to bring their expertise to Regina to help the cause of mentoring youth culture in North Central. (See Block, "Subject Matter of TV Series Hits Home with Actors," *Regina Leader Post*, 6 November 2003, B2).

7. Paula J. Massood, "Mapping the Hood: The Genealogy of City Space in *Boyz N the Hood* and *Menace II Society*," *Cinema Journal* 35, 2 (1996): 88.

8. Ibid., 88.

9. Rob Shields, *Places on the Margin: Alternative Geographies of Modernity* (London: Routledge, 1991), 3, 47, 57, 199.

10. Ibid., 20.

11. See also Christine Ramsay, "Made in Saskatchewan! Features Since Telefilm," *Self Portraits: The Cinemas of Canada Since Telefilm* (Ottawa: Canadian Film Institute, 2006), 203–235.

12. See Dave Margoshes, "Survey Results Show Regina Continues to Get No Respect: The City's Leaders and Residents Say this Poor Opinion is Based on Ignorance," *Vancouver Sun,* 8 August 1998, B1. As many readers will also know, "idol fever" hit Canada in November 2004 as CBC Television voted Tommy Douglas the "Greatest Canadian" of all time in a nationwide contest. "Over 1.2 million votes were cast in a frenzy of voting that took place over six weeks as each of 10 advocates made their case for the Top 10 nominees in special feature programs on CBC Television.... CBC Television received over 140,000 Greatest Canadian nominations from all corners of the country," declaring the following winners in order of most votes received: Tommy Douglas, Terry Fox, Pierre Elliott Trudeau, Sir Frederick Banting, David Suzuki, Lester B. Pearson, Don Cherry, Sir John A. Macdonald, Alexander Graham Bell, and Wayne Gretzky. (See Canada Broadcasting Corporation, "The Greatest Canadian" [Ottawa: CBC, 2004], www. cbc.ca/greatest/ [accessed 18 May 2005]). For a more critical look at Saskatchewan politics since the Douglas legacy, see John W. Warnock, "NDP a Pale Shadow of Pioneering CCF," *Regina Leader Post,* 2 November 2004, B8.

13. Jonathon Gatehouse, "Canada's Worst Neighbourhood," *Maclean's,* 8 January 2007, 25.

14. Iain Chambers, *Border Dialogues: Journeys in Postmodernity* (London: Routledge, 1990), 112.

15. See Angela Hall, "Regina Battles Reputation as Crime Capital: Queen City Tops Break-ins, Car Theft, Murder," *Calgary Herald,* 18 July 2002, A12. According to Statistics Canada data from 2001, "Regina has the dubious distinction of recording the highest crime rate, a rate that increased 10 per cent from the year before" (A12). However, as Mike O'Brien observes, quoting Regina police chief Cal Johnston, the problem must be considered in the context of the legacy of poverty and social problems, and, I would add, racism: "Regina is one of several Western Canadian cities that will continue to have a disproportionally high crime rate until it addresses the socio-economic issues facing our First Nations population.... 'Seventy-six per cent of the people we're putting in jail in this province are of aboriginal ancestry. Eight per cent of the province's population is aboriginal.'... Three-fourths of the province's young offenders are aboriginal, even though they make up only 15 per cent of the province's youth population." (See Mike O'Brien, "Crime Linked to Native Woes: High Rate will Stay until Problems Addressed: Police Chief," *Regina Leader Post,* 21 December 2000, A1.) See also John McCullough, "Regina: Capital of the 21st Century," *Regina's Secret Spaces* (Regina: Canadian Plains Research Centre, 2006), 155–164.

16. Marian Bredin, "Ethnography and Communication: Approaches to Aboriginal Media," *Canadian Journal of Communication* 18, 3 (1993): 306.

17. Ibid., 303.

18. Brenda Longfellow, "Counter-Narratives, Class Politics and Metropolitan." Dystopias: Representations of Globalization in *Maelström, waydowntown,* and *La Moitié gauche du frigo," Canadian Journal of Film Studies* 13, 1 (2004): 69.

19. Qtd. in Bruce Robbins, "Comparative Cosmopolitanism," *Social Text* 31–32 (1992): 181.

20. Paul Rabinow, "Representations Are Social Facts: Modernity and Postmodernity in Anthropology," in *Writing Culture: The Poetics and Politics of Ethnography,* ed. James Clifford and George E. Marcus (Berkeley: University of California Press, 1986), 258.

21. Longfellow, "Counter-Narratives," 70.
22. Ibid., 70.
23. Qtd. in Bredin, "Ethnography and Communication," 305.
24. Massood, "Mapping the Hood," 88.
25. Ibid., 87.
26. Another interesting point of comparison would be Lee Tamahori's 1994 *Once Were Warriors*, a portrait of a dysfunctional Maori family living in an Auckland ghetto for whom similar themes of alcoholism, sexual abuse, and misogyny arise. However, a deeper investigation is beyond the scope of this paper.
27. Massood, "Mapping the Hood," 89.
28. Ibid., 88.
29. Ibid., 89.
30. Margoshes, "Survey Results," B1. What I am taking issue with is not Regina's recent tendency to self-promotion (many of Margoshes's positive observations are true, and, given the city's reputation as the crime capital of Canada, it could do with some healthy self-esteem building) but the fact that North Central and Regina's Aboriginal citizens have been, more often than not, erased and made invisible in such booster discourse.
31. Ibid., B1.
32. Massood, "Mapping the Hood," 88.
33. Ibid., 93.
34. Qtd. in Massood, "Mapping the Hood," 89.
35. Massood, "Mapping the Hood," 88.
36. Edward Soja, *Postmodern Geographies: The Reassertion of Space in Critical Social Theory* (New York: Verso, 1993), 7.
37. bell hooks, *Outlaw Culture: Resisting Representations* (New York: Routledge, 1994), 168.
38. Ibid., 170.
39. Liam Lacey, "Sundance Film Festival 2003: Native Talent in a Gritty 'Hood," *Globe and Mail*, 24 January 2003, R1.
40. Ibid., R1.
41. Ibid., R1.
42. Jeremy Parnes, "North Central Community Partnership: Report on the Community Vision and Action Plan," Regina, May 2003, 5.
43. For coverage of the Saskatoon case, see Dion Spotted Eagle, "First Nations Want Fair Treatment," *Regina Leader Post*, 2 May 2005, B8; Tim Cook, "Hearing for Two Cops Fired in Neil Stonechild Case Begins in Saskatoon," *Canadian Press NewsWire*, Toronto, 4 May 2005. For coverage of the Edmonton cases, see Florence Loyie and Ryan Cormier, "Police Confirm Body in Field was Prostitute," *Calgary Herald*, 10 May 2005, A3; Jim Farrell, "Second Body in 3 Weeks," *Edmonton Journal*, 8 May 2005, A3; Muriel Stanley Venne, "Let's Lay off the Loaded Language: Missing Women Much More than Prostitutes," *Edmonton Journal*, 3 May 2005, A15. See also Regina-based filmmaker Sarah Abbott's 2008 *Out in the Cold*, a short poetic dramatization of the Saskatoon "starlight" tours, starring Gordon Tootoosis, Matthew Strongeagle, and Erroll Kinistino.

CHAPTER 7

Co-producing First Nations' Narratives:
The Journals of Knud Rasmussen

DORIS BALTRUSCHAT

As discussed in previous chapters in this collection, the Aboriginal Peoples
Television Network (APTN) licences media productions from a variety of
Aboriginal sources. The demand for new indigenous film and television
content and new markets for indigenous media have increased the opportunities for co-production and for the use of more sophisticated digital
production and distribution technologies. Increasingly, programs include
interactive features and multi-platform applications. These emerging attributes of indigenous screen production have led to greater local, national,
and international access to indigenous film and video. This chapter focuses
on Isuma Productions in Igloolik, Nunavut, as a case study in the changing
environment for indigenous cinema and the development of co-production
agreements and digital technologies in Inuit contexts. Beginning with a
brief history of colonial representations in the Arctic, the chapter goes on to
explore the roles new media and co-production play in indigenous filmmaking, with a particular focus on community-based media from an Inuit point
of view. The discussion of how Isuma makes use of the Internet to engage
viewers in the feature film *The Journals of Knud Rasmussen* through online
diaries, blogs, and historical maps[1] demonstrates how new media allow
Aboriginal filmmakers to educate the wider community about indigenous
history, culture, and rights.

Digital Media Production and Storytelling

Experience, which is passed on from mouth to mouth is the source from which all storytellers have drawn. And among those who have written down the tales, it is the great ones whose written version differs least from the speech of the many nameless storytellers.

—*Walter Benjamin,*
"The Storyteller"[2]

Digital and online media provide an accessible alternative to traditional, analog television production. APTN's website features promotional and educational materials, as well as live webcasts and video archives.[3] For example, the historical series about the Anishinaabe/Ojibwe of the Great Lakes region, titled Waasa-Inaabidaa ("We look In All Directions"), is linked to an elaborate and interactive site[4] that provides educational materials about the history and culture of this nation.[5] Digital technologies are also used in feature-film production, such as in the film *Atanarjuat, the Fast Runner*, which combined digital technology with traditional storytelling to recreate an Inuit legend. The accessibility of digital video, as a result of reasonable production costs and ease of use, allowed the filmmakers, Zacharias Kunuk and Norman Cohn, to produce a feature from an Inuit point of view: "Video [is] a different way of representing reality. It's a different form of narrative story telling. All this video experience has been invisible except in the art world and in remote regions where it's been an empowering tool for self-representation by getting inside-out points of view instead of the kind of authoritarian outside-in points of view. So this whole concept is a marriage of what was really a very experimental art form, video, with the richness of Inuit oral tradition."[6]

Igloolik Isuma Productions is Canada's first independent film and video production company to present stories from an Inuit perspective. Their latest film, *The Journals of Knud Rasmussen*, is a narrative about transition and change in the history of the Igloolik community. The film traces the fifth Thule expedition by the Danish explorers Knud Rasmussen, Peter Freuchen, and Therkel Mathiassen, who between 1921 and 1922 undertook an expedition to northern Baffin Island, including the Igloolik region. At the centre of the film lies a spiritual tale about the shaman Avva (played by Pakak Innuksuk) and his headstrong daughter Apak (Leah Angutimarik), who experience the dramatic impact of colonization on their nomadic way of life. Kunuk and Cohn present the story from an Inuit point of view; thereby reclaiming this narrative about the encounter with the explorers, who, as

Cohn describes, were the proverbial "accidental tourists" of their time.[7] The script is based on journals from explorers and missionaries, museum collections, government documents, and, most importantly, oral history accounts from Inuit Elders.[8] This combination of historical documents and eyewitness accounts offers a new perspective on the events that shaped the region and its people in the early twentieth century. Kunuk had wanted to make this film for a long time, in order to "recreate the misunderstanding and go after true stories."[9]

Kunuk began experimenting with media production in 1981 and created his first independent video in 1985, called *From Inuk Point of View*. In the 1980s, he managed the Inuit Broadcasting Corporation production centre in Igloolik.[10] Then, in 1990, he co-founded Igloolik Isuma Productions with screenwriter Paul Apak Angilirq, cinematographer Norman Cohn, and actor Paul Qulitalik. Their goal was to produce independent, community-based film, video, and Internet sites in order to enhance local culture and language traditions. In addition, the company provides economic opportunities in the region. Both their feature films employed predominantly local talent from the area, including actors, set builders, and costume designers. *The Journals of Knud Rasmussen* also features actors and producers from Denmark and Greenland because it was co-produced with Barok Film in Copenhagen.

The key to Isuma's philosophy is to create films and television programs that accurately reflect Inuit history and daily life. Kunuk states that the Inuit point of view in filmmaking is based on the authentic representation of Arctic settings, peoples, and environment: "In Igloolik we're working with families and documenting them. We could tell them what we want to do and they create their own lines. We've been working with these people for a long time and we've been training them so they are professional actors. In the Inuit way you learn by watching. The bottom line is that we're trying to show our culture the way it was, since it's been misunderstood a lot."[11] For *Atanarjuat*, Kunuk and Cohn used oral history accounts and museum exhibits to explore traditional ways of life. The filmmakers involved the entire community in every aspect of the production process. From costume making, set construction, and makeup, to actors, scriptwriters, and technicians, over 100 Igloolik residents took part in the film.[12] Paul Apak wrote the script, which Norman Cohn translated into English. Like *The Journals of Knud Rasmussen*, *Atanarjuat* received funding from government agencies such as Telefilm Canada. Its international success resulted in the recognition of Inuit filmmaking—including its unique aesthetic form of representation.[13] It also made it easier for Isuma to develop *The Journals of Knud Rasmussen*.

The script for *The Journals of Knud Rasmussen* includes stories from the entire Igloolik community. Collective storytelling practices are an essential cultural base for Inuit peoples, who, without a written language, have passed on their life's experience and histories in the form of stories for many generations. According to Kunuk:

> The Inuit style of filmmaking takes lots of teamwork. We work horizontally while the usual Hollywood film people work in a military style. Our entire team would talk about how to shoot a particular scene, from art directors to the sound man. We put the whole community to work. Costumes, props—we had a two-million-dollar budget [for *Atanarjuat*], and one million stayed with the people of Igloolik. The people learned to practice their own cultures, and language, although of course we had no Igloolik style of igloos. Everything was authentic, handmade. Inuit people are storytellers. Four thousand years we have been passing stories to our youth. We saw other films being made about the north where you could see a woman's seal oil lamp turned the wrong way around and the production people didn't care or know better. It is important we tell our stories from our Inuit point of view.[14]

Human beings create narratives to organize their experiences and to understand the world around them as well as their "inner world" of memory and emotions. As J. Bruner states, "A story must construct two landscapes simultaneously: the outer landscape of action and the inner of thought and intention."[15] In *The Journals of Knud Rasmussen,* the shaman Avva maps his personal experiences through stories and songs. In this way, stories become cultural markers of time and space because they encapsulate memories of historical events. When missionaries introduced Christian hymns to the region and forbade traditional songs, the result was the loss of an identity tied to these aural markers of time and space. Thus, the locus of control shifted to the colonizers.

The events described in *The Journals of Knud Rasmussen* attain greater significance when they are placed in the historical context of colonial aggression. In the early part of the twentieth century, photographic and filmic images constituted an important strategy for mapping the Canadian nation. They allowed for the documentation and archival preservation of the North while linking it to the authorities of the state, church, and corporation.[16]

Colonial Traces in the Arctic

> It was strange to us to meet with police in these regions; and we were at once impressed by the energy with which Canada seeks to maintain law and order in the northern lands. The mounted police, a service popular throughout the country, has here to relinquish its splendid horses and travel by dog sledge, making regular visits of inspection over a wide extent of territory.
>
> —*The Journals of Knud Rasmussen*[17]

Rasmussen's journals are filled with recollections and photographs of Canada's North. Visual documentation of the Arctic began as early as 1853 and 1854 in the form of calotype portraits and daguerreotyping,[18] which served to document, map, and demarcate the region in order to establish territorial and cultural sovereignty for the Canadian state, church, and corporate interests. Hudson Bay employees, for example, used wet-plate technology[19] to document and journal their experiences, thus leaving traces of early economic activity. By the turn of the century, Canadian sovereignty gained new importance, with Norwegian, American, and Scottish interest in the area. Even though Canada had received title from Great Britain for the Arctic archipelago in 1880, it had few means to enforce its claim to the North. However, after the Alaska–Canada boundary dispute, in which Canada ceded territory to the United States, the government pursued its sovereignty claims more actively. Under the command of A.P. Low, the *Neptune* expedition (1903–1904) and *Arctic* expedition (1904–1905) were launched to assert Canadian control over Hudson Bay and the eastern part of the Arctic. Low published an illustrated account of these voyages and gave slide lectures to the public, which contributed to the growing popular interest and, as Pamela Stern points out, created "a public sense of ownership"[20] of the region.

Missionary photography highlights the extent to which images of the Arctic were constructed to publicize and justify the church's presence in the North. The Anglican Church in particular, under the stewardship of Bishop Archibald Lang Fleming, provided visual documentation of the region between 1927 and 1948. Fleming held travelling slide shows of his photographs and films in North America and Great Britain, disseminating his views of the North to the general public. According to Peter Geller, Fleming presented Inuit peoples in a state of progressive cultural evolution and in need of missionary guidance.[21] His portraits depict Inuit peoples in a "before" and "after" fashion, signifying the missionary endeavour to transform "darkness" into "lightness." Similarly, he juxtaposed images of the exterior and interior of the All Saints' Cathedral in Aklavik to denote a "land of twilight." These photographs remain as disturbing reminders of the cultural dominance and colonization processes that church, government, and economic interests exerted in the region. Selective presentations of these images hide the tragic failures of native residential schools, displacement, and the wide impact colonial expansion had on traditional ways of life.[22]

In addition to photographs, several films were made to feature Arctic communities. The most famous is Robert Flaherty's documentary *Nanook of the North*, from 1922. The film created a romanticized image of an Inuit family living in a pre-industrial setting amidst a hostile natural world. Flaherty's dramatic scenes centred on the "happy Inuit," a constructed reality that was far removed from the social and political conditions of the time. As Alan Marcus points out, Alakariallak (who played Nanook) and his family were from the same Inukjuamiut community that would be relocated to the High Arctic by the Canadian government thirty years later.[23] The film had a tremendous impact on audiences around the world, even though it obscured Arctic realities and diversity. *Nanook* was released in London, Moscow, and New York, where it fuelled the popular imagination about Inuit life. Companies exploited this sentiment and designed marketing campaigns around different brands of ice cream, which sold as "Nanuks" in Germany and "Esquimaux" in France. It also led to more feature films, such as the German-American co-production *SOS Eisberg (SOS Iceberg)* in 1932, which was shot off the coast of Greenland. Directed by A. Fanck and Knud Rasmussen, the film focused predominantly on the exotic aspects of the location and included a scene in which a group of Inuit approach a village in their kayaks. Rasmussen directed this sequence in Nuugaatsiaq, where he had hired locals to act for the film.[24] In 1952, the character of Nanook was adapted once more for the Canadian Film Board documentary titled *Land of the Long Day*. The director, Doug Wilkinson, intentionally used Flaherty's "mythological mould" of the Inuit to perpetuate the stereotypical portrayal of the noble and stoic Native. However, in contrast to Flaherty's focus on a pre-industrial existence, Wilkinson depicted the Inummariit as an integrated cultural group who used modern tools in a naturalized and non-conflicted way, thus omitting the important historical context of colonization.[25]

The production of films and television programs from an Inuit perspective is a necessary intervention in the long history of stereotypical portrayals of Inuit peoples in order to balance representations of indigenous peoples.

Even though filmmakers such as Flaherty claimed that their actors participated in production—that is, Alakariallak contributed to reconstructing the pre-colonial *mise en scène*[26]—the editorial choices of any director determine how content is constructed through selecting, framing, and timing, as well as sequencing of events. In addition, the context of production sets parameters for content, mode of address, promotion, and licensing. Flaherty's dramatic interpretation of Inuit life, for example, was meant for cinematic exhibition with the aim to generate profit for its investors.[27] In comparison, Inuit documentaries, such as the works by the anthropologist Asen Balikci, were produced for use in school curricula. Even though Balikci notes that his approach to filmmaking is "holistic" and without "cinematic exaggerations,"[28] his documentaries are nonetheless defined by their purpose to provide educational lessons, from an anthropological point of view, for a predominant North American and European audience.[29]

Isuma's approach is therefore fundamentally different in that it starts with community involvement in all production processes. Also, Isuma's narratives are rooted in Inuit spirituality and symbolism, which are not "translated" to provide non-Inuit viewers easier access to their meaning. The films are as much a celebration of cultural continuity as they are mnemonic devices to reconnect to memories of the past. Their purpose goes beyond educational aims, as they allow Inuit participants and audiences to engage with and reflect upon issues that are important to the community. Within the context of colonial legacies and unresolved land claims, the films also represent a political voice for indigenous rights that extend beyond national borders.

In *The Journals of Knud Rasmussen*, the filmmakers used historical records to retrace events from the early twentieth century. Photographs served to map locations and to find peoples that came in contact with Rasmussen, Mathiassen, and Freuchen. Journals from explorers, missionaries, and whalers, government documents, and museum artifacts were researched to learn about previous customs, beliefs, facial adornment, and clothing. In reclaiming these artifacts and memorabilia for the creative interpretation of history, colonial traces were redrawn and used as a form of empowerment for the present. The result is a deeper understanding of the impact of colonial forces on the community and the reconnection of collective memory to its social world.

The Journals of Knud Rasmussen depicts the traumatic influence of missionaries on traditional belief systems, as is exemplified in a key moment in the film, when Apak's former lover Nuqallaq (Natar Ungalaaq) addresses a group of Inuit: "Turn away from your old way of life. Satan tempts us with old taboos, but Jesus saves us with only ten commandments. Sing only Jesus songs. Do not drum and sing Satan's songs that tempt Inuit to burn in hell forever. Shamans serve Satan and cannot heal us."[30] In *The Journals*, the impact of Christianity is interpreted through the shaman Avva and his daughter Apak, whose actions symbolize the transition between pre- and postcolonial times. Apak, in particular, acts as a bridge between the past and the present. Her departure from her family to join a Christian sect marks a break with tradition, which leaves her family unit ruptured and her father Avva isolated and powerless. The filmmakers re-tell this story by combining Rasmussen's recollections with oral history accounts, reclaiming the narrative of the encounter and highlighting colonial traces and painful dichotomies.

The Inuit Point of View

When I was growing up, we were learning about Jesus Christ who walked on water, ran out of wine, and made water into wine. To us, that was a shaman. I was brought up on the Anglican side, and our minister didn't allow us to dance or storytell. In the seventies, those things were totally banned.

—*Zacharias Kunuk*[31]

Video and lightweight camera equipment sparked a revolution in independent productions in the 1980s, which inspired Kunuk and Cohn to create their own works. It was their shared interest in video that led to initial collaborations and resulted in their twenty-five-year-long creative partnership. According to Cohn, Inuit storytelling values intersect with alternative video to create films that depict an "authentic world."[32] The third vector in this equation is video/digital technology and its evolution into user-friendly applications with easy access to portable recording and editing equipment. According to Cohn,

as a marriage of art and politics, Isuma's videomaking synthesizes several related themes in a new way. First, Inuit oral storytelling is a sophisticated mix of fact, fiction, performance, improvisation, past and future, which has maintained Inuit culture successfully through art from Stone Age to Information Age. Second, being colonized offers artists a fertile reality for original progressive self-expression. Third, the invention of low-cost video at the end of the

1960s enabled people from Harlem to the Arctic to use TV as a tool for political and social change in local communities. And finally, after thirty years on the margins, video, reincarnated as "digital filmmaking," finally moved to the mainstream.[33]

The Journals of Knud Rasmussen is shot on High Definition (HD), a format that allows for digital post-production on site. Rushes from the daily shoot could be screened in Igloolik and did not have to be sent to Montreal, which would have resulted in lengthy delays.[34] *Atanarjuat* and *The Journals of Knud Rassmussen* are Kunuk and Cohn's first "scripted" features. Their portrayal of Inuit life has a distinct "community-theatre" feel resulting from the reciprocal relationship between storytelling traditions, community theatre, improvisations, and collaborative film production.

Kunuk and Cohn chose to co-produce *The Journals* with Barok Film in Denmark since they wanted to "master" this aspect of the film industry.[35] *The Journals* is a "natural co-production" because the film recalls the historical encounter between different cultures. Since the explorers Rasmussen, Freuchen, and Mathiassen are important figures in Denmark, collaboration with a foreign production company made sense, even though differences in production styles (Isuma's community-based film practices versus Barok's business approach to production) required compromises from both partners.

International film and TV co-productions have been a focal point for filmmakers and television producers for over a decade, especially in Canada. Co-productions provide the means to pool financial, talent, and labour resources from more than one country and, even though they tend to be more elaborate, time consuming, and, in some instances, expensive, they are promoted as a way to access the global market through international distribution. Government incentives from Telefilm and Heritage Canada, in the form of workshops, international conferences, and participation at markets like MIPTV and MIPCOM in Cannes, have created a central place for this global production practice.[36]

Studies suggest that co-productions are suitable for "global stories" that transcend cultural boundaries. They are ideal for dramatic programs dealing with human emotions and the dynamics of close relationships[37] as well as for documentaries, which feature topics on nature, sports, international celebrities, or common histories.[38] In most instances, co-productions assume forms that are relatively culturally indistinct and that eschew political content. Some genres, such as drama, adventure, science fiction, and documentary, are preferred over others, and these tend to focus on human relationships and emotional storylines to increase their universal appeal. Co-production also affects the temporal organization and spatial reference of narrative structures, especially in science-fiction and adventure programs.[39] Although Jäckel emphasizes that even though co-productions tend to be identified as "mainstream products ... where maintaining cultural identity means losing profits," they also, in some instances, can be "symbolic bearers of national identity,"[40] especially when they are promoted as national productions, as is the case with Canadian feature films *Le Confessionnal* and *The Red Violin*.

In the case of *The Journals of Knud Rasmussen,* co-production caused little conflict in the development of the local narrative and its historical setting because the film is a Canadian majority co-production, and it therefore received most of its funding from the Canadian side.[41] This allowed the Canadian filmmakers to focus on the aesthetic style of Inuit filmmaking— single, continuously recorded performances shot with a particular camera set-up, careful attention to detail on how tools are used in daily life, and an emphasis on stories and myths that represented the transition between pre-colonial existence and the arrival of Christianity. Danish actors portrayed the explorers Rasmussen (Jens Jørn Spottag), Freuchen (Kim Bodnia), and Mathiassen (Jakob Cedergren). While they recreated historical personas, their casting also fulfilled the requirements for treaty co-production, namely to allocate talent and crew according to the financial participation of each co-producer. With a budget of nearly CDN $6.3 million, co-producing *The Journals* significantly increased the financing for the film. In comparison, the *Atanarjuat* budget was just under CDN $2 million.[42]

However, in co-producing *The Journals*, Isuma also linked the film to a global production technology, which, as many producers have noted, can potentially compromise the creative vision for a project.[43] Co-production is based on a financing model that is inherently unstable and does not guarantee long-term funding opportunities for local film and television industries. Furthermore, international co-productions are subject to the government policies of more than one country.[44] A shift in official mandates abroad can therefore impact production in Canada.[45] Co-production thus places *The Journals* firmly within the volatile global market; however, interestingly, it also creates a space for presenting an alternative film on an international platform at a time when Arctic themes are increasingly gaining media attention. Cohn comments on the multiple purposes of Isuma's films, which are determined by their particular contexts:

> The work we do has multiple, parallel identities. The very same film might exist in the film industry as entertainment. It might exist in the art world at Documenta or the Art Gallery of Ontario. It might

exist as materials that are discussed and written about by anthropologists doing a Ph.D. in the department of Anthropology, or, at the same time, be used to teach in schools about Inuit culture. So the entertainment media value, the artistic identity and the educational identity of what we do, and the cultural meaning of what we do, are all separate lives of the very same product.[46]

Digital Production and Online Access to Isuma Films

In spite of the international distribution and recognition of Isuma's films, the filmmakers' main focus remains on creating Inuit films for local audiences—especially because the ease of digital production promotes participatory forms of communication.[47] This decentralization of media practices is an exercise in empowerment, which at various points intersects with mainstream media to redirect nationwide foci.[48] Interest in northern communities, its lands and peoples, is intensifying in scientific research (into the environment and global warming) and international politics (with respect to Canada's sovereignty claim in the North) as well as in the popular imagination of the public (for example, concerning animal preservation and tourism), especially in light of the International Polar Year (IPY) of 2007–2008. IPY spotlights Canada's northern communities through research, news broadcasts, and documentaries. It is therefore necessary to promote media production opportunities from an Inuit point of view and to create connections between different organizations and communities, especially considering the existing pan-indigenous identity that spans the Canadian Arctic, Alaska, Greenland, and Russia.[49]

One of Isuma's goals is the development of educational initiatives such as the SILA project (SILA is the Inuit word for "all that surrounds us" as in the weather, the climate, and the world), which is linked to a comprehensive website that fulfills these multiple purposes:

- providing information about *The Journals of Knud Rasmussen*

- extending an invitation to participate in an online forum during the shoot of the movie

- including an educational project to engage the wider public in learning about Inuit culture and traditions.

The website acts like a narrative map, providing various entry points into traditional songs, stories, and the actual shooting of the movie. For example, during production in 2005, webcams allowed a glimpse into on-going production. Also, crew and actors posted diaries, blogs, and reflections to engage the local community (as well as the international press) in a dialogue about the film, exemplified by the following entry by Jobie Weetaluktuk on 6 April 2005:

> At least the first four scenes of the *Journals of Knud Rasmussen* were shot between 9pm and 9am overnight between Tuesday and Wednesday. To begin the production with a night shoot is a gruelling idea. This is a story about people who would do such a thing. Søren Bjørn, the Danish Production Assistant for Barok Films, stands at a road blockade in –20 C, keeping skidoos and other vehicles from getting near the set. At 11 pm, a bone chilling breeze keeps him constant company.

> This is an epic tale, the *Journals of Knud Rasmussen*. It is being told by creative people: actors, extras, writers, directors, producers, and many others. People with specific skills. People with multiple skills. Storytellers like Zacharias Kunuk, who's been up since 5 am. "We might need pills to keep us awake", he joked with Natar Ungalaaq. Normally producers shoot at night only when the production is well underway.

> Then to top it all off, at the last minute the co-director and cinematographer Norman Cohn has to play the role of Angakuq or Captain George Comer. Comer is known to the Inuit as Angakuq, or shaman because he had the particular skill of being able to take photographic images of people, record their voices, and making plaster impressions of their faces. For these things, he was known as Angakuq, a magician of skill. In the early 1900's, such feats were beyond imagination for the Inuit. Comer's archived collection has become a valuable resource for the production of the film.[50]

In addition to online diaries, the website features video clips, photographs, and radio-program archives. This open paradigm invites the site's visitors into an egalitarian setting and encourages engagement with educational materials, which through their non-linear construction and predominant visual and aural content accommodate varying literacy levels. The SILA project is also an e-learning forum for Inuit youth to learn about their past, explore traditional ideas, and create a record of life in their community. These activities anchor experiences in the present and facilitate the re-territorialization of knowledge that provokes positive action and hope for the future.[51]

In 2007, Isuma launched a new interactive initiative in the form of Isuma TV, an online video portal for indigenous filmmakers, who can upload their film and video to a designated website. The site provides a forum for filmmakers "to serve their own needs, within a powerful collective consciousness, to build a growing audience for indigenous productions, especially in remote communities."[52] One of the key aspects of Isuma TV, similar to the SILA project, is to create an archive of stories, cultural practices, and traditions for future generations, while promoting international access to indigenous media.

Conclusion

There are many different ways to tell the same story. In the empowering act of seizing the role of the narrator in *The Journals of Knud Rasmussen,* Isuma presents the Inuit way of life from an authentic perspective, which corrects as well as balances historical portrayals. The film engages the collective memory of the Igloolik community as it recalls the historic constellation of events that would shape the region for years to come. Kunuk and Cohn based their script on Rasmussen's journals but interpreted developments through their own lens. Oral history accounts and collective storytelling therefore created an ethnographic map that stands in stark contrast to mainstream depictions of Inuit communities. In addition, the filmmakers' use of co-production, digital media, and interactive websites expand the film's reach beyond the local community and invite international audiences to learn more about Inuit history and culture. The websites provide valuable background information, which highlights the importance of language, environment, and traditions for Inuit peoples. These educational outreach efforts are well timed as global interest re-emerges due to environmental, economic, and political developments that focus global media attention on Canada's North.

NOTES

1 *The Journals of Knud Rassmussen,* Homepage, 2005, http://www.isuma.ca/thejournals/en/ (accessed 20 June 2006).

2 Walter Benjamin, "The Storyteller: Observations on the Works of Nikolai Leskov," in *Walter Benjamin: Selected Writings Volume 3, 1935–1938,* ed. Howard Eiland and Michael W. Jennings (Cambridge, MA: Belknap Press of Harvard University, 2002), 144.

3 Aboriginal Peoples Television Network, "Homepage," APTN, http://www.aptn.ca (accessed 15 March 2006).

4 *Ojibwe,* "Waasa-Inaabidaa 'We look In All Directions,'" Homepage, http://www.ojibwe.org (accessed 20 June 2006).

5   Jim Compton, director of programming, APTN, in discussion with the author, 20 March 2003.

6   Norman Cohn, "Atanarjuat, the Fast Runner," *IndieWire*, http://www.indiewire. com/film/interviews/int_Cohn_Kunuk_020605.html (accessed 6 May 2002).

7   Norman Cohn, cinematographer, writer and director, Igloolik Isuma Productions, in discussion with the author, 27 February 2006.

8   Zacharias Kunuk, cinematographer, writer and director, Igloolik Isuma Productions, in discussion with the author, 2 February 2006.

9   Zacharias Kunuk, "Zacharias Kunuk on his film *Atanarjuat*," interview by Ian Reid, acting co-ordinator of the Aboriginal Arts Secretariat. *The Canada Council for the Arts*, June 2001, http://www.canadacouncil.ca (accessed 6 January 2006).

10 The Aboriginal Peoples Television Network (APTN) evolved out of broadcasting initiatives in the Canadian Arctic that date back to the late 1970s, when satellite transmissions provided health and educational programming to Inuit communities. A few years later, the implementation of successful projects such as "Inukshuk" in the Northwest Territories and "Naalakvik," an Inuit Association in Northern Quebec, laid the foundations for the Inuit Broadcasting Corporation in 1981.

11 Kunuk, interview by I. Reid.

12 Faye D. Ginsburg, "Atanarjuat Off-Screen: From 'Media Reservations' to the World Stage," *American Anthropologist* 105, 4 (2003): 828.

13 Shari Hunsdorf, "Atanarjuat, The Fast Runner: Culture, History, and Politics in Inuit Media, *American Anthropologist* 105, 4 (2003): 824.

14 Igloolik Isuma Productions, "The Inuit Style of Filmmaking," Isuma Teacher's Resource Guide, SILA, http://www.sila.nu/teachers (accessed 23 July 2006).

15 J. Bruner, *Actual Minds, Possible Worlds* (Cambridge, MA: Harvard University Press, 1986), quoted in H. McEwan and K. Egan, eds., *Narrative in Teaching, Learning, and Research* (New York: Teachers College, Columbia University, 1995), vii.

16 Peter Geller, "Pictures of the Arctic Night: Archibald Land Fleming and the Representation of Canadian Inuit," in *Imaging the Arctic*, ed. J.C.H. King and Henrietta Lidchi (Seattle: University of Washington Press and Vancouver: University of British Columbia Press, 1998).

17 Knud Rasmussen, *Across Arctic America. Narrative of the Fifth Thule Expedition* (New York: Greenwood Press, 1969), 41.

18 Calotype portraits were made following a method invented by F. Talbot, in which paper, sensitized with common salt and silver nitrate, created a negative from which positives could be rendered. Daguerreotyping was a photographic method developed by L.J. Mandé Daguerre.

19 Wet-plate technology required that the glass plates were coated with light-sensitive chemicals just prior to exposure. The photographs had to be developed right afterwards, in contrast to dry-plate photography, which allowed for delayed processing.

20 Pamela Stern, "The History of Canadian Arctic Photography: Issues of Territorial and Cultural Sovereignty," in King and Lidchi, *Imaging the Arctic*, 50.

21 Geller, "Pictures of the Arctic Night," 64–65.

22 Ibid., 67.

23 Alan R. Marcus, *Relocating Eden. The Image and Politics of Inuit Exile in the Canadian Arctic* (Hanover: University Press of New England, 1995).

24 Henrietta Lidchi, "Filmic Fantasies in Arctic Lands: Photographing the Inuit of North West Greenland in 1932," in King and Lidchi, *Imaging the Arctic*, 197–199.

25 Marcus, *Relocating Eden*, 14–15.

26 *"Mise en scène"* refers to the disposition of all visual elements in a film or video frame.

27 Jay Ruby, "A Re-Examination of the Early Career of Robert J. Flaherty," *Quarterly Review of Film Studies* 5, 4 (1980): 431–457.

28 Asen Balikci, qtd. in Paul Hockings, "Asen Balikci Films Nanook," *Visual Anthropology Review* 17, 2 (2001–02): 72.

29 Asen Balikci, "Anthropology, Film and the Arctic Peoples: The First Forman Lecture," *Anthropology Today* 5, 2 (1989): 5.

30 *The Journals of Knud Rasmussen*, DVD, directed by Norman Cohn and Zacharias Kunuk (Igloolik, Nunavut: Isuma Productions, 2006).

31 Zacharias Kunuk, qtd. in G. MacDonald, "Coming to a Screen Near You," *Globe and Mail*, 25 January 2006, R1–R2.

32 Cohn, in discussion with the author.

33 Norman Cohn, "The Art of Community-Based Filmmaking," SILA, 2005, http://www.sila.nu/teachers (accessed 15 March 2006).

34 Kunuk, in discussion with the author.

35 Cohn, in discussion with the author.

36 The director of the French Film Centre, Michel Fourré-Cormeray, is attributed with developing the idea for treaties that accredit films with a dual nationality. France and Italy were the first countries to sign an "experimental" co-production agreement in October 1946, which became official in 1949 (See Anne Jäckel, "Dual Nationality Film Productions in Europe," *Historical Journal of Film, Radio and Television* 23, 3 [2003]: 231–243). International co-productions became popular in the mid-1990s when changes to public broadcasting mandates and funding cut backs resulted in an industry-wide restructuring. Telefilm administers all international co-production treaties on behalf of the Canadian government. Today, Canada has 57 co-production treaties with 53 countries. Britain and France are the most important and prolific co-producers internationally.

37 Sharon Strover, "Recent Trends in Co-productions: The Demise of the National," in *Democracy and Communication in the New Europe*, ed. F. Corcoran and P. Preston (Cresskill, NJ: Hampton Press, 1995), 111.

38 C. Binning, "Special Report on Documentary Production and Distribution: Who's Shopping for Docs," *Playback Magazine*, 9 March 1998, http://www.playbackmag.com/articles/pb/20973.asp.

39 Doris Baltruschat, "International Film and TV Co-productions: A Canadian Case Study," in *Media Organization and Production*, ed. Simon Cottle (London: Sage Publications, 2003), 204.

40 Anne Jäckel, "The Search for the National in Canadian Multilateral Cinematographic Co-productions," *National Identities* 3, 2 (2001): 166.

41 *The Journals of Knud Rasmussen* is an 80:20 Canadian majority co-production with Denmark.

42 Igloolik Isuma Productions, "Independent Inuit Film. About Us," http://www. isuma.ca/about (accessed 29 May 2007).

43 Colin Hoskins and Stuart McFadyen, "Canadian Participation in International Co-productions and Co-ventures in Television Programming," *Canadian Journal of Communication*, 18, 2 (1993): 231.

44 The U.K. launched an official co-production review in 2003, which was followed by similar reviews in Canada and Australia. The primary objective: the balancing of economic and cultural benefits for each country and their respective industries.

45 For example, as a result of a shift in official policy in the U.K. in 2003, international co-producers temporarily had to spend at least 40 percent of their feature-film production budget in Britain, an increase from the previous 30 percent minimum. The impact of this change is noticeable in the decline of co-production activities between the two countries, as reported by the Canadian Film and Television Production Association in October 2004.

46 Cohn, in discussion with the author.

47 On 9 March 2006, *The Journals of Knud Rasmussen* was first shown to the Igloolik community in the local Ataguttaaluk high school before it began its travelling tour through northern communities, and before its southern premiere in Toronto, where it opened the International Film Festival in September 2006. The film was well received by critics and audiences alike and, according to *Playback Magazine* (qtd. in Toronto International Film Festival Group, 2008), became one of the highest grossing Canadian films in 2007.

48 R. Jain, "Video: For, by and with the People," in *Video the Changing World*, ed. N. Thede and A. Ambrosi (Montreal: Black Rose Books, Vidéazimut and Vidéo Tiers-monde, 1991).

49 Karla Jessen Williamson, "Celestial and Social Families of the Inuit," in *Expressions in Canadian Native Studies*, ed. Ron F. Laliberté et al. (Saskatoon: University of Saskatchewan Extension Press, 2000), 128.

50 Igloolik Isuma Productions, "Live from the Set," SILA, http://www.sila.nu/live/ (accessed 15 March 2006).

51 The Canadian government is planning to introduce broadband access to indigenous communities through public and private partnerships in the coming years in order to address the current digital divide in remote areas of Canada (see the First Nations Connectivity Research Team of the School of Communication at Simon Fraser University, http://arago.cprost.sfu.ca/smith/research).

52 Isuma Distribution International, "About Us," Isuma TV, http://www.isuma.tv/ (accessed 5 July 2008).

CHAPTER 8

Wearing the White Man's Shoes: Two Worlds in Cyberspace

MIKE PATTERSON

This chapter moves from the analysis of film and television to examine both the academic literature on and personal experiences in cyberspace with respect to Native peoples in Canada. It gives examples of the early emergence of Native cyber-communities in Canada and elsewhere and asks what is being gained and lost in exchanges between people and computers, in people communicating in new ways with information technology, and in new global dialogues. It then describes some visions for the future use of cyberspace, with a caution to be aware of its contradictory possibilities. The chapter concludes that Natives in Canada should take a proactive approach to developing indigenous cultures in this new territory still in the process of creation, to refine and redefine Native and non-Native priorities with regards to cultural survival, self-determination, and mutual recognition.

Emerging Native Cyber-communities

Over the last twenty years, I have seen myself, my friends and family, and now much of global society gravitate more and more to the new place called cyberspace. This is a place "where the forest meets the highway,"[1] where land-based people such as Natives[2] in Canada meet the landless world of e-commerce, dot-com, and global change. Also, in terms of inter-Native communications, it is the new "Moccasin Telegraph." I took a five-year extensive journey into emerging Native cyberspace starting in the late 1990s, and what follows are a series of case studies from different political, cultural, and economic perspectives. These examples represent emerging communities, some of which still exist, others of which have evolved to meet different needs, and still others of which have disappeared entirely.

The sharing and distribution of knowledge in cyberspace allows for distinct and free cyber-communities, where Natives and other users of the Net have access to all of Michel Foucault's "three great variables" of power: "territory, communication and speed."[3] It was the technology of the horse that enabled the Plains Indians to become the finest survivors and light cavalry of their day and place, commanding the Great Plains territory with the communication and speed of movement the horse made possible. These case studies examine how the new technology of cyberspace may similarly aid, and hinder, decolonization and self-determination for Native and other marginalized peoples.

In June 1998, Ottawa's SAW Gallery hosted an exhibition created by Iroquois artists exploring and using information technology (IT). The show visited those areas "At the Edge of the Woods: Along the Highway" and also explored "the notion of four states of awareness in Iroquoian culture, representing the progression from the edge of the woods, to the clearing around a village, the village itself and the inside of a longhouse."[4] Two exhibits struck me: one by William Powless, an installation consisting of lodge poles forming a tipi, with a computer where the fire would be, displaying a video of a fire; and the other by Melanie Printup Hope, an interactive web project that allowed people to remotely and virtually contribute beads toward the making of an Electronic Wampum Belt. Both suggested that cultural interaction was alive on many levels, reaching into the past and future, trying to find ways of reconciling the meeting of two distinct world views that, from many Native perspectives, were supposed to remain apart.

Natives in Canada have maintained their value systems through five hundred years of colonization policy in Canada, but cyberspace is a new territory. A strong movement toward self-determination has begun in this country, and tools brought by the Europeans and others have traditionally been used by Native peoples to allow them to overcome marginalization and resist colonization policies. Cyberspace now plays a central role in this decolonization process—it represents the territory, communication potential, and speed needed to help shift the balance of power and stratification in society today.

Where is Cyberspace?

Cyberspace is a place that brings together telecommunications, the Internet, the World Wide Web, and other communications technologies, a place virtually populated by a rapidly expanding group of people with disparate world views and objectives. William Gibson's fictional "cyberspace" is described as a place that contains all the information in the world and can be entered with disembodied consciousness with the aid of a computer. It is "an infinite cage" wherein the heights and depths of power, pleasure, culture, and survival are plumbed.[5]

Natives in Chiapas, Mexico, used the Net to publicize their plight over a decade ago, when they were under attack by government forces. According to Otto Froehling, "the success of Internet organizing in southern Mexico is due to the constant and reciprocal connections between cyberspace and other social spaces, which avoided the restriction of events to a contained space and scale."[6] As Vinay Lal has argued,

> If the conquest of the Americas furnished the Spaniards with a charter for conquest and colonization, the enthusiasts of cyberspace point ... to the Americas as the site for new forms of resistance to global capitalism, as the originary point from which a truly new world order can be envisioned ... The laboratories and universities of the United States may have seeded the script for the cyberspace revolution, but it was enacted in the relatively remoter areas of Mexico, when the Zapatista National Liberation Army led the people of Chiapas to an insurrection on New Year's Day 1994.[7]

The Zapatistas held six towns, forcing the government to the negotiating table through an international media campaign using a "new element of revolutionary warfare, the Internet. Mexico's foreign minister Jose Angel Gurria observed that after initial shots were fired, for 15 months 'the war has been a war of ink, of written word, a war on the Internet,' and the commander of the Zapatistas declared that 'one space ... so new that no one thought a guerilla could turn to it, is the information superhighway.... It was a territory not occupied by anybody.'" The irony of this victory is in the simultaneous threat and promise of cyberspace together: "Though the activists who staged the marvelous demonstration against the World Trade Organization in November 1999 ... were summoned to Seattle by messages widely dispersed on the Internet, it is doubtful that these activists, buoyed by their Internet successes, have reflected sufficiently on the ironic fact that the Internet is avowedly the most expressive realization of that very idea of 'globalization' against which they militate."[8] This may not be as ironic as it seems. The Spanish introduction of the horse to the Americas foreshadowed the colonizing imperative that followed, but at the same time, Plains Indians gained the speed and communication they needed to form alliances and to resist and evade the colonizers. What follows is a brief survey of key sites and online communities in the late 1990s and early 2000s that illustrate Native people's use of computer networks in the experience of, and strategies for, decolonization.

FrostysAmerindian

Ron (Frosty) Deere is a Mohawk from Kahnawake. I first ran across him in the late 1990s on Native listservs, where he often provided third-party material (newspaper articles, reports) on Native people and issues. At Yahoo, there are a thousand chat groups under the category "Native American," ranging from the largest at almost 3,000 subscribers to the smallest of fewer than five. Categories include powwow talk, recipes, general chat, languages such as Mohawk, Seneca, and Lenape, prophecies, crafts, politics and issues, music, native singles, women-only, two-spirited, gay Native women, black Native Americans, Métis issues, and sports. FrostysAmerindian Listserv provides volumes of information on a daily basis. It is not a chat group, although comments and dialogue can occur; it is more of a narrow cast of current news and events across Canada and around the world.

I joined in March 2002, and there are now around 300 people on the list, with perhaps a dozen regular contributors. This is patently a Native list—it is not moderated by Frosty, but I have yet to see the anti-Native arguments, insulting questions, or childish comments that I have seen on other lists. The list is "for and about Native American Indians/Aboriginals/Amerindians. The objective is to talk about nations and international subjects that are important to all people ... to keep us informed about what is going on in Indian Country." Frosty has also created a dozen or so other lists, related to Iroquois languages, politics, and culture, as well as a chat room.[9] The Mohawk language list alone generates thousands of messages, which is remarkable because the Mohawk-speaking population is estimated to include only 3,000 to 4,000 individuals. Frosty also publishes "Kahon:wes's Mohawk and Iroquois Index," a personal and humorous take on many subjects (Kahon:wes is Frosty's youngest son).[10] There are many websites linked to the information network designed by Frosty, ranging from mainstream sources (*Globe and Mail*) to local Native efforts (tuscaroras.com). These sources and others produce a flood of daily information directly relevant to indigenous cultures and politics.

The Fighting Whites

What started as an idea among some University of Northern Colorado students soon became a phenomenon in cyberspace and in the media. The Fighting Whites story says a lot about the power of the Net as host to dialogue on issues such as Nativeness, racism, and appropriation. In March 2002, the *Denver Post* reported that some university students had named their intramural basketball team, made up of American Indians, Hispanics, and whites, "The Fighting Whites." The satirical name was aimed at nearby Eaton High School for its nickname, "The Fightin' Reds," and the American Indian caricature on the team logo. The aim was to get Eaton to stop its offensive stereotyping. The Eaton High School mascot was a caricature of an Indian with a big crooked nose, loincloth, and feathers. The UNC team had tried talking to the high school, to no avail; their pleas for tolerance were misunderstood or discounted, so they decided to use some provocative humour to stir up the debate, and eventually it worked. "Walk in someone else's shoes, and then you can make a judgment," said Mohawk Ryan White, 22, a team member.[11]

The Whites printed up jerseys saying, "Every thang's going to be all white," with a caricature of a middle-aged white businessman on the front. Later, to clarify their position, the students put the message "Go Fighting Whites—Fighting the use of Native American Stereotypes" on the back. The intramural basketball team's official name had been "Native Pride," but soon after adopting the new name, the Fighting Whites became more widely known by the more in-your-face "Fightin' Whities," a name coined by the campus newspaper. Another misunderstanding occurred when some white people at the university took the Fighting Whites name to be an affirmation of the recognition of whites in sport.

Solomon Little Owl, director of Native American Student Services at UNC and a member of the team, said the Whities mascot is about education, not retaliation. His wife, non-Native Kacy Little Owl, taught special education at Eaton High School for two years, and he said that "as parents of a half-Anglo, half-American Indian son, we felt uncomfortable mingling with townspeople at school events, especially at ballgames where the large-nosed Indian caricature was the prominent team symbol."[12] He said Eaton was a convenient first target to raise the issue of how sports mascots used by teams ranging from high schools to professionals offend Indians, but not everyone was ready to take a stand on this issue. "When I put the team together, I didn't plan to make a political statement," said student Charles Cuny, another Native on the team. "I just wanted to play basketball on Tuesdays." He said that "most young Indians are more interested in larger issues, such as health care, tribal treaties with the federal government and mineral rights to their land, but offensive mascots are a starting point to deal with the weightier issues." He did not expect their T-shirts to cause Eaton to change its mascot. "Going to the school board is like going to Congress and asking for our land back," Cuny said. "It's not going to happen."[13] Like Ryan White, Little Owl said, "The Fighting Whities" issue is "to make people understand what it's like to be on the other side of the fence. If people get offended by it, then they know how I feel, and we've made our point."[14]

Team members got phone calls from around the country and invitations to appear on TV; they were mentioned by Jay Leno on the *Tonight Show*; and the American Indian Movement (AIM) announced support of the name. Within weeks, the team was selling T-shirts online and had started a chat room to discuss the issues. This thread on alt.native had evolved over several weeks, describing possible names and connotations. Whatever the intention of the Fighting Whites in adopting their name, the discussion quickly turned into a racist rant:

Listserve: alt.native
Thread: The Fightin' Whities mascott [sic]
Date: Fri, 15 Mar 2002 10:43
User: Jimmie

I was thinking maybe they could have a goofy cartoon of Hitler for their mascot, and everyone in the stands could chant Heil Heil Heil. Or maybe a silly Truman, riding a nuke down to ground zero with their slogan "Fighting Whities 'Bomb' their competition" Two very profound White racial images of power, I don't see why not.[15]

The Fighting Whites are part of a larger movement on the part of Natives to eliminate stereotyping, one that has gained momentum on the Internet. "Though Native American activists have made little progress at the highest level of pro sports—officials of the Atlanta Braves, Chicago Blackhawks, Cleveland Indians and Washington Redskins, for example, say they have no intention of changing their teams' names or mascots—their single-minded pursuit of the issue has literally changed the face of sports in the U.S."[16]

The Fighting Whites stepped into the centre of a storm when they decided to take their message to the press and into cyberspace. A basketball team from a small university became known worldwide on the Web. The team went on to lose its first season in basketball. The Eaton school, however, decided to drop its Fighting Red mascot, signalling a major victory. The Fighting Whites name is no longer necessary, perhaps, but has grown beyond its original purpose to exist in cyberspace as a forum and cybershop together, something like the old corner store with the pickle barrel.

Profits from shirt sales established a Native American Scholarship Fund. As of early December 2002, "more than 15,000 shirts and hats [had] been sold, raising at least $100,000" for the team and its scholarship fund, $10,000 of which has been given away yearly since 2003. A spokesperson for the American Indian Movement reinforced the importance of the Net in bringing a remote town to the mainstream: "It's actually kind of an amazing thing that happened there in Colorado. Not only did they raise the level of debate but they also turned it around and raised money for Native American scholarships," said Charlene Teters, vice president of the AIM's National Coalition on Race in Sports and Media, who also estimates that about 3,000 professional and amateur team names are offensive.[17]

Canada's SchoolNet

Over the past two decades, transfer-of-authority arrangements have given First Nations more control over education in their communities, and today over 500 Canadian schools are under First Nations management. *Gathering Strength*, the Government of Canada's action plan to implement the recommendations of the Royal Commission on Aboriginal Peoples (RCAP), emphasized the importance of investing in the acquisition of the education, skills, and training necessary for individual self-reliance, although funding for these efforts is just a fraction of what was called for by the RCAP. The plan identifies greater access to technology for Aboriginal schools as a primary means of enhancing learning, and initiatives such as Industry Canada's Native SchoolNet and Community Access Program (CAP) represent an initial response to this challenge. Today some 98 percent of First Nations schools in Canada are connected through SchoolNet, a federal-government initiative that was implemented in the mid-1990s, and 70 percent of communities have a Web access point.[18]

SchoolNet and broadband access are important tools to help First Nations deal with a long list of social and economic problems. Education and communication via the Net, and services such as Telehealth and videoconferencing, are essential to remote communities. Individual communities are now in search of alternatives in the absence of a clear national vision, and are being approached by suppliers of various low-band solutions. Infrastructure, in other words, is still so much patchwork. A host of Native enterprises is being spawned to provide solutions. Ottawa's Donna Cona Inc. concentrates on wireless high-speed Internet access via satellite to remote communities.

John Bernard (Abenaki/Maliseet and Italian from Edmundston, NB), majority owner and CEO of Donna Cona, was interviewed on TV Ontario's *Studio 2* on 21 November 2002 and was asked, "Why bring the Internet to Native communities?" He answered, "education, ecommerce, and enlightenment." The Net represents "a new economic way of life" in remote communities: "It's very plausible that somebody from Old Crow Yukon, where there are no roads, could have created eBay."[19]

Broadband access and community networks are more essential to Natives than to the mainstream. Native educators see computers, and cyberspace, as keys to the retention of language and oral culture. Distance education and tele-learning mean that older, top-down systems of learning are giving way to more inclusive and participatory environments. Table 1 shows a comparison between existing educational practices and the new model enabled by new information technologies and networks.

Table 1: Impact of Technology on Education and Training Delivery

The OLD System	merges with	the NEW System
Teacher as knowledge holder		Teacher as knowledge facilitator
Information dissemination		Information exchange
Standardization		Flexibility
Classroom learning	<—>	Any time, any place
Group learning		Self-directed and collaborative learning
One-to-one/one-to-many		Many-to-many

Sources: TeleLearning Network of Centres of Excellence, 1999; The Conference Board of Canada, 2000.[20]

In their essay "Cyberspace Smoke Signals: New Technologies and Native American Ethnicity," Larry J. Zimmerman, Karen P. Zimmerman, and Leonard R. Bruguier quote Betsy Buck, a Hodenausonee from Six Nations, who says that some school children learn to use computers before they learn to read or write, and the multimedia format fits well with a learning style based on oral tradition. The authors conclude, "Buck's comments about the use of the web for education are fairly typical. An emphasis on the relation of the medium to oral tradition is common, and it may be this that promotes Web use among many American Indian schools. It also provides a way for the tribal community to know what is going on in the classroom at the same time that it promotes key cultural practices and values."[21]

An innovator from Canada working in the midst of this development is Buffy Sainte-Marie, who started the Cradleboard Teaching Project in the mid-1990s.[22] It was born through her own experiences as a teacher (she has degrees in Oriental Philosophy and Education as well as a PhD in Fine Arts) travelling through Indian country constantly as both singer and educator. The project is aimed both at Native children and educators, and at non-Native students, and both groups can exchange perspectives and information. With lesson plans and an excellent curriculum, the Cradleboard Teaching Project is also live and interactive, and children learn with and through their long-distance peers.

Other examples of the potential of cyberspace for First Nations education include Aboriginal Digital Collections, an Industry Canada pilot program to allow Native Canadians to preserve, celebrate, and communicate their heritage, languages, and contemporary life by developing and accessing materials on the Web.[23] The website is largely non-Native, though, and it presents a distinctly federal perspective on First Nations. The program also pays Aboriginal youth to create websites featuring material ranging from information on businesses and entrepreneurship to traditional knowledge and contemporary issues, such as the preservation of Aboriginal languages. In contrast, the Aboriginal Youth Network is a website designed by and for Native youth in an effort to create and maintain an online youth community nationwide.[24]

Beyond SchoolNet and the digital libraries of cyberspace, Native education today depends on broadband access for communities, and personal access for youth and the community. The Aboriginal Peoples Television Network, for example, has launched DigitalDrum.ca to showcase Aboriginal culture, history, and people; it contains video content and user-generated discussion of shows that include video, audio, text, and images. Aboriginal learners have unique cultural needs, and cyberspace has the potential to significantly affect values, traditions, and language. Protection of culture is a critical issue for Natives, and cyberspace has shown itself to be a powerful tool for this. How we can ensure this protection is an important question. Each Aboriginal community is unique; there are differing stages of economic development and technology infrastructure (or lack thereof), varied locations, history, and languages, and disparate levels of technology adoption and community responsibility for educational programming. Native communities understand that the Net should serve learners and the community in general; they "want greater involvement in defining the relationship between technology and learning. They want to ensure that initiatives result in outcomes that are compatible with their reality."[25]

At the Mall

There are thousands of Native-run commercial websites in cyberspace today, in various stages of development. Hundreds are located in Canada. It is still too early in the game to be able to see how these sites will fare commercially, or to predict how e-commerce will affect those on remote reserves. Cyberspace has become a key location for change to consumption practices, however, and it is clear that online shopping and business networks represent increasingly significant economic value.

GoodMinds.com is a Native-owned and operated business located on the Six Nations of the Grand River Territory in Ontario. It sells Aboriginal and Native American educational resources for schools, libraries, and the general public, at kindergarten to post-secondary levels. They also produced and sell The Great Peace CD-ROM, which explores the history, culture, and spirituality of the Haudenosaunee. Iroqrafts, a long-established trading post in the heart of Six Nations, has a website that is understated yet powerful in that it reflects the wealth of traditional supplies to be found in the store, from rawhide to finished moccasins, hair combs to hatchets.[26] Moose hide and elk and deer skins are available, but one posting there stated that "Beavertails are currently unavailable," and horsetail is "temporarily not available (does anyone know a source for these? thank you)."[27]

The Turtle Island Native Network is a very comprehensive portal with an excellent resources section that includes the Royal Commission on Aboriginal Peoples reports, an Aboriginal People's Guide to the Records of the Government of Canada, the National Aboriginal Document Database, an overview of Aboriginal history in Canada, Aboriginal rights research resources, links to historical documents such as the Jesuit Relations, legal cases relating to Aboriginal and treaty rights, the Reconciliation and Social Justice Library, and more. It is like the bookstore at the mall. It is also an Iroquois site, well known in the Native cyber-community, that offers news and information on Native education, health and wellness, communities, business, and culture.[28]

Aside from all this business at the mall, the youth are also "hanging" there, of course. The official website of First Nations hip-hop artists WARPAR-TY gives access to the group's latest news, lyrics, pictures, music, and video downloads. It provides "a look into the world of hip-hop culture from the reservation." The group from Hobbema, Alberta, won Aboriginal Music Awards in 2001 and 2002, with songs such as "Feeling Reserved," which is anything but reserved. WARPARTY (which one member pronounces "Par-tay") knows that Web presence is crucial in the hip-hop world today. The band members rely on the web, and email from their fans, for feedback and support.[29] Linked to their site is a list of small hip-hop groups, associations, and clubs dotted throughout Western Canada, in rural Saskatchewan and Manitoba, all connected in cyberspace.

Questions of identity and issues regarding education of non-Natives are also seen at the mall. A couple of threads regarding identity, cultural appropriations, and racial ignorance on eBay appeared on the alt.native listserv in January 2003, shortly after a woman advertised an "Indian Squaw Dress" for sale. The following posting is from eBay:

VINTAGE NATIVE AMERICAN BUCKSKIN SQUAW DRESS

I AM LISTING BEADED NECKLACES AND MOCCASINS THAT GO WITH THIS DRESS SO PLEASE CHECK MY OTHER AUCTIONS FOR MORE ITEMS THAT CAME WITH THIS LOT. First I apologize for my lousy pictures - for some reason this dress was hard to photo. This auction is for a beautiful Authentic Native American Buckskin Squaw Dress. I got it from a lady who said it had been worn by a teacher who got it to wear for her students every year at their harvest celebration - she had it at least 30 years. It is beautifully made and the bodice and sleeves are lined with fabric. There is fringe going all the way down each side starting at the sleeves. For it's [sic] age it is very clean - no stains, no funky smells - I would have no qualms about wearing it as is...

Within days someone had notified the alt.native list of this item, and the "NDN" (politically affirmative Native self-description) anger erupted in cyberspace, moving all the way back to the seller.

Listserve: alt.native
Thread: S**** dress!

Date: Sat, 1 Feb 2003 11:38:01 –0600
User: Primitive Bubble

I have a specific question for the God damn prick ass seller!!! If you care to pass it along? What the hell is a {SQUAW DRESS}??? Is it red?

Do high heels come with it? And is the back of it a little worn out, from laying on the ground? Could you also ask if the disrespectful prick or ass wipe also has a few scalps hanging around that might possibly be for sale. Aloha ... Clam dip....

Another member commented on the volume of Native-appropriated items for sale, replying, "Get an ebay account and you can ask all these sellers the same." He did a search and found 212 items under "squaw," and posted this:

Listserve: alt.native
Thread: S**** dress!

Date: Sat, 01 Feb 2003 14:48
User: Joker & Harley at Arkham

This just goes to show, we have to educate people. And for many years, the term squaw was thought to mean NDN female by about 85 percent of U.S. population. They didn't know. It's only been recently brought to the average person's attention (that this term is insulting).

Now, the word is getting out there. And we have to make sure people hear the word and understand why they shouldn't use it.

Insulting people because they don't know won't make the message get across.
Harley

There are pages of listings for items with "Squaw" in the name on eBay. The group discussed notifying eBay of the connotation and asking that they refuse any further listings. On 31 January the seller added the following information to her eBay page:

Since listing this dress I have received over 12 emails from Native Americans bringing it to my attention that the term "Squaw" is an insult to the women of their culture. For this I apologize. I had no idea the term was a slam to women! The dress was sold to me as being called that so that's what I titled it. This has been enlightening to me and I am glad to have it brought to my attention so I can erase the term from my vocabulary because I in no way want to insult anyone of Native American descent. In the meantime Ebay does not allow me to change the title or the description of the auction because it has bids. All that is allowed is this addition to the description. To all those who have been offended I sincerely apologize. [30]

This incident was still under discussion when another item surfaced. A restored "Museum Quality Native American Indian Buck Skin Ceremonial Shirt" appeared, "made entirely of buckskin, the back adorned with a full coyote face and ermine tails," beadwork, bells, and tin cones (jingle dress cones). One list member wrote "a sucker is suckered again ... restored? my dogs hiney" to which Wolvbtch replied "well, didn't see your dog's hiney on that shirt ... lol ... but saw newer type cheap cones, and that strip of beadwork looks like the kind one buys from the trading posts pre-made ... the coyote face is also easily purchased from the same place one can buy the bead strips and cones ... well ... someone will pay $500, and then find out somewhere down the years, or even months they were ripped off." The list was less concerned with the hawking of Native tradition than with the inauthenticity of the shirt. Primitive Jim, another list regular, put it this way:

> I go to eBay daily and buy things there from time to time. Anything that's hawked as "real" Indian or even better "vintage" or "old" real Indian commands a hefty premium and causes ferocious bidding. Find some worn moccasins, put some beads on them from Grey Owl Indian Crafts, label them "vintage Lakota Sioux," and you've suddenly got $125 or more in your pocket. "Used" is important since it implies that Sioux feet were once in them.

Replies from some others on the Native-L listserv:

> Meanwhile, I agree w Jim, and am thinking about going into ebusiness, sure need the money. I have some used Mohawk jeans, an old workshirt, and some genuine leather Mohawk winter boots (they leak, but OK for display purposes).
> -Mike

> Hi Mike,

> I think you're on to something. I've got a few quarts of used motor oil. From my Pontiac, a true "rez rocket."
> -bill

> GREAT IDEA!!! You mean used is better? Holy crap man, I just happen to have a very used snake skin jock strap. "Great." Since I used it for bagging my "native" balls, it should bring in a wad of money on e-bay, right? Hot damn, this is surely my lucky day.
> -Red [31]

At the mall, everything is available. There are thousands of Native (and non-Native) websites selling arts, crafts, and artifacts—all overshadowed by the e-tail giant eBay. It remains to be seen how successful Native enterprises will be, and whether they will allow Natives to see some measure of independence through ecommerce. As it stands, the tools and momentum are in the hands of the mall owners, and they are most definitely non-Native.

Two Worlds

Cyberspace is a forum in which to expand upon issues central to Native people, to communicate in all the four directions, and, not least, to make fun and have a few laughs in the new territory. Much of this, as with Frostys and the Fighting Whites, has to do with drawing attention to the obstacles and risks faced by Natives in their everyday lives. It is just this correcting and challenging of vital issues that make cyberspace an increasingly central forum for the meeting of two worlds, Native and non-Native. In this virtual space, a dialogue is emerging. The Native community on the Internet is growing fast, and now more Native bands, companies, and organizations are using websites to reach their clients, associates, and members. People who have moved away from their home communities can feel connected by accessing an online resource from the community. People can access their local news publication on the Net. And they can speak to the world, from home.

At the same time, as Canada's economy becomes more knowledge based, there is significant danger that under-skilled Natives, and other marginalized peoples, will be excluded from new economic opportunities and will be pushed farther toward the margins of society. They could be left behind and increasingly disenfranchised as the pace of technology adoption and integration in the economy increases. Most Native communities lack the money, technical infrastructure, and human and technical resources needed to get to cyberspace, the new global territory. Getting there will not solve the serious social and economic challenges that many communities face, but it is a piece of the puzzle. The solution to such complex problems requires holistic and coordinated approaches on the part of all in the communities. Natives must prioritize the adoption of information technology to avoid falling deeper into the digital divide in Canada, and in cyberspace. This new territory is just as real as the physical space we inhabit and travel through. There is a lot of opportunity there, but there is also the danger described in the "Funny Moon Message," found on a Native listserv:

Listserve: alt.native
Thread: NASA and Dine'

Date: 30 August, 1999 3:00am
User: sjerry

When NASA was preparing for the Apollo Project, it took the astronauts to the Navajo Nation in Arizona for training.

One day, a Navajo elder and his son came across the space crew walking among the rocks. The elder, who spoke only Navajo, asked a question. His son translated for the NASA people: "What are these guys in the big suits doing?"

One of the astronauts said that they were practicing for a trip to the moon. When his son relayed this comment the Navajo elder, he got all excited and asked if it would be possible to give to the astronauts a message to deliver to the moon?

Recognizing a promotional opportunity when he saw one, a NASA official accompanying the astronauts said, "Why certainly!" and told an underling to get a tape recorder. The Navajo elder's comments into the microphone were brief. The NASA official asked the son if he would translate what his father had said.

The son listened to the recording and laughed uproariously. But he refused to translate. So the NASA people took the tape to a nearby Navajo village and played it for other members of the nation. They too laughed long and loudly but also refused to translate the elder's message to the moon.

Finally, an official government translator was summoned. After he finally stopped laughing the translator relayed the message: "Watch out for these pricks. They have come to steal your land."[32]

Are we doomed to revisit the colonial experience in cyberspace? Yes, if access is denied to most of the Native community. No, if First Nations can make a leap forward into the digital world. The challenge in Canada is to develop strategies that build its overall level of technological development and competitiveness, while creating an equitable distribution of resources and benefits among all communities. Natives are increasingly participating in the global economy and in the knowledge economy. Building technological skills is key to education, employment, and self-sustainability. Communities need help and support to make it to cyberspace in time, before the IT revolution sweeps by. Today, many Natives in Canada might agree with Iroquois artist William Powless, who said, "The information highway is criss-crossing the earth, and I am roadkill by the ditch."[33]

Still, cyberspace is rapidly becoming the central communication medium for Natives in remote communities, on the reserves, and in the cities. It remains to be seen how the people will fare in this new territory, but it is essential to find ways of providing access to digital technologies and the education necessary to use those technologies. Native peoples have to adopt this new technology, as they did the horse, and move into this new space. It is another case of needing to adopt the white man's ways, while maintaining Native traditions—balancing and moving between two worlds, forging new relationships and understandings. These teachings are not new, but they are finding a new home in cyberspace.

William Redhawk writes on his website:

> Many Horses was an Oglala Sioux medicine man, a friend of Sitting Bull, and a promoter of the Ghost Dance as the last protection against the white man's incursions. He organized the final Ghost Dance at Standing Rock Reservation in the Spring of 1890, to dance away the white soldiers camped at the foot of the hills. At dawn the white tipis of the U.S. Army were still visible, and Many Horses, with a heart full of grief, knew that the magic had failed. But the Great Spirit spoke to him. Turning his back on the rising sun, he addressed the assembled warriors:

> "I will follow the white man's trail. I will make him my friend, but I will not bend my back to his burdens. I will be cunning as a coyote. I will ask him to help me understand his ways, then I will prepare the way for my children, and their children. The Great Spirit has shown me—a day will come when they will outrun the white man in his own shoes."

> All other recorded prophecies of Many Horses have come to pass. The nations of the People see the beginnings of this final prophecy today. We have the white man's shoes.[34]

Foucault's three variables, territory, communication, and speed, all exist in cyberspace. We are walking, and running, to get there. As with the horse, Natives have the chance to work with this new force, tame it, and use it to support dialogue, education, and self-determination. Buffy Sainte-Marie expressed it this way:

> The digital scene in Indian country at the moment is a microcosm of the way it is most everywhere else, with people at various stages of expertise and enthusiasm going through the big shift.

Issues of sovereignty are often the first to come up among Native intellectuals, and the spectre of digital colonialism frightens some and challenges others. Questions of control and ownership arise of course, as they do in the mainstream, but with perhaps a sharper edge, given the facts of Native American history. Indian educators, artists, elders, women, tribal leaders and business people have plenty on our minds when it comes to counterbalancing past misinterpretations with positive realities, and past exploitations with future opportunities.

The reality of the situation is that we're not all dead and stuffed in some museum with the dinosaurs: we are Here in this digital age. We have led the pack in a couple of areas (digital music and online art). Although our potential at the moment exceeds the extensiveness of our community computer usage, our projects are already bearing fruit, we expect to prosper and to contribute, and we will defend our data.

If I have a message in this scant overview, it is this: real Indian people are rising to the potential of the technology, in school and out. We were born for this moment and we are solidly behind our pathfinders.[35]

NOTES

1   Mike Patterson, "Where the Forest Meets the Highway," *Alternate Routes* 16 (2000), 9.

2   Although the term preferred by governments today is "Aboriginal," most people I know still say "Native." I use this term to refer to all people who are descendants of or related to the original inhabitants of Turtle Island (North America). This includes Inuit, Métis, and First Nation (both status and non-status) peoples. It reflects an incredible diversity of languages, culture, values, and worldviews. The term also includes the concept of "indigenous" as being "the tribal peoples ... whose distinctive identity, values, and history distinguishes them from other sections of the national community, [who] despite their legal status, retain some or all of their social, economic, cultural and political institutions" (Willie Ermine, Raven Sinclair, and Bonnie Jeffery, *The Ethics of Research Involving Indigenous Peoples. Report of the Indigenous Peoples Health Research Centre to the Interagency Advisory Panel on Research Ethics.* (Saskatoon: Indigenous Peoples Health Research Centre, 2004), 5.

3   Michel Foucault, "Space, Knowledge, and Power," in *The Foucault Reader*, ed. Paul Rabinow, (London: Penguin, 1984), 239–255.

4   Chari Marple, "First People's Show on the Road," *Ottawa XPRESS*, 25 June 1998, 14.

5 William Gibson, *Mona Lisa Overdrive* (New York: Bantam, 1988), 49.

6 Otto Froehling, "The Cyberspace War of Ink and Internet in Chiapas, Mexico," *Geographical Review* 87, 2 (1997): 291. Also see Harry Cleaver, "The Zapatistas and the Electronic Fabric of Struggle," 1998, http://www.eco.utexas.edu/Homepages/Faculty/Cleaver/zaps.html; Jerry W. Knudson, "Rebellion in Chiapas: Insurrection by Internet and Public Relations," *Media, Culture and Society* 20 (1998): 507–518; M.E. Martinez-Torres, "Civil Society, the Internet, and the Zapatistas," *Peace Review* (2001): 347–355.

7 Vinay Lal, "The Politics of History on the Internet: Cyber-Diasporic Hinduism and the North-American Hindu Diaspora," *Diaspora* 8, 2 (1999): 132.

8 Ibid., 140.

9 Kahon:wes, "Onelist Groups," http://www.kahonwes.com/onelist.htm.

10 Kahon:wes, "Mohawk and Iroquois Index," http://www.kahonwes.com/index1.htm.

11 Cornelius Coleman, "Fightin' Whities Swamped with T-shirt Requests," *Denver Post*, 13 March 2002, B1.

12 Ibid.

13 Joe Garner, "'Whities' Mascot Is About Education, Not Retaliation: Intramural Basketball Team Takes Shot At Indian Caricature Used By Eaton High School," *Rocky Mountain News*, 12 March 2002, 4A.

14 Ibid.

15 Alt.native archives for this discussion are available at http://groups.google.com/group/alt.native/browse_frm/month/2002-3?start=1750&sa=N

16 S.L. Price, "The Indian Wars: The Campaign Against Indian Nicknames and Mascots Presumes That They Offend Native Americans—But Do They? We Took a Poll, and You Won't Believe the Results," *Sports Illustrated*, 4 March 2002, 70.

17 MSNBC.com, "'Whites' Team Spoof Raises $100,000," 2 December 2002.

18 Paul Barnsley, "Native Groups Ponder Life after Tobin," *Windspeaker*, 22 March 2002, http://www.itbusiness.ca/it/client/en/Home/News.asp?id=21844&bSearch=True.

19 John Bernard, interview by Steve Paikin, *Studio 2*, TV Ontario, 21 November 2002.

20 David Greenall and Stelios Loizides, *Aboriginal Digital Opportunities: Addressing Aboriginal Learning Needs Through the Use of Learning Technologies* (Ottawa: Conference Board of Canada, 2001).

21 Larry J. Zimmerman, Karen P. Zimmerman, and Leonard R. Bruguier. "Cyberspace Smoke Signals: New Technologies and Native American Ethnicity," in *Indigenous Cultures in an Interconnected World*, ed. Claire Smith and Graeme Ward (Victoria: University of British Columbia Press, 2000), 79.

22 Cradleboard Teaching Project, http://www.cradleboard.org/main.html.

23 http://aboriginalcollections.ic.gc.ca.

24 Aboriginal Youth Network, http://www.ayn.ca (accessed 8 April 2003, site currently offline).

25 Greenall and Loizides, *Aboriginal Digital Opportunities*, 19.

26 Iroqrafts, http://www.iroqrafts.com.

27 Iroqrafts, http://www.iroqrafts.com (accessed 8 April 2003).

28 Turtle Island Native Network, http://www.turtleisland.org.

29 WARPARTY now has an active presence on the Myspace social networking site at http://www.myspace.com/officialwarparty.

30 Sellers response is quoted at http://groups.google.com/group/alt.native/browse_ thread/thread/1ca7da3f73d5ab07/a5ab79dd4ac90094?q=Jan+2003+squaw+dress &lnk=ol&#.

31 Native-L list is no longer active, partial archives can be found at http://listserv. tamu.edu/archives/native-l.html.

32 Archives for this discussion are at http://groups.google.com/group/alt.native/ about.

33 Marple, "First People's Show," 14.

34 William Redhawk, "Many Horses," Redhawk's Lodge, http://siouxme.com/ manyhors.html.

35 Buffy Sainte-Marie, "Cyberskins," 1998, http://www.aloha.net/~bsm/cybersk.htm.

CHAPTER 9

Taking a Stance: Aboriginal Media Research as an Act of Empowerment

YVONNE POITRAS PRATT

I better get going, says Coyote. I will tell Raven your good story. We are going to fix this world for sure. We know how to do it now. We know how to do it right.

So, Coyote drinks my tea and that one leave. And I can't talk anymore because I got to watch the sky. Got to watch out for falling things that land in piles. When that Coyote's wandering around looking to fix things, nobody in this world is safe.

—*Thomas King, "The One About Coyote Going West"*[1]

Like the transformational Coyote figure of Native mythology, anyone attempting to "fix things" or to "give back" to community through developmental work should possess a certain amount of reckless fortitude and some transformational qualities. As a graduate student of Métis ancestry undertaking my Master's degree in Communications, I adopted several of these trickster-like qualities when I undertook a communications development project that explored Aboriginal community participation in the planning for broadband technology. However, unlike our often ill-fated hero, I opted to have others join me on my journey of discovery. After all, this was an adventure that was best taken in the company of others.

This chapter considers the potential of broadband access for indigenous cultures and communities in Canada. But, more centrally, it explores key questions about how future Aboriginal communication needs and priorities can be articulated using participatory research models. Finally, this chapter outlines the unique position of the "native ethnographer" within indigenous media scholarship.

Soon after hearing that virtually every one of the 429 communities in Alberta was to receive a SuperNet broadband connection that would be the envy of the nation, I was immediately intrigued by the question of what this network would mean to the Aboriginal communities of Alberta. This was especially important to me, considering the large number of relatives I have who reside either on the Métis settlements in northern Alberta or in and around the Edmonton area. As part of my research design, I developed research partnerships with three distinct and representative Aboriginal groups in Alberta: the Kikino Métis Settlement, the Red Crow Community College on the Blood (Blackfoot) Reserve, and the Sturgeon Lake (Cree) First Nations community. In the initial stages of planning, the project was viewed as a way to educate and raise the awareness of local community people concerning the potential applications of broadband technology. It was also important to me from the onset of the project that the principles inherent in a participatory and action-based approach informed its overall design. However, as the project progressed, it was the unique research processes that evolved in each community through collaboration that proved to be of particular interest to me. This interest in the overall research process justified my eventual use of ethnography, and in particular the use of action ethnography, to frame my research findings.

There were a number of compelling reasons why I chose the more demanding and participatory methodology of action ethnography over the standard academic interpretation of events. The strongest of these reasons was my belief that the active involvement of these Aboriginal groups in planning for the Alberta SuperNet broadband technology would empower them to fully realize their own development initiatives. It was my hope that the active involvement of community people in the research process would not only ensure that the adoption of this new technology in their everyday lives would be relevant and meaningful, but also help ensure that each community's unique cultural needs would be met. What I found as we worked collaboratively through the project was that the process of community empowerment is a highly complex and challenging process. There are complex social and structural issues, such as ongoing colonization, inherent in Aboriginal communities; in addition, both the incoming researcher and the community members involved in the project must be motivated to take risks outside the conventions of normal research, as well as outside their familiar boundaries of knowing, to realize any positive and lasting social change. Thus, positive risk-taking by all stakeholders was essential to any attempt to enact positive and lasting social change. While the challenges in this type of work loom large, it remains my belief that, if these risk-taking attempts prove successful, there is great potential for positive social change to extend well beyond the scope of any project. In my mind, this makes the attempts worth the extra efforts.

Giving Back

As an Aboriginal scholar, I was and remain personally motivated to make a positive difference in some of our nation's most disadvantaged communities. While Canada is often touted as a country of great wealth and prosperity, it is a less recognized reality that the majority of Aboriginal groups in Canada subsist in what has been termed "Fourth World" conditions.[2] The national statistics that paint these stark realities have been repeated in comments from political leaders who concur that circumstances are "shameful" for many Aboriginal people residing in Canada.[3] Moreover, the persistent attempts made by Aboriginal groups in Canada to gain equal footing with their non-Aboriginal counterparts often result in only small and precarious advances.

Statistical evidence for this inequality is reiterated within the *Aboriginal Peoples Survey 2001,* which reports that Aboriginal people residing in Canada, both rural and urban, continue to place well below national averages in terms of family income levels, educational achievement, and an overall standard of living.[4] A recent analytical paper entitled "Aboriginal Conditions in Census Metropolitan Areas,[5] 1981–2001" concludes that despite some improvements in the past twenty years or so, "huge challenges still face urban Aboriginal peoples, especially those in western CMAs, and large gaps with their non-Aboriginal counterparts remain."[6] Notably, this disparity is most perceptible in western Canada, where recent trends of urban relocation are on the rise. Without negating the important strides that have been made in raising educational levels and income earnings within certain Aboriginal populations, a substantial and growing number of Aboriginal people also barely subsist at poverty levels.[7] When coupled with the debilitating effects of colonization, this rampant poverty creates fertile ground for a crop of related social ills within the everyday life of the Aboriginal person.

Taking into account the excessive levels of suicides, a higher-than-average incidence of chronic diseases, and a staggering incarceration rate, it is evident that many Aboriginal people contend with severe and often relentless challenges throughout their lives. The presence of extreme life challenges also means that an excessive amount of energy is expended in trying to rebalance and reorient family members to a standard, or non-crisis, level of functioning. The extra energy and attention that is focused on dealing with crises can have a cumulative negative impact on a person's work, school, and day-to-day activities. Without question, the time and energies spent handling these situations represent a very real and persistent impediment to individual attainment. Tragically, those populations that require the greatest support in terms of closing the quality-of-life divide are also those most distracted from their future aspirations by the overwhelming realities of day-to-day survival. This current state of affairs may be all too familiar to most Aboriginal readers. But it is also these types of realities that further impel concerned citizens and scholars to create an agenda for social change. While colonization has played, and continues to play, a major role in this dismal state of affairs, a number of committed groups have been working to rectify this unfortunate situation through scholarly activities.[8] My recognition of the situation similarly impels me to enact positive social change using the privilege of my education.

An Aboriginal Communication Tradition

Interestingly, even while the indigenous people of the Americas have long demonstrated the skills and the capacity necessary to take control of their communication activities,[9] the limiting stereotype of traditionalism appears to persistently hinder more proactive efforts in the realm of new media. In fact, finding literature on the topic of new-media use by Aboriginal people proves a difficult task; furthermore, the scant literature that does exist on the topic has historically focused on national connectivity interests. For instance, quantitative studies such as the "2003 Report on Aboriginal Community Connectivity Infrastructure" afford readers a rather linear accounting of who is and who is not connected.

Still, some recent studies have started to focus on issues beyond techni-cal infrastructure to those of social infrastructure needs, including policy and privacy concerns, globalization concerns, community activism, com-munity informatics, and issues of representation.[10] While these studies add a qualitative richness to the conventional survey approach, inquiries that move beyond a critical or resistance-based approach to a more action-based one are even harder to find. Commendable efforts to reposition technology as an ally for oppressed peoples began as far back as the 1970s, with groups such as NWICO and the MacBride Commission, and continue today with a variety of scholars working in diverse fields.[11] Nevertheless, an argument persists for a more proactive approach within development communication to implement lasting and positive social change. As a result, I deliberately situated my re-search as an action-based inquiry within a circle of community partnerships, with the hope of empowering some of our most marginalized citizens to take an active role in planning for broadband implementation.

As Faye Ginsburg and others have argued, the need for transformative action within the realm of indigenous use of new media is necessary if indigenous groups are to realize new social and cultural possibilities. With a burgeoning Aboriginal youth population increasingly exposed to and skilled in the use of new technologies, we have reached a critical crossroads in how new-media forms might best be used to support the health of future generations. Indigenous groups must realize that the choice of how we shape technology to suit our needs remains ours. In other words, we can choose to remain passive bystanders while the mainstream engine of progress rolls over us, or we can take hold of this new technology to realize its full potential in supporting our cultural needs and desires. History has shown us that adopting a proactive stance toward the adoption of new technology can serve a multitude of community needs, including the reclamation of voice and vision and the equally important cultural preservation of a threatened lifeworld. Just as importantly, the ability to "talk back" to a hegemonic mainstream discourse renders this two-way, interactive new-media form a potentially powerful tool of decolonization. The choice remains ours, but there must be a willingness on the part of community members to engage in positive risk-taking ventures.

Standing as we are at this critical crossroads, the various authors in this book have similarly argued for a cultural-activist stance whereby indigenous people are encouraged to take hold of new media to advance their own interests. Interestingly, in the world of academe, researchers are typically granted the academic freedom to take on a research approach of their preference. While many take this privilege for granted, such freedom is arguably not available for all researchers. It is my contention that researchers from disadvantaged or marginalized backgrounds are often more motivated than others to adopt an action-oriented approach, as a result of their past or present life experiences. Indeed, when a person has experienced first hand the loathsome effects of colonization, that experience can exert an influence that is far more compelling than might ever be imagined. In fact, faced with the ongoing realities of accelerated suicide rates, above-average rates of domestic abuse, and dysfunctional behaviours such as rampant alcoholism, gambling addictions, and drug abuse—often within their immediate family environments—Aboriginal researchers may have many significant reasons to want to initiate a change in this status quo. Not too surprisingly, research becomes imbued with an importance, and even urgency, that negates a passive and solely objective approach. Ultimately, the hope for many Aboriginal scholars is that an action-oriented research approach might help to bring about positive and lasting change within some of our more disadvantaged communities.

Significantly, social scientists in Canada are also increasingly being put to task by federal funders to consider how, and even if, their work "gives back" to fellow Canadians.[12] This call to give back to communities supports the ethos of researchers working within the turbulent waters of community development and empowerment, who maintain that in a distinctively unjust world of haves and have-nots, there is little question that action research is the appropriate methodology for enacting positive social change.[13] Moreover, while the rationale for action-based research is often rooted in socio-political inequalities, indigenous researchers may be motivated to bring about positive social change for other, equally provocative reasons.

Knowledge Acquisition through Ethnography

For far too many Aboriginal people, the hardest life lessons have come from outside the classroom. Yet for the fortunate few who have managed to move beyond these negative events to seek another life path, education provides a new lens of understanding through which to view their lives. By learning to understand the long-standing and cumulative effects of colonization upon their home communities, many scholars have been able to attain a higher level of self and community awareness. With this new level of insight, scholars are strategically positioned to decide for themselves which path they will choose for their future. Many will certainly feel obliged to communicate the genuine concerns and realities of Aboriginal groups to others who may be willing to take up the challenge of initiating change. Some scholars may simply find the situation hopeless and retreat back to the comfort of familiar research methods. Finally, an intrepid few will decide that they are the ones best equipped to take on the challenge of motivating social change.

In questioning and coming to terms with their own unique positioning as insider-outsiders, a number of indigenous scholars are making important new inroads into both participatory and ethnographic research. In truth, the "indigenous or native ethnographer" offers a unique perspective and even new levels of understanding within media projects. At the same time, this ethnographer's unique positioning poses many challenges. As Maori scholar and researcher Linda Tuhiwai Smith sees it, not only are indigenous scholars attempting to offer "solutions to the real-life dilemmas that indigenous communities confront ... [they are also] trying to capture the complexities of being indigenous."[14] Theirs is a dual burden, says Tuhiwai Smith: Aboriginal scholars must not only justify their research but also defend their unique perspective, which tends to fall outside the norms of conventional research theory and methodology in the Western canon.

An anthropologist of mixed Chicano origins, Mónica Russel y Rodríguez describes the indigenous ethnographer's position rather fittingly as "the newcomer in academe, the overeducated at home."[15] Coupled with this disconcerting, shifting identity are the equally demanding ethical and moral challenges demanded by the duality of roles. Indeed, Russel y Rodríguez is adamant that she will not use theories that "require me to silence myself or the women I know."[16] Similarly, I have come to accept that my positioning places me in a continual state of questioning, of both my approach and its underlying assumptions. While I am well aware that my training and the resources available to me are designed for use within a Western perspective, I am also confident that there is another way that is just now emerging. As one indigenous scholar notes, there is oftentimes a real impasse in trying to bridge the gap between two contrary worlds: "I would have to objectify women I knew and with whom I identified to save this social science. No, it wasn't just the scientific paradigm I had to watch out for; it was las comadres [my friends]."[17] Likewise, I worried that the community people that I worked alongside would resent my version of this ethnography while I also fretted about whether or not my ethnographic account would meet the academic rigours of the university. This is the very real tension that results when differing epistemologies and cultures meet in the research arena.

As a critical point of inquiry, Marian Bredin questions "the extent to which a largely non-Native body of thought on social change, political economy, communication, and cultural resistance can legitimately address issues in aboriginal culture."[18] Indeed, based on an examination of past ethnographic efforts within the Aboriginal mediascape, Bredin argues that considerable methodological changes are now required to make the process more respectful and representative of the Aboriginal perspective. As one possible alternative, Bredin recommends that ethnographers take on "committed research"—in which the political position of the researcher as well as the intent of the project is made clear, from the beginning through to the end of the study. There should be little room for political neutrality when assuming the mantle of social change. It is for this reason that I detail my positioning and my experience as fully as possible.

All in all, the process of working as an Aboriginal researcher within Aboriginal communities was not only the most interesting aspect of my work, it was also the element of my work that I felt could, through detailed description, most help to advance similarly placed projects. In fact, even though shared cultural backgrounds helped to initiate the critical phase of trust and relationship building, the sharing of communal ties also brought forth a unique set of challenges. The shared experiences of working (and living) within communities that endure ongoing oppression create some of the most heart-rending situations imaginable. As Nancy Naples sees it, the goal of ethnographic study is not so much a generalization to the larger population, but rather a highlighting of some of the "inconsistencies, limits, and contradictions, as well as possibilities"[19] that may surround research activities within specific communities. In deciding on an ethnographic approach, I was in reality only midway through my methodological decision-making. A spiralling of events brought me from traditional ethnography, to critical ethnography, to, eventually, my final choice of action ethnography.

Changing Roles of and within Ethnography

The use of ethnography, once solely the domain of anthropologists, to empower and enact positive change within populations of study is a comparatively recent move. Douglas Foley provides his readers with insight into his own experience as an ethnographer during the transition in the 1970s from an "anthropology [that] was founded upon liberal, humanist doctrines of ameliorism, orientalism, colonialism, and racism"[20] to the more current neo-Marxist approach of cultural critique. The conflicting tensions that reside within an ethnographic approach become apparent through its various descriptions. While Gerry Philipsen describes an ethnographic approach to communication as "descriptive, cultural, focused, comparative, and theoretical,"[21] other scholars see ethnography as a hopeless attempt to "get round the un-get-roundable fact that all ethnographical descriptions are homemade, that they are the describer's descriptions, not those of the described."[22] Issues around representation of voice and final authority over textual representations continue to perplex the field of ethnography.

Moreover, ethnography has earned itself a bad reputation within indigenous communities. Tuhiwai Smith admits that the "ethnographic 'gaze' of anthropology has collected, classified and represented other cultures to the extent that anthropologists are often the academics popularly perceived by the indigenous world as the epitome of all that is bad with academics."[23] James Clifford also notes how Aboriginal authors such as Vine Deloria have further villainized the ethnographer as the "ambitious social scientist, making off with tribal lore and giving nothing in return, imposing crude portraits on subtle peoples, or (more recently) serving as a dupe for sophisticated informants."[24] Others, including Johannes Fabian, claim that anthropology has helped to legitimize and rationalize colonialism.[25] Thus, as a mainstay methodology of anthropology, it seems rather ironic that ethnography is being appropriated as a fitting form of methodology within my project.[26]

Academics such as Clifford and Bredin are also careful to remind us that ethnographies are only ever a partial retelling of the entire story.[27] Indeed, these carefully constructed stories exemplify relations of power and knowledge. By any account, ethnographies tell us as much in what they reveal as what they conceal. Clifford maintains that "Ethnographers are more and more like the Cree hunter who (the story goes) came to Montreal to testify in court concerning the fate of his hunting lands in the new James Bay hydroelectric scheme. He would describe his way of life. But when administered the oath he hesitated: 'I'm not sure I can tell the truth ... I can only tell what I know.'"[28] As of late, ethnographies are becoming less celebratory in their accounts, less visually based on so-called objective and authoritarian accounts, and thereby more polyvocal in their textual production. Mainstream ethnographers have, of necessity, become much more critical of their approach. However, a "crisis of representation" remains a primary roadblock as mainstream ethnographers strive to reconcile their positions of authority outside a given culture and over the production of the text. Since this outsider dilemma was one that I could lay only partial claim to, the open-critique philosophy of critical ethnography offered an interesting alternative.

As Michael Crotty describes it, critical ethnography, in striving to "unmask hegemony and address oppressive forces,"[29] is a distinct move away from the scientific haze of cultural relativism in yesteryears. Critical approaches have instead "sought to produce studies that helped win legal battles, rent strikes, and various political actions."[30] Similarly, scholars including James Clifford, Shirley Grundy, Richard Quantz, Roger Simon and Don Dippo,[31] contend that ethnographic work can be both counter-hegemonic and emancipatory. Michael Campbell describes the critical ethnographer as a collaborator and activist who adopts an openly political stance in what Lather once termed an "openly ideological" position. [32]

Yet in spite of these well-intentioned efforts, Margery Wolf and Elizabeth Bird dispute the overall outcome of these endeavours. In fact Wolf and Bird, in their critical assessments, suggest that "much of this current self-reflection on the part of a white male elite has not resulted in a very significant alteration of structures of ethnographic and academic power."[33] For these academics, this newly critical approach is seen as woefully inadequate; real and lasting change must occur through action. In truth, I hold the same belief. Thankfully, action ethnography offers particular promise as a constructive research methodology that strategically and deliberately moves beyond reflection and criticism to a place of active change.

In looking for a more purposeful way to research, Jo Tacchi, Don Slater, and Greg Hearn have creatively combined action research and ethnography to arrive at an approach that enables them to examine a "big picture" of the community's overall communication activities, the local resources available, and an examination of how local people understand these media within their particular social setting. These scholars maintain that a holistic understanding of the communicative ecology is integral in the study of information and communication technologies (ICTs) as "these are new media which do not yet have a fixed form. We need to, and can, adapt them to local ways of communicating."[34] Interestingly, the mapping of local communication practices demonstrates a potential means of identifying people who could act as "targets" for interventionist efforts. Once an effective target group is identified, the ways in which ICTs could be best used to effect positive social change can be explored from a number of different angles. The all-important question can finally be asked: "How might ICTs help them?"[35] For these international scholars, ethnography is seen as the critical first stage in developing an understanding of the local communicative ecology, even when there is evident potential for creative appropriation of new media.

Tacchi further maintains that "the challenge is to educate people in content creation, to allow them to engage in more active ways with the new network economy."[36] The hope is that these target groups will be better able to direct and shape the new-media networks coming to their communities by working within an applied ethnographic setting. Because I was situated in a preliminary stage of broadband arrival, yet I still wanted to initiate some reflection on the best possible uses of this new media, this approach had much appeal and apparent utility for my work within Alberta's Aboriginal communities.

"All My Online Relations": An Action Ethnographic Study

The research project "All My Online Relations: Aboriginal Community Participation in Planning for Alberta SuperNet Broadband Technology" was designed to help empower some of Canada's most disadvantaged citizens through their active involvement in planning and research activities focused on the Alberta SuperNet. In choosing to work in a participatory project with three communities, representing Blackfoot, Cree, and Métis, I drew inspiration from the seminal work of Paulo Freire with Brazilian peasants.[37] Additionally, a decision was made early in the project to concentrate efforts on planning interventionist activities that would actively involve community members throughout the process. The ultimate goal of this emancipatory project was to mobilize these Aboriginal groups into self-sustaining, and potentially self-actualizing, modes of operation.

Adopting the use of ethnography meant that I was engaged with these communities for an extended period of time while attempting to draw out what broadband technology means, or more rightly could mean, to them. As an exploratory study before the actual light-up of the broadband network, my study spanned some two years, with a total of eighteen community visits to the three different communities. During this time, I worked alongside key contacts and other interested community members in articulating the principles of participatory-action research to curious community members. I also collaborated in developing an online survey of community needs around broadband technology and held a number of focus-group sessions in an effort to stimulate dialogue around the topic of the Alberta SuperNet. All in all, this intense work reflected my desire and commitment to meet the needs of groups who are traditionally left behind in mainstream communication initiatives, yet my interest could also be perceived as self serving. After all, these communities are *all my relations*.[38]

The Marginal Native/Facilitator Position

Traditionally, the positioning of the observer as "the primary research instrument," standing "at the heart of ethnography and of its open-ended nature,"[39] sets ethnography distinctly apart from most other methodologies. However, my positioning as an insider-outsider, although problematic at times, is one of the more potentially engaging aspects of my ethnographic work. While Raymond Gold once noted that "observer" roles can take a variety of positions, ranging from complete participant to complete observer, David Walsh contends that the position of "marginal native" is the prime position for an ethnographer to adopt within traditional ethnography.[40] In this preferred role, the ethnographer is strategically balanced between an over-familiarity with the community and a too-distant positioning outside the community—either of which could jeopardize the final research findings. While this marginal role is seen as one of optimal positioning for Walsh, he also counsels that this role "creates considerable strain on the researcher as it engenders insecurity, produced by living in two worlds simultaneously, that of participation and that of research ... [the marginal native] researcher will be physically and emotionally affected by this."[41] Interestingly, these words of caution are appreciated by those working within the ethnographic tradition, but the situation they describe seems to be further complicated by those researchers hailing from indigenous or multifarious heritages.[42]

As a matter of fact, in doling out advice on the importance of *impression management*, whereby careful attention to appropriate dress, demeanour,

Red Crow Community College (site of critical ethnographic study related to Alberta SuperNet, Red Crow, Alberta). Photographer Neal Shade. Used with permission of Red Crow Community College.

speech, and habits must be taken in order to fit into the community, Walsh further cautions, "the researcher must prevent sociability, rapport and trust from deteriorating into exploitation or 'going native.'"[43] With due respect to this cautionary note, there was no risk of "going native" in my project—in fact, no amount of impression management could alter the reality of already being Native. Despite well-intentioned efforts, there can be no simple intellectual dismissal of culturally shared background and history just to prove a methodological point. We are who we are by way of birth, and no amount of strategic positioning will be able to erase the reality of our ethnic origins.

Thus, the position that I adopted within this project was that of a facilitator, or organizing co-researcher, who self-identified early on as an Aboriginal person of Métis heritage. I was deliberately upfront that the intent of this research project was to create a possible avenue for community empowerment. Yet, the move to frame my work within ethnography was solely my decision. As a scholar I knew full well that I was solely accountable for the analysis and writing of this project. However, the fact that I was open and honest about the need for a collaborative research process and about my own role within the project undoubtedly helped to establish both access to the field and continued good working relations.[44] But even while I felt I was being open and honest in my approach to the research, it was evident that I had to pass through a series of ongoing evaluations of my belief and value systems—first, as an Aboriginal, and second, as a scholar. These "tests" took a number of varying forms but are best envisioned as an ongoing process demonstrated by appropriate conduct with community members.

While my cultural heritage gained me a certain advantage, my role as an Aboriginal scholar/researcher brought with it its own set of challenges. In fact, even though it may hold true that the sharing of a cultural heritage can open doors otherwise inaccessible to outside researchers, there is a great deal more involved in gaining and maintaining access to a community than the ethnic or cultural label that one straps on. Indeed, scholars such as Walsh maintain that "the success of observational work depends on the quality of relations with the people under study."[45] As a mixed-blood anthropologist, Kirin Narayan further contends that it is the intent of the researcher in their dealings with the communities that should prevail over any cultural identity of the researcher: "What we must focus our attention on is the quality of relations with the people we seek to represent in our texts; are they viewed as mere fodder for professionally self-serving statements about a generalized Other, or are they accepted as subjects with voices, views, and dilemmas— people to whom we are bonded through ties of reciprocity and who may even be critical of our professional enterprise?"[46]

As Narayan suggests, it is not enough for indigenous researchers to sit comfortably on the laurels of our cultural identity. We must constantly be cognizant of how our cultural connection is perceived within the community and how our actions as an insider-researcher will affect the responses of the community members. Narayan, who is herself of mixed East Indian, Germanic, and American descent, articulates the challenges that surround researchers from mixed backgrounds, as "different aspects of identity became highlighted at different times."[47] Once again, questions of identity often go well beyond racial definitions to that of countries and regions of origin, religions, classes, educational backgrounds, and even gender. The Métis community and I share close cultural and even familial connections, so in my own work my background became an item of some interest and discussion, particularly during my community work at the Métis settlement. Whereas outsider-researchers are likely to have a community judge them primarily around their scholarly intentions and conduct, insider-researchers must be aware that questions directed at their family connections and origins can appear to take precedence over the professional role that we assume. Without question, it is here that one makes or breaks the case for professionalism.

Tuhiwai Smith concurs that indigenous researchers must contend with a different set of insider dynamics than non-indigenous researchers. Regrettably, home communities can judge indigenous researchers quite harshly for their ascribed status—including their family background, politics, and religious preferences—something that researchers have very little, if any, control over.[48] Further exacerbating these inner-circle judgments is the fact that "non-indigenous teachers and supervisors are often ill prepared to assist indigenous researchers in these areas and there are so few indigenous teachers that many students simply 'learn by doing,'"[49] or fail in the trying. In breaking trail in a new field of study, albeit in often-familiar home territory, many Aboriginal researchers find that they must fend for themselves and, more often than not, learn through their mistakes. Certainly as time goes on and more Aboriginal people take up the challenge of this type of work, it will be essential to share experiences and knowledge with one another so that fewer errors will occur at the expense of the community and the researcher.

The Issue of Trust

Trust is undoubtedly one of the pillars to any good partnership, and ideally it should be the glue that binds disparate communities together in a mutual bond of goodwill and rapport. However, the issue of trust, defined by the Encarta World English Dictionary as "confidence in and reliance on good qualities, especially fairness, truth, honour, or ability," becomes particularly poignant within Aboriginal communities. Indeed, gaining trust with people who have had little opportunity to experience the same, at least from the outside world, is a very critical and sensitive endeavour. Knowing this from insider experience, I modelled my community research work on the principle that trust is not given out freely but should be diligently earned through a researcher's integrity, honesty, and openness with the participating community. Stories from my own childhood and upbringing as an Aboriginal person were a key component of this trust-building process and were vital in establishing and maintaining connections with community members.

From a similar standpoint, Tuhiwai Smith asserts that access to an indigenous community is best seen as gained and maintained through the attributes of a specific researcher. She writes, "Consent is not so much given for a project or specific set of questions, but for a person, for their credibility. Consent indicates trust and the assumption is that the trust will not only be reciprocated but also constantly negotiated—a dynamic relationship rather than a static decision."[50] Tuhiwai Smith further cautions that negotiating entry to a community can be complex and even somewhat overwhelming for indigenous researchers because "the skills and reflexivities required to mediate and work with these [insider] dynamics are quite sophisticated."[51] She suggests that indigenous researchers should think carefully and critically through the larger concept of research and its associated ideologies, and also be highly reflexive of their own role as a researcher within their communities, before attempting access.

Just as Tuhiwai Smith suggests, I found that the important work of community involvement leading to empowerment is certainly one that requires much investment. In truth, the work of empowerment cannot be accomplished in a few scattered days, or even weeks, of well-intended work. This is difficult and deeply intense work that requires the commitment of mind, body, emotions, and spirit. Furthermore, it is quite supercilious to assume that people will simply jump on board the research bandwagon because it has pulled into town for a short visit. I firmly believe that community members must see real benefit for themselves before they will become genuinely engaged in research activities. Interestingly enough, even though remuneration and acknowledgement can be effective motivators, I found that one of my most successful motivational strategies was talking to a youth group about how research can become a tool of decolonization. This talk seemed to incite a collective sense of ownership and responsibility around the topic of community knowledge and traditions in several members of the youth group. In fact, if we do not make this empowering aspect of research evident at the onset, we are asking community members to accept a substantial risk with little prospect of concrete payback. As researchers, we must be willing to participate in the risk-taking by sharing our own values and belief systems around often-contentious issues with community members.[52]

Lessons Learned from the Research Process within Communities

From the beginning, participation from the various Aboriginal communities ranged from lesser involvement to full, authentic involvement. For instance, the involvement of all three key community facilitators within this project must be rightfully considered full and authentic participation. Their activities were seen as politically motivated, and their participation was active and involved elements of influence. Undoubtedly, this research project was viewed by these key facilitators as beneficial for increasing community awareness and participation in the SuperNet technology, and thus deserving of their extra efforts. In all three cases, I presented my research approach in detail and was then asked to answer questions on the process until these community leaders felt satisfied that they understood the process enough to present it to Council on my behalf. At the level of community organizations, there was a more diverse range of participation levels displayed. Each organization's involvement appeared to directly coincide with its specific mandate, which is not altogether surprising. Those organizations that could be viewed as fairly autonomous and acting in their community's best interests were much more involved in research participation than those that operated under either a regional or a provincial governance structure, which tend to superimpose their own terms of control upon community people. It is for this reason that the larger, macro-level structures, such as government departments, are often regarded as somewhat restrictive and limiting to the real and perceived needs of community people. Throughout the course of this project, a deliberate attempt was made to engage people in dialogue on the topic of the Alberta SuperNet and, more specifically, on how this new form of media could positively influence their lives. Overall, it was found that although conversing one-on-one with community participants could be quite informative, conversation in a group setting was felt to have greater impact and potential for community empowerment. As a number of authors have mentioned, the sharing of knowledge with one another and the recognition of unity based on common concerns are valid and credible means of community empowerment.

Conclusion

This candid account of my work within the ethnographic tradition was intended to give the reader a sense of the complicated role and processes that accompany an action ethnography performed by an Aboriginal person in Aboriginal communities. In searching for the right fit for my work, I was motivated by the need to make social change as well as the need to explore alternative methodological approaches that could potentially make a lasting difference within Aboriginal communities. Although the principles and the process that formed the foundation of this research project were intended to be empowering, there were certainly a number of unintended consequences—not the least of which was the eventual framing of the project within ethnography.[53]

Despite the deliberate focus of this chapter, it should be noted that this heightened sense of responsibility to improve conditions within Aboriginal communities is not just felt by Aboriginal people. In *Aboriginal Conditions: Research as a Foundation for Public Policy*, editors Jerry White, Paul Maxim, and Dan Beavon call on strategic partnerships between Aboriginal people, government policy makers, and other scientists to find effective solutions to the ongoing social problems of Aboriginal people. Although that specific triad is the focus of their current endeavours, the editors also acknowledge that true capacity building includes the eventual formation of Aboriginal-led research institutions where, "hopefully, some of these Indigenous scholars will use their greater cultural understanding and personal histories and join with us to address many of the data and analytical gaps that plague the Aboriginal policy domain."[54] Thus, at least during this critical time of transitioning, the important work of empowering disadvantaged populations will benefit from respectful partnerships between government, community members, and researchers willing to share and learn from one another.

In summary, the introduction of new-media technologies into Aboriginal communities has been deemed a "double-edged sword" by a number of observers. This new-media form undoubtedly has a dual nature. On the one hand, the collection of oral traditions, the preservation and restoration of indigenous languages, and the re-invigoration of indigenous knowledge traditions through broadband-enabled multimedia could certainly help to rebuild and strengthen many of our disadvantaged communities. On the other hand, it is apparent that new media brings in new risks of the outside world luring a youthful population away from cultural traditions. At day's end, the best solution is likely to rest in the committed involvement of community members in designing proactive media projects in tandem with academics who are willing to take an action-oriented approach to research. Those of us who are committed to making a positive difference in the Aboriginal world should continue setting our research sights on "fixing the world," knowing full well that the sky's the limit if you are ever-vigilant about learning from your mistakes.

NOTES

1   Thomas King, "The One About Coyote Going West," in *All My Relations: An Anthology of Contemporary Canadian Native Fiction,* ed. Thomas King (Toronto: McClelland and Stewart, 1990), 105–106.

2   Various scholars, including Sally Jane Norman, in "Culture and the New Media Technologies" (UNESCO Working Paper presented at the Power of Culture Conference, Stockholm, Sweden, 1995), define the "Fourth World" as those groups who reside at a very low socio-economic level within an otherwise highly developed nation.

3   Paul Martin, *Speech from the Throne to Open the Third Session of the Session of the 37th Parliament of Canada,* Privacy Council Office, 2 February 2004, http://www.pco-bcp.gc.ca/index.asp?lang=eng&page=information&sub=publications&doc=sft-ddt/2004_1_e.htm

4   Canada, Statistics Canada, *Aboriginal Peoples Survey Community Profiles,* 2001, http://www12.statcan.ca/english/profilo1aps/home.cfm.

5   Census Metropolitan Areas, or CMAs, are defined by Statistics Canada as those areas where "the census population count of the urban core is at least ... 100,000." http://www12.statcan.ca/english/censuso1/Products/Reference/dict/geo009.htm

6   Rosalinda Costa and Andrew Siggner, "Aboriginal Conditions in Census Metropolitan Areas, 1981–2001," in *Trends and Conditions in Census Metropolitan Areas* 8 (Ottawa: Statistics Canada, The Online Catalogue, 2005), 5.

7   An annual median income of less than $26,015 (for a family of four, before taxes, and in a rural community) is considered "living in poverty," according to a compilation of national statistical standards. (See Community Low Income Centre, "Low Income Cutoff Levels," http://www.weyburnclic.com/index.php?page=low_income_cutoff_levels.)

8   One of the most important lessons to be learned by any Aboriginal person is that of our colonized history. Postcolonial studies have contributed important discussions to this topic (see the works of Gayatri Chakravorty Spivak and Homi Bhabha) but have also benefited from discussions by Canadian scholars such as Marie Battiste.

9   See, for example, Shannon Avison and Michael Meadows, "Speaking and Hearing: Aboriginal Newspapers and the Public Sphere in Canada and Australia," *Canadian*

Journal of Communication 25, no. 3 (2000): 347-355; George Baldwin, "Public Access to the Internet: American Indian and Alaskan Native Issues," in *Public Access to the Internet*, ed. Brian Kahin & James Keller, (Cambridge, MA: MIT Press, 1995), 137-153; Kathleen Buddle, "Aboriginal Cultural Capital Creation and Radio Production in Urban Ontario," *Canadian Journal of Communication* 30, 1 (2005): 7–40; James May, "Information Technology for Indigenous Peoples: The North American Experience, " in *Digital Democracy: Policy and Politics in the Wired World, ed.* Cynthia Alexander & Leslie A. Pal, (Toronto: Oxford University Press, 1998), 220-237; Lorna Roth, *Something New in the Air: The Story of First Peoples' Television Broadcasting in Canada* (Montreal: McGill Queen's University Press, 2005); Claire Smith, Heather Burke, and Graeme K. Ward, "Globalisation and Indigenous Peoples: Threat or Empowerment?" In *Indigenous Cultures in an Interconnected World*, ed. Claire Smith and Graeme K. Ward (Vancouver: UBC Press, 2000), 1-26; K. Tallbear (2001, February), Racialising Tribal Identity and the Implications for Political and Cultural Development, paper presented at the Indigenous Peoples and Racism Conference, Sydney, Australia.

10 See, for example, Cynthia Alexander, "Wiring the Nation! Including First Nations? Aboriginal Canadians and Federal E-Government Initiatives," *Journal of Canadian Studies* 35, no. 4 (2001): 277-96; Cynthia Alexander and Leslie Pal, eds. *Digital Democracy: Policy and Politics in the Wired World* (Toronto: Oxford University Press, 1998); Valerie Alia, "Scattered Voices, Global Vision: Indigenous Peoples and the New Media Nation," in *The Media of Diaspora*, ed. Karim Karim (New York: Routledge, Taylor & Francis Group, 2003), 36-50; Yale Belanger, "Northern Disconnect: Information Communications Technology Needs Assessment for Aboriginal Communities in Manitoba," *Native Studies Review* 14, 2 (2001): 43-69; Judy M. Iseke-Barnes, "Aboriginal and Indigenous People's Resistance, the Internet, and Education," *Race, Ethnicity and Education* 5, 2 (2002): 171-98; William J. McIver, "A Community Informatics for the Information Society," in *Communicating in the Information Society*, ed. Bruce Girard and Seán O Siochru (Geneva: United Nations Research Institute for Social Development, 2003), 33-64.

11 See, for example, Manuel Castells, *The Rise of the Network Society*, Malden, Mass.: Blackwell Publishers, 1996; Fals-Borda, Orlando, and Muhammad Anisur Rahman, *Action and Knowledge: Breaking the Monopoly with Participatory Action-Research*, New York: Apex Press, 1991; Faye D. Ginsburg, "Mediating Culture: Indigenous Media, Ethnographic Film, and the Production of Identity," in *Fields of Vision: Essays in Film Studies, Visual Anthropology, and Photography*, ed. Leslie Devereaux and Roger Hillman (Berkeley: University of California Press, 1995), 256–291, and "Screen Memories: Resignifying the Traditional in Indigenous Media," in Ginsburg, Abu-Lughod, and Larkin, *Media Worlds*, 39–57; Srinivas R. Melkote and H. Leslie Steeves, *Communication for Development in the Third World: Theory and Practice for Empowerment*, 2nd ed. (New Delhi: Sage Publications, 2001); M. Tehranian, M., "Communication and Development," in *Communication Theory Today*, ed. D. Crowley & D. Mitchell , 274-306 (Stanford: Stanford University Press, 1994).

12 Social Sciences and Humanities Research Council of Canada, *From Granting Council to Knowledge Council*, 2004, http://www.sshrc.ca/web/whatsnew/ initiatives/transformation/consultation_framework_e.pdf.

13 See, for instance, the communications development work of Srinivas Melkote and H. Leslie Steeves in *Communication for Development in the Third World* and the participatory action-based work of Susan Smith in "Deepening Participatory

Action-Research," in *Nurtured by Knowledge: Learning to Do Participatory Action-Research*, ed. Susan E. Smith, Dennis George Willms, and Nancy A. Johnson (New York: The Apex Press, International Development Research Centre, 1997), 173–263.

14 Linda Tuhiwai Smith, *Decolonizing Methodologies: Research and Indigenous Peoples* (London: Zed Books, 1999), 151.

15 Mónica Russel y Rodríguez, "Confronting the Silencing Praxis in Anthropology: Speaking of/from a Chicano Consciousness," *Qualitative Inquiry* 4, 1 (1998): 347.

16 Ibid., 361.

17 Ibid., 353.

18 Marian Bredin, "Ethnography and Communication: Approaches to Aboriginal Media," *Canadian Journal of Communication* 18, 3 (1993): 311. For further discussion in this area, see Susanne Dabulskis-Hunter, *Outsider Research: How White Writers "Explore" Native Issues, Knowledge and Experiences* (Bethesda, MD: Academica Press, 2002).

19 Nancy Naples, *Feminism and Method: Ethnography, Discourse Analysis, and Activist Research* (New York: Taylor and Francis, 2003), 146.

20 Douglas E. Foley, "Critical Ethnography: The Reflexive Turn," *Qualitative Studies in Education* 15, 5 (2002): 470.

21 Gerry Philipsen, "An Ethnographic Approach to Communication Studies," in *Rethinking Communication*, Vol. 2, ed. Brenda Dervin (New Brunswick, NJ: International Communication Association, 1989), 265.

22 Clifford Geertz, *Works and Lives: The Anthropologist as Author*, Harry Camp Lectures at Stanford University (Stanford, CA: Stanford University Press, 1988), 144–145.

23 Tuhiwai Smith, *Decolonizing Methodologies*, 67.

24 James Clifford, introduction to *Writing Culture: The Poetics and Politics of Ethnography (a School of American Research Advanced Seminar)*, ed. James Clifford and George E. Marcus (Berkeley: University of California Press, 1986), 9.

25 Johannes Fabian, *Time and the Other: How Anthropology Makes Its Object* (New York: Columbia University Press, 1983).

26 For those on the inside of Aboriginal knowing, the Trickster has definitely come out to play.

27 Clifford, introduction to *Writing Culture*; Bredin, "Ethnography and Communication."

28 Clifford, introduction to *Writing Culture*, 8.

29 Michael Crotty, *The Foundations of Social Research: Meaning and Perspective in the Research Process* (London: Sage Publications, 1998), 12.

30 Foley, "Critical Ethnography," 470.

31 James Clifford, Introduction to Writing Culture; Shirley Grundy, *Curriculum: Product or Praxis*, Deakin Studies in Education Series (London: Falmer, 1987); Richard Quantz, *The Handbook of Qualitative Research in Education*, ed. W.L. Millroy, M.D. LeCompte, J. Preissle (San Diego, CA: Academic Press, 1992); Roger I. Simon and Donald Dippo, "On Critical Ethnographic Work," *Anthropology and Education Quarterly* 17, 4 (1986): 195–202.

32 Michael Campbell, "Young Workers Becoming Critical: A Critical Ethnographic Study of the Theory and Practice of the Young Christian Workers' Movement as

Lived by a Group Young Workers in 'Workington.'" M Ed. diss, University of South Australia, 1994; Patti Lather, "Research as Praxis." *Harvard Educational Review* 56, 3 (1986): 258.

33   Bredin, "Ethnography and Communication," 302.

34   Jo Tacchi, Don Slater, and Greg Hearn, *Ethnographic Action Research Handbook* (New Delhi: UNESCO, 2003), 8.

35   Ibid., 9.

36   Jo Tacchi, "Researching Creative Applications of New Information and Communication Technologies," *International Journal of Cultural Studies* 7, 1 (2004): 95.

37   Paulo Freire, *Pedagogy of the Oppressed*, trans. Myra Bergman Ramos, rev. ed. (New York: Continuum Publishing, 1992).

38   The use of the phrase "all my relations" is not to be taken literally (although in many cases it could be) but should instead be thought of as representing the interconnectedness and interrelatedness aspect of those adhering to indigenous belief systems. Importantly, this phrase is also used to end prayer in much the same way that "Amen" is used within the Catholic regime.

39   David Walsh, "Doing Ethnography," in *Researching Society and Culture*, ed. Clive Seale (London: Sage Publications, 1998), 221..

40   Ibid., 223.

41   Ibid., 226–227.

42   Indeed, there is a strong likelihood that such researchers may find this awkward positioning inherently familiar—especially if they are from Métis heritage.

43   Walsh, "Doing Ethnography," 226.

44   Ibid., 221.

45   Ibid., 225.

46   Kirin Narayan, "How Native Is a 'Native' Anthropologist?" *American Anthropologist* 95, 3 (1993): 672.

47   Ibid., 674–676.

48   Tuhiwai Smith, *Decolonizing Methodologies*, 10.

49   Ibid., 10

50   Ibid., 136.

51   Ibid., 136–137.

52   The protection and preservation of indigenous knowledge traditions is one such politically contentious topic as indigenous groups work to find the right balance between sharing knowledge and maintaining appropriate boundaries around cultural disclosure, a balance that respects both protocols and traditions.

53   I struggled with the choice that I made in choosing ethnography simply because this decision was made on my own—without consultation with community members. Yet the production of my thesis was also a responsibility that I knew was mine alone to bear. Still, it remains true that the work that I performed was done with the best of intentions and with what I believe were the right motives. I can only hope that the right message comes across.

54   Jerry P White, introduction to *Aboriginal Conditions: Research as a Foundation for Public Policy*, ed. Jerry P. White, Paul S. Maxim, and Dan Beavon (Vancouver: University of British Columbia Press, 2003), xxiv.

SELECTED BIBLIOGRAPHY

Aboriginal Peoples Television Network. *APTN Journalistic Policy.* Winnipeg: APTN, 2004.

_____. *APTN Promotional Brochure.* Winnipeg: APTN, n.d.

_____. "APTN Viewing Audience Continues to Grow," news release, 2004. http://www.aptn.ca/index.php?option=com_content&task=view&id=39&Itemid=39 (accessed 16 February 2006).

_____. "About APTN," http://www.aptn.ca (accessed 2 May 2005).

_____. *APTN Media Sales Package.* Toronto: APTN Media Sales, 2006.

_____. *Aboriginal Urban Population and APTN.* Winnipeg: Brave Strategy, 2005.

Alexander, Cynthia "Wiring the Nation! Including First Nations? Aboriginal Canadians and Federal E-Government Initiatives." *Journal of Canadian Studies* 35, no. 4 (2001): 277-96.

Alexander, Cynthia, and Leslie Pal, eds. *Digital Democracy: Policy and Politics in the Wired World.* Toronto: Oxford University Press, 1998.

Alia, Valerie. *Un/covering the North: News, Media, and Aboriginal People.* Vancouver: University of British Columbia Press, 1999.

Alia, Valerie "Scattered Voices, Global Vision: Indigenous Peoples and the New Media Nation." In *The Media of Diaspora,* edited by Karim Karim, 36-50. New York: Routledge, Taylor & Francis Group, 2003.

Appadurai, Arjun. "Deep Democracy: Urban Governmentality and the Horizon of Politics." *Public Culture* 14, 1 (2002): 21–47.

_____. *Modernity at Large: Cultural Dimensions of Globalization.* Minneapolis: University of Minnesota Press, 1996.

Asch, Timothy, Jesus Ignacio Cardozo, Hortensia Cabellero, and Jose Bortoli. "The Story We Now Want to Hear Is Not Ours to Tell: Relinquishing Control over Representation: Toward Sharing Visual Communication Skills with the Yanomami." *Visual Anthropology Review* 7, 2 (1991): 102–106.

Assembly of First Nations. "June 27, 2005—AFN National Chief Phil Fontaine Meets with Federal-Provincial-Territorial Ministers to Discuss First Ministers Meeting: National Chief Challenges Ministers to 'Close the Gap' Between First Nations and the Canadian Population within Ten Years." http://www.afn.ca/article.asp?id=1546 (accessed 30 September 2005).

_____. "Release of Report Card on Royal Commission on Aboriginal Peoples." Ottawa: Assembly of First Nations, 2006. http://www.afn.ca/cmslib/general/afn_rcap.pdf (accessed 11 January 2007).

Avison, Shannon, and Michael Meadows. "Speaking and Hearing: Aboriginal Newspapers and the Public Sphere in Canada and Australia." *Canadian Journal of Communication* 25, 3 (2000): 347-56.

Belanger, Yale. "Northern Disconnect: Information Communications Technology Needs Assessment for Aboriginal Communities in Manitoba." *Native Studies Review* 14, 2 (2001): 43-69.

Balikci, Asen. "Anthropology, Film and the Arctic Peoples: The First Forman Lecture." *Anthropology Today* 5, 2 (1989): 4–10.

Baldwin, George. "Public Access to the Internet: American Indian and Alaskan Native Issues." In *Public Access to the Internet*, edited by Brian Kahin & James Keller, 137-53. Cambridge, MA: MIT Press, 1995.

Baltruschat, Doris. "International Film and TV Co-productions: A Canadian Case Study." In *Media Organization and Production*, edited by Simon Cottle, 181–207. London: Sage Publications, 2005.

_____. "Television and Canada's Aboriginal Communities: Seeking Opportunities Through Traditional Storytelling and Digital Technologies." *Canadian Journal of Communication* 29, 1 (2004): 47–59.

Barnsley, Paul. "Native Groups Ponder Life after Tobin." *Windspeaker*, 22 March 2002, http://www.itbusiness.ca/it/client/en/Home/News.asp?id=21844&bSearch=True.

Battiste, Marie. "Maintaining Aboriginal Identity, Language, and Culture in Modern Society." In *Reclaiming Indigenous Voice and Vision*, edited by Marie Battiste. Vancouver: University of British Columbia Press, 2000.

Benjamin, Walter. "The Storyteller: Observations on the Works of Nikolai Leskov." In *Walter Benjamin: Selected Writings, Volume 3, 1935–1938*, edited by Howard Eiland and Michael W. Jennings, 143–166. Cambridge, MA: Belknap Press of Harvard University, 2002.

Bernard, John. Interview by Steve Paikin, *Studio 2*, TV Ontario, 21 November 2002.

Bhabha, Homi K. *The Location of Culture*. London: Routledge, 1994.

Binning, C. "Special Report on Documentary Production and Distribution: Who's Shopping for Docs." *Playback Magazine*, 9 March 1998. http://www.playback-mag.com/articles/pb/20973.asp.

Bird, S. Elizabeth. *The Audience in Everyday Life*. New York: Routledge, 2003.

_____. "Travels in Nowhere Land: Ethnography and the 'Impossible' Audience." *Critical Studies in Mass Communication* 9 (1992): 250–260.

Block, Sheri. "North Central Gets $6M Federal Boost." *Regina Leader Post*, 31 January 2004, B1.

———. "Subject Matter of TV Series Hits Home with Actors." *Regina Leader Post*, 6 November 2003, B2.

Bredin, Marian. "Aboriginal Peoples Television Network." In *Encyclopedia of Television*, 2nd ed., edited by Horace Newcomb, 6–8. New York: Routledge, 2004.

———. "Ethnography and Communication: Approaches to Aboriginal Media." *Canadian Journal of Communication* 18, 3 (1993): 297–313.

Browne, Donald R. *Electronic Media and Indigenous Peoples: A Voice of Our Own?* Ames: Iowa State University Press, 1996.

Buddle, Kathleen. "Aboriginal Cultural Capital Creation and Radio Production in Urban Ontario." *Canadian Journal of Communication* 30, 1 (2005): 7–40.

———. "From Birchbark Talk to Digital Dreamspeaking: A History of Aboriginal Media Activism in Canada." PhD diss., McMaster University, 2002.

Campbell, Michael. "Young Workers Becoming Critical: A Critical Ethnographic Study of the Theory and Practice of the Young Christian Workers' Movement as Lived by a Group Young Workers in "Workington." " M. Ed. diss, University of South Australia, 1994.

Canada, Department of Canadian Heritage. *Report of the Standing Committee on Canadian Heritage: Our Cultural Sovereignty*. Ottawa: Department of Canadian Heritage, 2004.

Canada, Department of Justice. *Broadcasting Act*. Ottawa: Queen's Printer for Canada, 1991.

Canada, Federal Government. "The Northern Broadcasting Policy." News release, 10 March 1983.

Canada, Indian and Northern Affairs. "Canada's Position: United Nations Draft Declaration on the Rights of Indigenous Peoples—29 June 2006." http://www.ainc-inac.gc.ca/nr/spch/unp/06/ddr_e.html.

———. *Report of the Royal Commission on Aboriginal Peoples, Volume 1: Looking Forward, Looking Back*. Ottawa: Minister of Supply and Services, 1996.

———. *Report of the Royal Commission on Aboriginal Peoples, Volume 3: Gathering Strength*. Ottawa: Minister of Supply and Services, 1996.

———. *Survey of First Nations People Living on-Reserve, Integrated Final Report*. Ottawa: Ekos Research Associates, 2003.

Canada, Industry Canada. *The New National Dream: Networking the Nation for Broadband Access*. Ottawa: Industry Canada, 2001.

Canada, Office of the Languages Commissioner, Northwest Territories. "Annual Report, 2000–2001." Yellowknife, Office of the Languages Commissioner, 2001.

Canada, Parliament. *Report of the Task Force on Broadcasting Policy*. Ottawa: Minister of Supply and Services, 1986.

———. *Statement of the Government of Canada on Indian Policy Presented to the First Session of the Twenty-eighth Parliament by the Honourable Jean Chrétien,*

Minister of Indian Affairs and Northern Development. Ottawa: Minister of Supply and Services, 1969.

Canada, Royal Commission on Aboriginal Peoples. "Last Words." In *People to People: Nation to Nation: Highlights from the Report of the Royal Commission on Aboriginal Peoples.* Ottawa: Minister of Supply and Services Canada, 1996. http://www.ainc-inac.gc.ca/ap/pubs/rpt/rpt-eng.asp.

Canada, Senate Committee on Transport and Communications. *Proceedings of the Standing Senate Committee on Transport and Communications. Issue 9–Evidence.* Winnipeg, 4 February 2005, http://www.parl.gc.ca/38/1/parlbus/commbus/senate/com-e/tran-e/09cv-e.htm?Lanugage=E&Parl=38&Ses=1&comm_id=19 (accessed 8 January 2006).

Canada, Social Sciences and Humanities Research Council. "Aboriginal Research: A Pilot Program." In *Dialogue on Research and Aboriginal Peoples.* Ottawa: Government of Canada, 2004.

_____. *From Granting Council to Knowledge Council,* 2004. http://www.sshrc.ca/web/whatsnew/initiatives/transformation/consultation_framework_e.pdf.

Canada, Statistics Canada. *Aboriginal Peoples Survey Community Profiles,* 2001. http://www12.statcan.ca/english/profil01aps/home.cfm.

Canada, Statistics Canada. *Selected Dwelling Characteristics and Household Equipment.* 2008. http://www40.statcan.gc.ca/l01/cst01/famil09c-eng.htm.

_____. *The Daily,* 13 January 1998.

_____. *The Daily,* 21 November 2003.

_____. *The Daily,* 9 July 2004.

_____. *The Daily,* 18 December 2009.

Canadian Broadcasting Corporation, "The Greatest Canadian." Ottawa: CBC, 2004. www.cbc.ca/greatest/ (accessed 18 May 2005).

_____. "Intervention Letter to CRTC." Ottawa: CBC, 19 October 1998.

_____. "Saving Native Languages up to First Nations: Chief," 14 November 2006. http://www.cbc.ca/canada/manitoba/story/2006/11/14/language-conference.html (accessed 24 November 2006).

Canadian Cable Television Association. "Intervention Letter to CRTC." Ottawa: CTCA, 12 November 1998.

Canadian Radio-television and Telecommunications Commission. *Decision CRTC 91–826.* Ottawa: CRTC, 28 October 1991.

_____. *Decision CRTC 99–42.* Ottawa: CRTC, 22 February 1999.

_____. *Mandate,* 1 November 2007. http://www.crtc.gc.ca/eng/cancon/mandate.htm.

_____. "Native Broadcasting Policy," Public Notice, 20 September 1990. Ottawa: CRTC 1990.

_____. *The 1980s: A Decade of Diversity, Report of the Committee on the Extension of Service to Northern and Remote Communities.* Ottawa: Minister of Supply and Services, 1980.

Carroll, William K., and Robert A. Hackett. "Democratic Media Activism through the Lens of Social Movement Theory." *Media, Culture and Society* 28, 1 (2006): 83–104.

Castells, Manuel. *The Rise of the Network Society*. Malden, Mass.: Blackwell Publishers, 1996.

Centre for Research and Information on Canada. "Canadians Want Strong Aboriginal Cultures But Are Divided on Aboriginal Rights." Press release, 26 November 2003.

Chambers, Iain. *Border Dialogues: Journeys in Postmodernity*. London: Routledge, 1990.

Chwialkowska, Luiza. "Coming Soon to Your Living Room." *National Post*, 23 February 1999, A3.

Cleaver, Harry. "The Zapatistas and the Electronic Fabric of Struggle," 1998. http://www.eco.utexas.edu/Homepages/Faculty/Cleaver/zaps.html.

Clifford, James. Introduction to *Writing Culture: The Poetics and Politics of Ethnography*, edited by James Clifford and George E. Marcus. Berkeley: University of California Press, 1986.

Cobb, Chris. "Aboriginal TV Goes Canada-wide." *Gazette*, 23 February 1999, F5.

Cohn, Norman. "The Art of Community-Based Filmmaking." SILA. 2005. http://www.sila.nu/teachers (accessed 15 March 2006).

_____. "Atanarjuat, the Fast Runner." *IndieWire*. http://www.indiewire.com/film/interviews/int_Cohn_Kunuk_020605.html.

Community Low Income Centre. "Low Income Cutoff Levels," 2005. http://www.weyburnclic.com/index.php?page=low_income_cutoff_levels (accessed 10 January 2007).

Consilium. *Aboriginal Languages Initiative (ALI) Evaluation, Final Report*. Ottawa: Department of Canadian Heritage, 2003.

_____. *An Audience Survey Conducted for Taqramiut Nipingat Inc*. Ottawa: Consilium Consulting Group, 2003.

_____. *Evaluation of the Urban Multipurpose Aboriginal Youth Centres*. Ottawa: Consilium Consulting Group, 2004.

_____. *Northern Native Broadcast Access Program Evaluation*. Ottawa: Consilium Consulting Group, 2003.

_____. *Northern Native Broadcasting: A Policy Survey*. Prepared for the Northern Native Broadcast Access Program, Native Citizens' Directorate, Department of Canadian Heritage, January 1995.

"Consumers Should Decide What They Want to Watch." *Vancouver Province*, 2 September 1999, A36.

Cook, Ray. "Native Community Radio, Its Function and Future." *Akwe:kon Journal*, 1985.

Cook, Tim. "Hearing for Two Cops Fired in Neil Stonechild Case Begins in Saskatoon." *Canadian Press NewsWire*, 4 May 2005.

Cortes, Carlos E. *The Children are Watching: How the Media Teaches About Diversity.* New York: Teachers College Press, 2000.

Costa, Rosalinda, and Andrew Siggner. "Aboriginal Conditions in Census Metropolitan Areas, 1981–2001." In *Trends and Conditions in Census Metropolitan Areas 8.* Ottawa: Statistics Canada (The Online Catalogue), 2005. http://www.statcan.ca/english/research/89-613-MIE/89-613-MIE2005008.htm.

Couldry, Nick. "The Extended Audience: Scanning the Horizon." In *Media Audiences,* edited by Marie Gillespie, 183–222. New York: Open University Press, 2005.

Cowl, Terrence. *Models of Aboriginal Broadcasting: An International Comparative Review.* International Comparative Research Group, Strategic Research and Analysis Directorate, Corporate and Intergovernmental Affairs Branch, Department of Canadian Heritage, October 1995.

Crotty, Michael. *The Foundations of Social Research: Meaning and Perspective in the Research Process.* London: Sage Publications, 1998.

Dabulskis-Hunter, Susanne. *Outsider Research: How White Writers "Explore" Native Issues, Knowledge and Experiences.* Bethesda, MD: Academica Press, 2002.

Daley, Patrick J., and Beverly A. James. *Cultural Politics and the Mass Media: Alaska Native Voices.* Urbana: University of Illinois Press, 2004.

David, Jennifer. *Aboriginal Language Broadcasting in Canada. An Overview and Recommendations to the Task Force on Aboriginal Languages and Cultures, Final Report.* Ottawa: Debwe Communications Inc and APTN, 2004.

Deger, Jennifer. *Shimmering Screens: Making Media in an Aboriginal Community.* Minneapolis: University of Minnesota Press, 2006.

Dornfeld, Barry. "Envisioning Reception." In *The Construction of the Viewer,* edited by Peter Ian Crawford and Sigurjon Baldur Hafsteinsson, 229–243. Højbjerg, Denmark: Intervention Press, Nordic Anthropological Film Association, 1996.

Environics Research Group. *North of 60° and Remote Community Monitor 2006: APTN Omnibus Report.* Ottawa: Environics, September 2006.

Ermine, Willie, Raven Sinclair, and Bonnie Jeffery. *The Ethics of Research Involving Indigenous Peoples. Report of the Indigenous Peoples Health Research Centre to the Interagency Advisory Panel on Research Ethics.* Saskatoon: Indigenous Peoples Health Research Centre, 2004

Evans, Michael Robert. "Frozen Light and Fluid Time: The Folklore, Politics and Performance of Inuit Video." PhD diss., Indiana University, 1999.

_____. *Isuma: Inuit Video Art* (Montreal: McGill - Queen's University Press, 2008).

_____. "Sometimes in Anger: The Struggle of Inuit Video." *Fuse Magazine* 22, 4 (2000): 13–17.

Fabian, Johannes. *Time and the Other: How Anthropology Makes Its Object.* New York: Columbia University Press, 1983.

Fairchild, Charles. "Below the Hamelin Line: CKRZ and Aboriginal Cultural Survival." *Canadian Journal of Communication* 23, 2 (1998): 163–87.

Fals-Borda, Orlando, and Muhammad Anisur Rahman. *Action and Knowledge: Breaking the Monopoly with Participatory Action-Research.* New York: Apex Press, 1991.

Faris, James. "Anthropological Transparency: Film, Representation and Politics." In *Film as Ethnography*, edited by Peter Ian Crawford and David Turton, 171–82. Manchester: Manchester University Press, 1992.

Farmer, Gary. "Listen! Native American Language Revival in Radio." *Native Americas* 13, 1 (1996): 22.

Farrell, Jim. "Second Body in 3 Weeks." *Edmonton Journal*, 8 May 2005, A3.

Fleras, Augie. "Racializing Culture/Culturizing Race: Multicultural Racism in a Multicultural Canada." In *Racism, Eh? A Critical Inter-disciplinary Anthology of Race and Racism in Canada*, edited by Carmille A. Nelson and Charmaine A. Nelson, 429–443. Concord, ON: Captus Press, 2004.

Foley, Douglas E. "Critical Ethnography: The Reflexive Turn." *Qualitative Studies in Education* 15, 5 (2002): 469–490.

Foucault, Michel. "Space, Knowledge, and Power." In *The Foucault Reader*, edited by Paul Rabinow. London: Penguin, 1984.

Freire, Paulo. "Cultural Action and Conscientization." *Harvard Educational Review* 40, 3.

_____. *Pedagogy of the Oppressed*. Translated by Myra Bergman Ramos. Revised edition. New York: Continuum Publishing, 1992.

Froehling, Otto. "The Cyberspace War of Ink and Internet in Chiapas, Mexico." *Geographical Review* 87, 2 (1997): 291.

Gatehouse, Jonathon. "Canada's Worst Neighbourhood." *Maclean's*, 8 January 2007.

Geertz, Clifford. *Works and Lives: The Anthropologist as Author*. Harry Camp Lectures at Stanford University. Stanford, CA: Stanford University Press, 1983.

Geller, Peter. "Pictures of the Arctic Night: Archibald Land Fleming and the Representation of Canadian Inuit". In King and Lidchi, *Imaging the Arctic*, 60–68.

Gibson, William. *Mona Lisa Overdrive*. New York: Bantam, 1988.

Ginsburg, Faye D. "Aboriginal Media and the Australian Imaginary." *Public Culture* 5 (1993): 20.

_____. "Atanarjuat Off-Screen: From 'Media Reservations' to the World Stage." *American Anthropologist* 105, 4 (2003): 827–831.

_____. "Embedded Aesthetics: Creating a Discursive Space for Indigenous Media." In *Internationalizing Cultural Studies: An Anthology*, edited by M.A. Abbas and John Nguyet Erni, 277–294. Malden, MA: Blackwell Publishing, 2005.

_____. "From Little Things Big Things Grow: Indigenous Media and Cultural Activism." In *Between Resistance and Revolution: Cultural Politics and Social Protest*, edited by Richard G. Fox and Orin Starn. New Brunswick, NJ: Rutgers University Press, 1997.

_____. "Indigenous Media: Faustian Contract or Global Village?" *Cultural Anthropology* 6, 1 (1991): 92–112.

_____. "Mediating Culture: Indigenous Media, Ethnographic Film, and the Production of Identity." In *Fields of Vision: Essays in Film Studies, Visual Anthropology, and*

Photography, edited by Leslie Devereaux and Roger Hillman, 256–291. Berkeley: University of California Press, 1995.

_____. "Resources of Hope: Learning from the Local in a Transnational Era." In *Indigenous Cultures in an Interconnected World*, edited by Claire Smith and Graeme K. Ward, 27–48. Vancouver: University of British Columbia Press, 2000.

_____. "Screen Memories: Resignifying the Traditional in Indigenous Media." In Ginsburg, Abu-Lughod, and Larkin, *Media Worlds*, 39–57.

Ginsburg, Faye D., Lila Abu-Lughod, and Brian Larkin, eds. *Media Worlds: Anthropology on New Terrain*. Berkeley: University of California Press, 2002.

Graburn, Nelson H.H. "Television and the Canadian Inuit." *Etudes Inuit Studies* 6, 1 (1982): 7–19.

Granzberg, Gary. "Television as Storyteller: The Algonkian Indians of Central Canada." *Journal of Communication* 32, 1 (1982): 43–52.

Granzberg, Gary, and Jack Steinbring. *Television and the Canadian Indian: Impact and Meaning among Algonkians of Central Canada*. Winnipeg: University of Winnipeg, 1980.

Granzberg, Gary, Jack Steinbring, and John Hamer. "New Magic for Old: TV in Cree Culture." *Journal of Communication* 27, 4 (1977): 154–157.

Greenall, David, and Stelios Loizides. *Aboriginal Digital Opportunities: Addressing Aboriginal Learning Needs Through the Use of Learning Technologies*. Ottawa: Conference Board of Canada, 2001.

Greene, Shane. "Indigenous People Incorporated? Culture as Politics, Culture as Property in Pharmaceutical Bioprospecting." *Current Anthropology* 24, 2 (2004): 211–237.

Greyson, John, and Lisa Steele. "The Inukshuk Project—Inuit TV: The Satellite Solution." In *Video re/View: The (best) Source for Critical Writings on Canadian Artists' Video*, edited by Peggy Gale and Lisa Steele, 57–63. Toronto: Art Metropole and V tape, 1996.

Grundy, Shirley. *Curriculum: Product or Praxis*. Deakin Studies in Education Series. London: Falmer, 1987.

Gupta, Akhil, and James Ferguson. "Beyond Culture: Space, Identity, and the Politics of Difference." In *Culture, Power, Place: Explorations in Critical Anthropology*, edited by Akhil Gupta and James Ferguson, 33–74. Durham, NC: Duke University Press, 1997.

Hall, Angela. "Regina Battles Reputation as Crime Capital: Queen City Tops Break-ins, Car Theft, Murder." *Calgary Herald*, 8 July 2002, A12.

Hall, Stuart. "Encoding/Decoding." In *Popular Culture: Production and Consumption*, edited by C. Lee Harrington and Denise D. Bielby, 123–132. Oxford: Blackwell, 2001.

Hartley, John. "Television, Nation, and Indigenous Media," *Television and New Media* 5, 1 (2004): 7.

Himpele, Jeff. *Circuits of Culture: Media, Politics and Indigenous Identity in the Andes*. Minneapolis: University of Minnesota Press, 2008.

Hockings, Paul. "Asen Balikci Films Nanook." *Visual Anthropology Review* 17, 2 (2001–02): 71–80.

hooks, bell. *Outlaw Culture: Resisting Representations.* New York: Routledge, 1994.

Hoskins, Colin, and Stuart McFadyen. "Canadian Participation in International Co-productions and Co-ventures in Television Programming." *Canadian Journal of Communication* 18, 2 (1993): 219–236.

Hudson, Heather. "The Role of Radio in the Canadian North." *Journal of Communication* 27, 4 (1977): 130–139.

Hunsdorf, Shari. "Atanarjuat, The Fast Runner: Culture, History, and Politics in Inuit Media." *American Anthropologist* 105, 4 (2003): 822–826.

Igloolik Isuma Productions. "The Inuit Style of Filmmaking." Isuma Teacher's Resource

Guide. SILA, http://www.sila.nu/teachers (accessed 23 July 2006).

_____. "Live from the Set." SILA, http://www.sila.nu/live/ (accessed 15 March 2006).

Iseke-Barnes, Judy M. "Aboriginal and Indigenous People's Resistance, the Internet, and Education." *Race, Ethnicity and Education* 5, 2 (2002): 171-98.

Jäckel, Anne. "Dual Nationality Film Productions in Europe." *Historical Journal of Film, Radio and Television* 23, 3 (2003): 231–243.

_____. "The Search for the National in Canadian Multilateral Cinematographic Co-productions." *National Identities* 3, 2 (2001): 155–167.

Jain, R. "Video: For, by and with the People." In *Video the Changing World*, edited by N. Thede and A. Ambrosi, 40–47. Montreal: Black Rose Books, Vidéazimut and Vidéo Tiers-monde, 1991.

Johnson, A. "*Fast Runner* Crew Fumes over Slow Subsidies." *Nunatsiaq News*, 18 March 2005. http://www.nunatsiaq.com/archives/50318/news/nunavut/50318_06.html (accessed 6 January 2006).

Johnson, D. "Connection, Community, Content. The Challenge of the Information Highway." Final Report of the Information Highway Advisory Council, 1995.

The Journals of Knud Rasmussen, DVD. Directed by Norman Cohn and Zacharias Kunuk. Igloolik, Nunavut: Isuma Productions, 2006.

King, J.C.H., and Henrietta Lidchi, eds. *Imaging the Arctic.* Seattle: University of Washington Press and Vancouver: University of British Columbia Press, 1998.

King, Thomas. "The One About Coyote Going West." In *All My Relations: An Anthology of Contemporary Canadian Native Fiction*, edited by Thomas King, 95–106. Toronto: McClelland and Stewart, 1990.

Knudson, Jerry W. "Rebellion in Chiapas: Insurrection by Internet and Public Relations." *Media, Culture and Society* 20 (1998): 507–518.

Koebberling, U. *Communication and Culture in the Western Arctic—A Case Study on the Growth of Inuvialuit-Controlled Broadcasts.* Inuvik: Inuvialuit Communications Society, 1986.

Koopmans, Ruud. "Movements and Media: Selection Processes and Evolutionary Dynamics in the Public Sphere." *Theory and Society* 33 (2004): 367–391.

Kunuk, Zacharias. "Zacharias Kunuk on his Film *Atanarjuat:*" Interview by Ian Reid, acting co-ordinator of the Aboriginal Arts Secretariat. *The Canada Council for the Arts,* June 2001. http://www.canadacouncil.ca (accessed 6 January 2006).

Lacey, Liam. "Sundance Film Festival 2003: Native Talent in a Gritty 'Hood." *Globe and Mail,* 24 January 2003, R1.

Lal, Vinay. "The Politics of History on the Internet: Cyber-Diasporic Hinduism and the North-American Hindu Diaspora." *Diaspora* 8, 2 (1999): 137–172.

LaRocque, Emma. "The Colonization of a Native Woman Scholar." In *Women of the First Nations: Power, Wisdom, and Strength,* edited by Christine Miller and Patricia Chuchryk. Winnipeg: University of Manitoba Press, 1996.

Lassiter, Luke Eric. "Authoritative Texts, Collaborative Ethnography, and Native American Studies." *American Indian Quarterly* 24, 4 (2000).

Lather, Patti. "Research as Praxis." *Harvard Educational Review* 56, 3 (1986): 257–277.

Levo-Henrikssen, Ritva. *Media and Ethnic Identity: Hopi Views on Media, Identity and Communication.* New York: Routledge, 2007.

Lewis, Peter. "Alternative Media in a Contemporary Social and Theoretical Context." In *Alternative Media: Linking Global and Local,* edited by Peter Lewis, 15–21. Paris: UNESCO Publishing, 1993.

_____. Preface to *Alternative Media: Linking Global and Local,* ed. Peter Lewis. Paris: UNESCO Publishing, 1993

Lidchi, Henrietta. "Filmic Fantasies in Arctic Lands: Photographing the Inuit of North West Greenland in 1932." In King and Lidchi, *Imaging the Arctic,* 197–206.

Longfellow, Brenda. "Counter-Narratives, Class Politics and Metropolitan Dystopias: Representations of Globalization in *Maelström, waydowntown,* and *La Moitié gauche du frigo.*" *Canadian Journal of Film Studies* 13, 1 (2004): 69–83.

Lougheed, Kendall, et al. "An Evaluation of the Northern Native Broadcast Access Program." Report to the Native Citizens' Directorate, Department of the Secretary of State, 1986.

Loyie, Florence, and Ryan Cormier. "Police Confirm Body in Field was Prostitute." *Calgary Herald,* 10 May 2005, A3.

Lutz, Hartmut. "Images of Indians in German Children's Books." In *Approaches: Essays in Native North American Studies and Literatures,* edited by Harman Lutz. Beiträge zur Kanadistik Bd. 11. Augsburg: Wissner, 2002, 13–47.

Lyons, Tom. "Young Aboriginals Flock to Hip-hop, Acting work." *Toronto Star,* 30 August 2003, H4.

MacDonald, G. "Coming to a Screen Near You." *Globe and Mail,* 25 January 2006, R1– R2.

Mackey, Eva. *The House of Difference: Cultural Politics and National Identity in Canada.* Toronto: University of Toronto Press, 2002.

Madden, Kate. "Video and Cultural Identity: The Inuit Broadcasting Corporation Experience." In *Mass Media Effects across Cultures,* edited by Felipe Korzenny, Stella Ting-Toomey, and Elizabeth Schiff, 130–49. Newbury Park, CA: Sage Publications, 1992.

Marcus, Alan R. *Relocating Eden. The Image and Politics of Inuit Exile in the Canadian Arctic.* Hanover: University Press of New England, 1995.

Marcus, George. Introduction to Marcus, *Connected: Engagements with Media*, 1–18.

Marcus, George, ed. *Connected: Engagements with Media.* Chicago: University of Chicago Press, 1996.

Margoshes, Dave. "Survey Results Show Regina Continues to Get No Respect: The City's Leaders and Residents Say this Poor Opinion is Based on Ignorance." *Vancouver Sun*, 8 August 1998, B1.

Marple, Chari. "First People's Show on the Road." *Ottawa XPRESS*, 25 June 1998.

Martin, Paul. *Speech from the Throne to Open the Third Session of the Session of the 37th Parliament of Canada.* Privacy Council Office, 2 February 2004, http://www.pco-bcp.gc.ca/index.asp?lang=eng&page=information&sub=publications&doc=sft-ddt/2004_1_e.htm

Martinez-Torres, M.E. "Civil Society, the Internet, and the Zapatistas." *Peace Review* (2001): 347–355.

Massood, Paula J. "Mapping the Hood: The Genealogy of City Space in *Boyz N the Hood* and *Menace II Society*." *Cinema Journal* 35, 2 (1996): 85–97.

May, James. "Information Technology for Indigenous Peoples: The North American Experience." In *Digital Democracy: Policy and Politics in the Wired World*, edited by Cynthia Jacqueline Alexander and Leslie Alexander Pal. Toronto: Oxford University Press, 1998.

Maxim, Paul S., Jerry P. White, and Dan Beavon, eds. *Aboriginal Conditions: Research as a Foundation for Public Policy.* Vancouver: University of British Columbia Press, 2003.

McEwan, H., and K Egan, eds., *Narrative in Teaching, Learning, and Research.* New York: Teachers College, Columbia University, 1995.

McGregor, Alex. *Report on the Needs of Northern Aboriginal Broadcasters, Department of Canadian Heritage*, June 2000.

McIver, William J. "A Community Informatics for the Information Society." In *Communicating in the Information Society*, edited by Bruce Girard and Seán O Siochru, 33-64. Geneva: United Nations Research Institute for Social Development, 2003.

McLuhan, Marshall. *Understanding Media.* Toronto: McGraw-Hill, 1964.

Meadows, Michael. "Broadcasting in Aboriginal Australia: One Mob, One Voice, One Land." In *Ethnic Minority Media*, edited by Harold Stephen Riggins, 82–101. Newbury Park, CA: Sage Publications, 1992.

_____. "Ideas from the Bush: Indigenous Television in Australia and Canada." *Canadian Journal of Communications* 20, 5 (1995): 197–212.

_____. "Indigenous Media Responses to Racism." Paper delivered to Post Colonial Formations Conference, Griffith University, Nathan, Australia, July 1993.

_____. "Voice Blo Mipla All Ilan Man: Torres Strait Islanders' Struggle for Television Access." In *Public Voices, Private Interests: Australia's Media*, edited by J. Craik, J. James Bailey, and A. Moran. Sydney: Allen and Unwin, 1993.

Media Awareness Network. "The Impact of Stereotyping on Young People." http://www.media-awareness.ca/english/issues/stereotyping/aboriginal_people/aboriginal_impact.cfm. (Accessed 26 November 2003.)

Melkote, Srinivas R., and H. Leslie Steeves. *Communication for Development in the Third World: Theory and Practice for Empowerment.* 2nd ed. New Delhi: Sage Publications, 2001.

Michaels, Eric. *The Aboriginal Invention of Television in Central Australia 1982–1986.* Canberra: Australian Institute of Aboriginal Studies, 1986.

_____. *For a Cultural Future: Francis Jupurrurla Makes TV at Yuendumu.* Sydney: Art and Text Publications, 1989.

Miller, Lyla. "First Nations' New Wave Taking Art to the Edge." *Ottawa Citizen,* 29 February 2004, A3.

Milloy, John. S. *"A National Crime": The Canadian Government and the Residential School System, 1879–1986.* Winnipeg: University of Manitoba Press, 1999.

Molnar, Helen, and Michael Meadows. *Songlines to Satellites: Indigenous Communication in Australia, the South Pacific and Canada.* Annandale, Austr.: Pluto Press, 2001.

Morris, Nancy, and Silvio R. Waisbord, eds. *Media and Globalization: Why the State Matters.* Lanham, MD: Rowman and Littlefield, 2001.

Naples, Nancy. *Feminism and Method: Ethnography, Discourse Analysis, and Activist Research.* New York: Taylor and Francis, 2003.

Narayan, Kirin. "How Native Is a 'Native' Anthropologist?" *American Anthropologist* 95, 3 (1993): 671–686.

"The Native Media." *Globe and Mail,* 24 February 1999, A16.

New Zealand, Ministry of Maori Development. "Te Tuaoma, The Maori Language: The Steps That Have Been Taken." http://www.tpk.govt.nz/publications/docs/tetuaomaeng.pdf.

Nordenstreng, Kaarle, and Herbert I. Schiller. *National Sovereignty and International Communication, Communication and Information Science.* Norwood, NJ: Ablex Publishing, 1979.

Norman, Sally Jane. "Culture and the New Media Technologies" UNESCO Working paper, presented at the Power of Culture Conference, Stockholm, Sweden, 1995.

Norris, Mary Jane, and L. Jantzen. "Aboriginal Languages in Canada's Urban Areas: Characteristics, Considerations and Implications." In *Not Strangers in These Parts: Urban Aboriginal Peoples,* edited by David Newhouse and E. Peters, 93–118. Ottawa: Policy Research Initiatives, 2003.

Northern Native Broadcasting, Yukon. *An Intervention of Conditional Support of Application 199804068 to the CRTC.* Whitehorse, YK: NNBY, 19 October 1998.

O'Brien, Mike. "Crime Linked to Native Woes: High Rate will Stay until Problems Addressed: Police Chief." *Regina Leader Post,* 21 December 2000, A1.

Parnes, Jeremy. "North Central Community Partnership: Report on the Community Vision and Action Plan." Regina, May 2003.

Patterson, Mike. "Where the Forest Meets the Highway." *Alternate Routes* 16 (2000): 9.

Paulson, Joanne. "Top Native Talent in City for Symposium." *Saskatoon Star Phoenix,* 19 May 2004, A1.

Petten, Cheryl. "All-Aboriginal Television Drama Set to Air." *Wind Speaker* 21, 8 (2003): 21.

Philipsen, Gerry. "An Ethnographic Approach to Communication Studies." In *Rethinking Communication,* Vol. 2, edited by Brenda Dervin, 258–268. New Brunswick, NJ: International Communication Association, 989.

Price, S.L. "The Indian Wars: The Campaign Against Indian Nicknames and Mascots Presumes that They Offend Native Americans—But Do They? We took a poll, and you won't believe the results." *Sports Illustrated,* 4 March 2002.

Philipsen, Hans Henrik, and Birgitte Markussen, eds. *Advocacy and Indigenous Film-Making.* Aarhus, Denmark: Intervention Press, 1995.

Prins, Harald. "Visual Media and the Primitivist Perplex: Colonial Fantasies, Indigenous Imagination, and Advocacy in North America." In Ginsburg, Abu-Lughod, and Larkin, *Media Worlds,* 58–74.

Pruden, Jana G. "Aboriginal TV Series Set in Regina Neighbourhood." *Saskatoon Star Phoenix,* 7 September 2004, C3.

Quantz, R.A. *The Handbook of Qualitative Research in Education.* Ed. W.L. Millroy, M.D. LeCompte, J. Preissle. San Diego, CA: Academic Press, 1992.

Quebec, Secretariat a la politique linguistique. "Living in French in Quebec," 2002.

Rabinow, Paul. "Representations Are Social Facts: Modernity and Postmodernityin Anthropology." In *Writing Culture: The Poetics and Politics of Ethnography,* edited by James Clifford and George E. Marcus, 241–261. Berkeley: University of California Press, 1986.

Ramsay, Christine. "Made in Saskatchewan! Features Since Telefilm." In *Self Portraits: The Cinemas of Canada Since Telefilm,* 203–235. Ottawa: Canadian Film Institute, 2006.

Rasmussen, Knud. *Across Arctic America. Narrative of the Fifth Thule Expedition.* New York: Greenwood Press, 1969.

Retzlaff, Steffi. "Tradition, Solidarity and Empowerment: The Native Discourse in Canada. An Analysis of Native News Representations." Paper presented at the third interdisciplinary Graduate Studies symposium, "Aboriginal Peoples in Canada in the 21st Century," University of Greifswald, 13–15 April 2005.

Robbins, Bruce. "Comparative Cosmopolitanism." *Social Text* 31–32 (1992):169–186.

Rollins, Peter C., and John E. O'Connor, eds. *Hollywood's Indian: The Portrayal of the Native American in Film.* Lexington: University Press of Kentucky, 1998.

Roth, Lorna. "The Delicate Act of 'Colour Balancing': Multiculturalism and Canadian Broadcasting Policies and Practices." *Canadian Journal of Communication* 23, 4 (1998): 487–505.

_____. "First Peoples' Television Broadcasting in Canada." http://www.museum.tv/ archives/etv/F/htmlF/firstpeople/firstpeople.htm

_____. "Mohawk Airwaves and Cultural Challenges: Some Reflections on the Politics of Recognition and Cultural Appropriation after the Summer of 1990." *Canadian Journal of Communications* 18, 3 (1993): 315–332.

_____. "Northern Voices and Mediating Structures: The Emergence and Development of First Peoples' Television Broadcasting in the Canadian North." PhD diss., Concordia University, 1994.

_____. *Something New in the Air: The Story of First Peoples Television Broadcasting in Canada.* Montreal: McGill-Queen's University Press, 2005.

_____. "Television Broadcasting North of 60." In *Images of Canadianness: Visions on Canada's Politics, Culture, Economics,* edited by Leen d'Haenens, 148–166. Ottawa: University of Ottawa Press, 1998.

Ruby, Jay. *Picturing Culture: Explorations of Film and Anthropology.* Chicago: University of Chicago Press, 2000.

_____. "A Re-Examination of the Early Career of Robert J. Flaherty." *Quarterly Review of Film Studies* 5, 4 (1981): 431–457.

Rudden, Terry. *Aboriginal and Public Broadcasting in Canada: An International Comparative Review.* Aboriginal Peoples Program, Department of Canadian Heritage, 2003.

Russel y Rodriguez, Monica. "Confronting the Silencing Praxis in Anthropology: Speaking of/from a Chicano Consciousness." *Qualitative Inquiry* 4, 1 (1998).

Santo, Avi. "Inuit Television and Cultural Citizenship." *International Journal of Cultural Studies* 7, 4 (2004): 379.

Schramm, Wilbur Lang, and Daniel Lerner. *Communication and Change in the Developing Countries.* Honolulu: University of Hawaii Press, East-West Center, 1972.

Scott, A.O. "Reel Change." *New York Times Magazine,* 7 July 2002, 11–12.

Shields, Rob. *Places on the Margin: Alternative Geographies of Modernity.* London: Routledge, 1991.

Shohat, Ella, and Robert Stam. *Unthinking Eurocentrism: Multiculturalism and the Media.* London: Routledge, 1994.

Simon, Roger I., and Donald Dippo. "On Critical Ethnographic Work." *Anthropology and Education Quarterly* 17, 4 (1986): 195–202.

Smith, Claire, Heather Burke, and Graeme K. Ward. "Globalisation and Indigenous Peoples: Threat or Empowerment?" In *Indigenous Cultures in an Interconnected World* edited by Claire Smith and Graeme K. Ward, 1-26. Vancouver: UBC Press, 2000.

Smith, Susan E. "Deepening Participatory Action-Research." In *Nurtured by Knowledge: Learning to Do Participatory Action-Research,* edited by Susan E. Smith, Dennis George Willms, and Nancy A. Johnson, 173–263. New York: Apex Press (International Development Research Centre), 1997.

Spotted Eagle, Dion. "First Nations Want Fair Treatment." *Regina Leader Post,* 2 May 2005, B8.

Stanley Venne, Muriel. "Let's Lay off the Loaded Language: Missing Women Much More than Prostitutes." *Edmonton Journal*, 3 May 2005, A15.

Stern, Pamela. "The History of Canadian Arctic Photography: Issues of Territorial and Cultural Sovereignty." In King and Lidchi, *Imaging the Arctic*, 46–52.

Stiegelbauer, Suzanne M. "What Is an Elder? What Do Elders Do? First Nation Elders as Teachers in Culture-based Urban Organizations." *The Canadian Journal of Native Studies* 16, 1 (1996): 37–66.

Strategic Inc. *APTN: Brand Equity Measure, Programming and Promotional Test.* Winnipeg: APTN, 2002.

Strover, Sharon. "Recent Trends in Co-productions: The Demise of the National." In *Democracy and Communication in the New Europe*, edited by F. Corcoran and P. Preston, 97–123. Cresskill, NJ: Hampton Press, 1995.

Tacchi, Jo. "Researching Creative Applications of New Information and Communication Technologies." *International Journal of Cultural Studies* 7, 1 (2004): 91–103.

Tacchi, Jo, Don Slater, and Greg Hearn. *Ethnographic Action Research Handbook.* New Delhi: UNESCO, 2003.

Tallbear, K. (2001, February). Racialising Tribal Identity and the Implications for Political and Cultural Development. Paper presented at the Indigenous Peoples and Racism Conference, Sydney, Australia.

Tehranian, M. (1994). Communication and Development. In *Communication Theory Today*, edited by D. Crowley & D. Mitchell, 274-306. Stanford: Stanford University Press.

Television Northern Canada. *North Link* [TVNC Newsletter]. Ottawa: TVNC, 1998-1999.

———. *Replies to Interventions Submitted with Respect to an Application by TVNC Inc. for a National Aboriginal Television Network Application #199804068. TVNC Letter to the CRTC.* Ottawa: TVNC, 30 October 1998.

———. *Response to CRTC Public Notice 1992-13.* Ottawa: TVNC, 10 March 1993.

Toronto International Film Festival Group. "By the Numbers". *Film Circuit Newsletter*, Summer 2008: 4. http://www.filmcircuit.ca/images/fc_newsletter_spring008.pdf.

Tuhiwai Smith, Linda. *Decolonizing Methodologies: Research and Indigenous Peoples.* London: Zed Books, 1999.

Turner, Stephen. "Sovereignty, or the Art of Being Native." *Cultural Critique* 51 (2002): 74–100.

Turner, Terence. "Representation, Politics, and Cultural Imagination in Indigenous Video: General Points and Kayapo Examples." In Ginsburg, Abu-Lughod, and Larkin, *Media Worlds*, 75–89.

UNESCO, Management of Social Transformation Programme. "Multiculturalism: A Policy Response to Diversity." Paper presented at the 1995 Global Cultural Diversity Conference, Sydney, Australia, 26–28 April 1995.

Valaskakis, Gail. "Communication, Culture and Technology: Satellites and Northern Native Broadcasting in Canada." In *Ethnic Minority Media*, edited by Stephen Harold Riggins. Newbury Park, CA: Sage Publications, 1992.

_____. "Communication and Control in the Canadian North: The Potential of Interactive Satellites." *Etudes Inuit Studies* 6, 1 (1982): 19–28.

_____. "Restructuring the Canadian Broadcasting System: Aboriginal Broadcasting in the North." In *Canadian Broadcasting, the Challenge of Change*, edited by Colin Hoskins and Stuart McFadyen. Edmonton: University of Alberta and ACCESS, 1985.

_____. "The Role, Development and Future of Aboriginal Communications." Research Report for the Royal Commission on Aboriginal Peoples. Ottawa, Government of Canada, 1995.

Valaskakis, Gail, and Thomas Wilson. *The Inuit Broadcasting Corporation: A Survey of Viewing Behaviour and Audience Preferences Among the Inuit of Seven Communities in the Baffin and Keewatin Regions of the Northwest Territories.* Montreal: Concordia University, 1985.

Valentine, Lisa Philips. *Making It Their Own: Severn Ojibwe Communicative Practices.* Toronto: University of Toronto Press, 1994.

Walker, Morley. "Aboriginal TV Deserves Better Spot on Dial." *Winnipeg Free Press*, 4 September 1999, B7.

Walsh, David. "Doing Ethnography." In *Researching Society and Culture*, edited by Clive Seale, 217–232. London: Sage Publications, 1998.

Warnock, John W. "NDP a Pale Shadow of Pioneering CCF." *Regina Leader Post*, 2 November 2004, B8.

WETV. *Intervention Transcript from CRTC Hearing of Application #199804068 to the CRTC.* Ottawa: CRTC, 12 November 1998

White, Jerry. Introduction to *Aboriginal Conditions: Research as a Foundation for Public Policy*, edited by Paul S. Maxim, Jerry P. White, and Dan Beavon, 222–247. Vancouver: University of British Columbia Press, 2003.

Whiteduck Resources Inc. and Consilium. *Northern Native Broadcast Access Program (NNBAP) and Northern Distribution Program (NDP) Evaluation. Final Report.* 25 June 2003. http://www.pch.gc.ca/pgm/em-cr/evaltn/2003/index-eng.cfm.

Wiley, Stephen B.C. "Rethinking Nationality in the Context Of Globalization." *Communication Theory* 14, 1 (2004): 78–96.

Williamson, Karla Jessen. "Celestial and Social Families of the Inuit." In *Expressions in Canadian Native Studies*, edited by Ron F. Lalibert, Priscilla Settee, James B. Waldram, Rob Innes, Brenda Macdougall, Lesley McBain, and F. Laurie Barron. Saskatoon: University of Saskatchewan Extension Press, 2000.

Wilson, Pamela, and Michelle Stewart, eds. *Global Indigenous Media: Cultures, Poetics, and Politics.* Durham, NC: Duke University Press, 2008.

Wolf, Margery. *A Thrice Told Tale: Feminism, Postmodernism and Ethnographic Responsibility.* Stanford, CA: Stanford University Press, 1992.

Worth, Sol. *Through Navajo Eyes; an Exploration in Film Communication and Anthropology.* Bloomington: Indiana University Press, 1972.

Yahyahkeekoot, Gabriel. "Problems behind Problems: A Young Person from 'The 'Hood' Endeavors to Stop the Ripple Effect of Cultural Genocide." *Briar Patch* 31, 6 (2002): 8.

Zimmerman, Larry J., Karen P. Zimmerman, and Leonard R. Bruguier. "Cyberspace Smoke Signals: New Technologies and Native American Ethnicity." In *Indigenous Cultures in an Interconnected World,* edited by Claire Smith and Graeme Ward. Victoria: University of British Columbia Press, 2000.

CONTRIBUTORS

Sigurjón Baldur Hafsteinsson, University of Iceland

Sigurjón Baldur Hafsteinsson is assistant professor at the University of Iceland. He has a doctoral degree from Temple University. His dissertation research is an ethnographic analysis of Aboriginal Peoples Television Network, called "Unmasking Deep Democracy: Aboriginal Peoples Television Network and Cultural Production."

Doris Baltruschat, Simon Fraser University

Doris Baltruschat combines research and scholarship with extensive professional experience in the film and television sectors. She has a PhD in Communication and focuses her research on globalization and culture, media ecologies, film and TV co-production, interactive and alternative media, and social movements. She has published articles on these topics in Canada, the U.S., England, Australia and China. Her latest book is titled *Global Media Ecologies: Networked Production in Film and Television* (Routledge, 2010).

Marian Bredin, Brock University

Marian Bredin is Associate Professor in the Department of Communication, Popular Culture and Film, and Director of the Centre for Canadian Studies at Brock. Her main research interests include Aboriginal and indigenous media, communications policy and cultural politics, and Canadian television. Her work has been published in the *Canadian Journal of Communication*, the *Canadian Journal of Native Studies* and elsewhere.

Jennifer David, Stonecircle Consulting.

Jennifer David is a member of the Chapleau Cree First Nation in northern Ontario. Jennifer has spent her career working in and supporting Aboriginal communications in Canada, first at Television Northern Canada, then as Director of Communications for the Aboriginal Peoples Television Network (APTN). She currently manages an Aboriginal management consulting company in Ottawa called Stonecircle Consulting.

Kerstin Knopf, University of Greifswald, Germany

Kerstin Knopf holds an MA in American/Canadian, Hispanic and Scandinavian Studies and a PhD from the University of Greifswald in Germany. Her dissertation *Decolonizing the Lens of Power: Indigenous Films in North America* was published with Rodopi Press in Amsterdam. Kerstin Knopf is assistant professor to the Chair of North American Studies at the University of Greifswald. Her main research interests are Indigenous literature, film, and media and women and gender studies.

Mike Patterson, Carleton University

Mike Patterson (Métis) has a PhD from Carleton University and has worked with many First Nations Elders, communities and NGOs in fields as diverse as Native music, prophecies (Seventh Fire), HIV/AIDS and injury prevention, research capacity building and networking in cyberspace, and the syncretic weaving of Western and Aboriginal worldviews. He hosted *Spirit Voice* Native radio for seven years, and was music editor for *Aboriginal VOICES* magazine. He developed the first graduate seminar in Aboriginal health at the School of Nursing at University of Ottawa. Currently he is Adjunct Research Professor at Carleton, focusing on online community research networks.

Yvonne Poitras Pratt, University of Calgary

Yvonne Poitras Pratt is a doctoral candidate and Canada Graduate Scholar at the University of Calgary working within the area of Aboriginal communications development. Her Masters research ethnographically explored the participation of three Aboriginal communities, including Cree, Blackfoot and Métis, in planning for the Alberta SuperNet broadband network. Yvonne is now collaborating with several stakeholders on the development of a digital media project that will involve youth and Elders in meaningful uses of media, including digital storytelling.

Christine Ramsay, University of Regina

Christine Ramsay teaches Media Studies and is Head of the Department of Media Production and Studies at the University of Regina. Her research is in the areas of Canadian and Saskatchewan cinemas, philosophies of identity, masculinities in contemporary cultures, and the culture of cities. She has published in various journals and anthologies and is currently working on two anthologies: *Making It Like a Man! Canadian Masculinities in Practice* and *Mind the Gap: Saskatchewan Cultural Spaces.*

Lorna Roth, Concordia University

Lorna Roth is Professor and former Chairperson of the Department of Communication Studies, Concordia University in Montréal. She is author of *Something New in the Air: The Story of First Peoples Television Broadcasting in Canada* (McGill-Queen's University Press, 2005) and is currently working on her second book entitled: *Colour-Balance: Race, Technologies, and "Intelligent Design."* She has a long-standing interest in issues related to minorities in public and private broadcasting sectors, and has written extensively about the construction of cultural and racial diversity in the media.